Long Journeys Home

NUMBER 156

Williams-Ford Texas A&M University Military History Series

Long Journeys Home

AMERICAN VETERANS OF WORLD WAR II, KOREA, & VIETNAM

Michael D. Gambone

TEXAS A&M UNIVERSITY PRESS | COLLEGE STATION

First edition

This paper meets the requirements
of ANSI/NISO Z39.48-1992 (Permanence of Paper).
Binding materials have been chosen for durability.
Manufactured in the United States of America

Library of Congress Cataloging-in-Publication Data

Names: Gambone, Michael D., 1963– author.
Title: Long journeys home : American veterans of World War II, Korea, and Vietnam / Michael D. Gambone.
Other titles: Williams-Ford Texas A&M University military history series ; no. 156.
Description: First edition. | College Station : Texas A&M University Press, [2017] | Series: Williams-Ford Texas A&M University military history series ; number 156 | Includes bibliographical references and index.
Identifiers: LCCN 2017010416| ISBN 9781623495800 (book/cloth : alk. paper) | ISBN 9781623495817 (ebook)
Subjects: LCSH: Veterans—United States—Social conditions—20th century. | Veteran reintegration--United States. | World War, 1939–1945—Veterans--United States. | Korean War, 1950–1953—Veterans--United States. | Vietnam War, 1961–1975—United States.
Classification: LCC UB357 .G36 2017 | DDC 305.9/0690973—dc23 LC record available at https://lccn.loc.gov/2017010416

DEDICATED TO

Louis A. Rodriquez

Republic of Vietnam, 1969–1970

and

Ryan Nolan

Iraq, 2005–2006, 2009

My brothers,

separated by time,

but no distance

CONTENTS

PREFACE

Coming home from a war can be a strange experience. It is a study in contrasts. Many of the clichés we apply to it are true. War is dirty, exhausting, and alternately filled with crushing boredom and periodic tension. Over time, the sights, sounds, and odors of war all combine into a kind of negative background noise on the periphery of a day-to-day contingency existence, tainting every moment of it. Back home, the atmosphere is abundantly more relaxed, clean, safe, convenient, and focused on the future, although most civilians seem unaware of it. Even the air seems to taste better.

My own homecoming happened in 2006, when I returned from Iraq after a tour as an army contractor. While there, I was part of a team charged with force protection at a forward operations base in Mosul. A few days after returning home, I decided to attend my university's commencement ceremony. I was excited and apprehensive about being there. Watching students graduate is a time-honored ritual that seemed to offer the prospect of returning to the civilian fold with some ease. Looking back, I assumed that an old conventional practice might displace my more recent experience in Iraq.

It didn't quite work out that way. As I carried my regalia through the crowds of faculty, I encountered many responses to my presence, surprise for the most part, and happiness. But I also saw flickers of apprehension on some of my colleagues' faces. That surprised and unsettled me. As much as I wanted to return to the fold, it was fairly obvious that it wasn't going to happen as I expected it. Like it or not, I brought the war home with me, and I could see it reflected in some of my friends' eyes. I had new baggage. It was one thing to participate in campus forums about the "Global War on Terror" or join Historians against the War. It was another experience entirely to actually be the subject of the debate. At the time, I lacked a clear understanding of the distinction. All I knew was how awkward it felt.

Until another colleague approached me. Lou Rodriquez is a member of my department who teaches American history. He was also a Vietnam veteran, with service in the Mekong Delta. Lou saw far more combat than I ever did, but I think he understood my predicament. Maybe he was just curious.

"So how was it?" he asked. Those four words felt like a breached dam. What I had in front of me was a person ready to talk about the war but, more important, someone with the capacity to understand what I was about to say.

I learned two things that day. I don't think time matters when it comes to veterans. War can be a common denominator that bridges gaps, sometimes crossing decades. Wars shape and define a common community within society, a subculture that Sebastian Junger recently wrote about in his 2016 book *Tribe: On Homecoming and Belonging*. I am grateful for my tribe.

Coming home takes many steps, some of which are helped or hindered by both the veterans and the folks back home. It navigates the crosscurrents of social mores, politics, gender, physical and mental wounds, and more complicated features than I could possibly recognize or name.

I don't think that the journey is ever completed.

ACKNOWLEDGMENTS

My academic career has benefited from the kindness of many individuals over almost three decades, and this project is no exception.

I thank the staff and archivists at the American Legion Library and Museum, the Army Heritage and Education Center, the Dwight David Eisenhower Library, the Gelman Library at George Washington University, the Hagley Museum and Library, the Library of Congress, the National Archives and Records Administration, and the Swarthmore College Peace Collection.

I also thank the many students whom I have taught over the years who were veterans. Their work, experiences, and humor constantly reminded me that there are stories to tell long after military service is over. I am particularly indebted to Ryan Nolan, a veteran of two tours in Iraq, one of which took him out of my classroom to Baghdad before final exams. We finished his incomplete while he was deployed. He is one of the finest people I have ever known.

I want to thank my good friend and colleague Patricia Kelleher for expressing her doubts about a basic assumption that I made in my first manuscript about veterans. She took me to task over my penchant toward triumphalism and the topic of veterans, a comment that stuck fast and guided my subsequent search for a more balanced perspective to this particular part of American history.

Special thanks also go to Michael Gabriel and Maureen Harp for their extensive, insightful, and extremely useful comments on my early drafts of the manuscript. I am grateful for the success in rescuing me from my own writing at key points in the process.

Finally, I want to recognize the two most important people in my life. To my wife and editor of nearly 30 years, Rachel, I want to again recognize her herculean patience and ability to present questions that guide me toward answers. My son, Michael, also deserves special thanks. He is on his way to college to explore an interest in writing. It has been an inspiration to watch someone at the beginning of his own story with so many more parts yet to find, understand, and express.

Long Journeys Home

Introduction

It's almost as if there had been no war, unless you happen to be kin to one of the town's thirty-eight dead. Folks who stayed behind haven't changed. The kids who came back—and almost all of the 1,800 who went away are back—are nowhere near as different as townsfolk thought they might be.

—New York Times article on veterans in St. Albans, Vermont, September 1946[1]

Fuck you—fuck you one and all.

—American soldier wounded in Vietnam on discovering he had lost his leg, 1971[2]

Defining a Veteran

Although the definition of a veteran seems self-evident, it is in fact fluid and subject to many interpretations.[3] We most often like to think of the veteran as a hero. People celebrate the soldier returning from war for his sacrifice in the defense of all the best virtues of society and polity. Commemorations to this bravery are part of the national calendar. They are woven into an ever-expanding list of public events from political speeches and parades to air force flyovers during the Super Bowl.

We also recurrently see veterans as victims. We commemorate death in the defense of the greater good because the sacrifice imparts an intangible but critical sense of gravity to service. Monuments to sacrifice are part of the public landscape. Town centers and old battlefields possess statuary and architecture that mark a glorious and poignant historical cadence of loss over decades and centuries of American history.

A number of veterans remain living victims of their wars. The wounded, disabled or otherwise, are a continuing testament to the cost of conflict.[4] Men wounded in battle and returned to the fight receive the accolades of both the military and society. The institution rewards persistence over suffering and dedication to duty. More to the point, a soldier who continues fighting also has the potential to function as a returned veteran. With the assistance of modern medicine and technology, the wound becomes a finite problem, an interruption on the path to postwar civilian normalcy.

Some of these wounds are permanent reminders of what it means to be a veteran. There are injuries to the mind and body that no amount of science can fix. Persistent suffering has a twofold impact. It significantly alters an individual's life in ways that are personal and subjective. More broadly, suffering also challenges the myths created in the process of commemoration. The disabled veteran is a living contradiction to glory and celebration. He is a reality that no amount of pomp and circumstance can mitigate and a constant reminder of the human costs of war. In this contradiction exists an important historical trend. While public memory appears well suited to veterans for the sake of glory, the same cannot be said with respect to their suffering. Contemporary scandals surrounding posttraumatic stress disorder, increasing suicide rates within the military, and seemingly unfixable levels of incompetence within the Veterans Administration have long-standing precedents in American history.[5]

The history of American veterans reflects a constant tension between myth and reality. As much as historians, politicians, or society as a whole would like to invest the group with its own special meanings, the process is difficult to define and often hotly contested by all parties. Veterans spend a great deal of energy attempting to define the meaning of their service. Part of this encompasses the important role that veterans and veterans' organizations play in public commemorations of service. Modern war has inspired veterans around the world to demand public recognition. Parades and testimonials are now an embedded part of culture thanks to their direct efforts. Perhaps more important is veterans' success at shaping public policy. Kind rhetoric may assuage the cost of war in some cases, but government budgets, policies, and programs carry more weight. Throughout the twentieth century, groups like the American Legion and Veterans of Foreign Wars have been extremely effective lobbyists, not only expanding funding but also dramatically advancing government entitlements in the dawning age of the welfare state. The 1944 Serviceman's Readjustment Act (GI Bill) is the most famous of an extensive social safety net built in the modern era.[6]

Veterans, however, did not wholly "own" their history. American society has provided its own fickle historical context for war and service. There are moments when, at least on the surface, the public rallied around American conflicts and returning veterans. This appears to be the case after World War II. In subsequent wars, however, a sense of public ambiguity bordering on open hostility at times is apparent. This transition was certainly evident during the Korean War and later Vietnam.[7] Ambiguity persists in the modern day, where a complex montage of unconventional global conflicts, political partisanship, and the legacies of past wars combine to make ambivalence the rule rather than the exception. Today, it is possible to be "for the troops, but against the war."[8]

The first goal of this book is to recognize that a more truthful history of veterans lies somewhere in between myth, reality, and the various contending parties attempting to understand and define both. Separating out actors, events, and interpretations is a delicate and complex task. The approximately 30 million veterans produced by World War II, Korea, and Vietnam certainly were not a monolithic bloc. Their wars separated them, as did race, gender, and a host of other factors. The America welcoming these 30 million home also evolved over three decades, witnessing sea changes in the national consensus present after World War II. What it meant to be a veteran, an agglomeration of hopes, fears, and unrealized potential, was a constant part of the domestic discourse. Would they be an economic asset or a burden? Did war make them a danger to society? Questions like these move far beyond the definitions of heroes and victims. They deserve detailed examination of their component parts to separate myth and the truth. A necessary first step in this process is to examine some of the broad, largely accepted assumptions that currently separate veterans of World War II and Vietnam.

Veterans, World War II and Vietnam: Between Myth and Reality

For the most part, histories of World War II and Vietnam veterans have been a study in polar opposites. Authors tend to lionize World War II veterans. One of the best and most recent forms of this testimonial approach came from Tom Brokaw and his 1998 book *The Greatest Generation*. Brokaw makes his intent clear in an early passage. His personal revelation came during a trip to Normandy that was part of the fortieth-anniversary celebrations of D-Day. Reflecting on the many veterans who accompanied him, Brokaw said, "I was deeply moved and profoundly grateful for all they had done. I realized that they had been all around me as I was growing up and that I had failed to appreciate what they had been through and what they had accomplished."[9] Hero worship guides *The Greatest Generation* and its categorization of war and military service from that point onward. Looking back at 1940, his birth year when the "storms of war in Europe and the Pacific" threatened, Brokaw writes: "The nation turned to its young to carry the heaviest burden, to fight in enemy territory and to keep the home front secure and productive. These young men and women were eager for the assignment. They understood what was required of them, and they willingly volunteered for their duty."[10] There is more than a touch of oversimplification and triumphalism in this approach. Taking a longer view of the historiography of World War II, Brokaw resides in a long line of writers and historians to do so. More than a decade before *The Greatest Generation*, Studs Terkel coined the term "good war."[11] Scholars have, for decades, picked up the refrain that World War II represented the apogee of American civilization, buttressed by global power and domestic consensus, drawing a sharp contrast between it and the later tumultuous sixties.[12] The same prevailing seamlessness appears in histories of the era. World War II thus appears as a great "crusade," to use Warren Hassler's term.[13] The postwar transition to peace reflected this consensus and predicated the greatness of the veterans who won the war. In the 1969 edition of *The Growth of the American Republic*, Samuel Eliot Morison, Henry Steele Commager, and William E. Leuchtenberg note: "Veterans had little difficulty finding work, and unemployment remained low; reconversion to civilian economy was swift; the dammed-up demand for consumer goods seemed insatiable."[14]

The traditional history of Vietnam and its veterans is a study in painful contrasts to the "good war." Writers commonly describe Vietnam as a badly flawed effort that left its veterans as victims of both mistaken policies and an American society divided against the war. In *The Nightingale's Song*, Robert Timberg captures Vietnam's contrast with World War II in stark terms: "For those who served in Vietnam, the war and its aftermath ushered in troubled times. Unlike veterans of other wars, they came home to hostility, contempt, ridicule, at best indifference. Their experiences were at first disorienting, then alienating."[15] Timberg focuses specifically on the chasm between the men who served and their baby boomer peers who did not. From this alternative "generation gap" emerged a sense of disillusionment and alienation that followed baby boomers for years after Vietnam. Yale psychiatrist Robert Jay Lifton, who worked with Vietnam veterans experiencing mental trauma, addressed another darker outcome inherent in this process in *Home from the War* (1973): "Unresolved death guilt can also be expressed through feelings of rage and impulses toward violence. These are prominent in survivors of any war, but the binds, betrayals, and corruptions experienced by the Vietnam veteran fuel those tendencies to the point where they invade large zones of his psyche."[16] Lifton suggested, and many Americans believed, that the alienation created by Vietnam service would eventually present a danger to society as a whole.

There is no question that many Vietnam veterans experienced the feelings of alienation and rage mentioned by Timberg and Lifton, but what is lost is a sense of proportion and historical context. Were these individuals the exception or the rule among Vietnam veterans? More important, were these tendencies unique to Vietnam veterans or could they be found in other past wars? For the most part, Vietnam and World War II veterans form the dichotomy of historical triumph and tragedy.

The Historical Dilemma of Korean War Veterans

For decades, Korean War veterans were as forgotten as their war. Public recognition was rare in the many years following the 1953 armistice. Congress did not approve a Korean War Memorial until 1986, and construction took almost a decade to complete.[17]

While excellent military and diplomatic histories of the Korean War acknowledge the immensely important place that this conflict had in the postwar period, this scholarship has never been matched by similar attention to Korean War veterans.[18]

Korean War veterans lived on uncertain historical footing. They fought at what was an important transitory time in modern America. They arrived to their service from a generation defined by the privations of the Great Depression and the sacrifices demanded by World War II. Patriotism, a binding sense of duty for the sake of the common good, and a general trust in the government shaped their outlook. As David Kennedy notes in his excellent study of the period, *Freedom from Fear*, "The war had shaken the American people loose and shaken them up, freed from a decade of economic paralysis and flung them around their country into new regions and new ways of life."[19] From this sea change came an era of unparalleled optimism. Veterans of Korea were as much a part of the great, post-1945 American consensus as anyone at that time.

Yet the relationship between war and society was anything but certain when North Korean forces crossed the 38th parallel in June 1950. Outwardly, in the newsreels shown back home, Americans deploying to Korea looked very much like the forces going overseas to Europe and Asia. With the exception of a few modern innovations, such as jet fighters and helicopters, there was a sense of continuity with World War II. However, most Americans alive at the start of the fifties understood the basic realities of atomic war and the constant possibility of escalation beyond the conventional conflict in Korea. Just how the United States might control this escalation temporarily eluded policy makers, as Douglas MacArthur discovered to his regret. This process of groping toward containment terrified the public. The accumulating sense of ambiguity, frustration, and fear tainted the Korean War and its veterans. Service in Korea carried a stigma, another form of guilt by association at a time when McCarthyism dominated the public discourse.

Contemporary American society was never fully vested in Korea. Although in the polls the public initially rallied behind President Harry Truman at the start of the conflict, people soon retreated from the war, fearful of escalation and distracted by the postwar economic boom taking hold of the country. The draft continued throughout the Korean War, but that proved to be the limit of national mobilization.

Americans at home did not have to worry about rationing, wage or price controls, "no strike" pledges, or the myriad other shared sacrifices of World War II. The main burden of the war, separation, wounds, and death, fell to nearly four million citizens, a tiny fraction of the population.

Stigma and separation may explain the lack of historical attention to Korean War veterans. In recent histories of post-1945 America, their absence is conspicuous. Studies of the American family, masculinity, gender relations, and social justice movements, to name but a few, almost never mention veterans.[20] Historian Melinda Pash is a recent new entry in what remains a sparsely populated field of study.[21] It seems almost counterintuitive to believe that nearly four million people who lived through a war had no role in shaping American postwar normalcy.

A dedicated, systematic study of these three wars and their veterans is necessary to challenge the World War II/Vietnam dichotomy and provide needed attention to Korea. It is important to understand the root sources of misapprehensions about veterans that hardened into conventional wisdom and, finally, history. It is equally important to find the points of commonality that connect veterans of World War II, Korea, and Vietnam and to discover the points of departure in their respective experiences.

This work has already begun. Andy Rooney took *The Greatest Generation* to task because it "was flawed in its basic concept" and had "tailored the evidence to fit Tom's theory that our generation was special."[22] Similarly, scholars have also challenged persistent misconceptions that cling to Vietnam veterans. Jerry Lembke's research has largely debunked the popularly accepted image of protesters who spat on returning Vietnam veterans.[23] Russell W. Glenn has questioned the "grossly unjust stereotype of the Vietnam veteran as a social misfit and malcontent."[24] Eric T. Dean argues that most Vietnam veterans successfully adjusted to civilian life despite exaggerations to the contrary. More important, Dean believes that "far from being *unique*, the Vietnam veteran is *typical* in many respects to the veteran throughout American history."[25]

My intent is to expand the approach taken by these authors. Rather than focus on veterans of one war in isolation, the book adopts a comparative approach to the large mass of men and women who served in World War II, Korea, and Vietnam. It illustrates many common assumptions that followed veterans from war to peace and test not only their validity but also their continuing application over time. Essentially, the book picks up the thread established by Eric T. Dean and follows two separate but related paths. It attempts to determine the distance between myth and reality applied to American veterans after 1945. As it proceeds, I also see whether or not the Vietnam veteran's experience was the exception or the rule during this time.

CHAPTER 1
Joining Up

I grew out of one war into another. My father came from leaden ships of sea, from the Pacific theater; my mother was a WAVE. I was the offspring of the great campaign against the tyrants of the 1940s, one explosion of the Baby Boom, one of millions come to replace those who had just died. My bawling came with the first throaty note of a new army in spawning. I was bred with the haste and dispatch and careless muscle-flexing of a nation giving bridle to its own good fortune and success. I was fed by the spoils of 1945 victory.

—*Tim O'Brien, If I Die in a Combat Zone, 1969*[1]

Introduction

Who should serve? The question begins the discussion on terms of military service and, subsequently, the nature of the veteran. Historically, the question travels back to the early colonial period when universal military service equaled survival on the frontier. In seventeenth-century America, it was not unusual for local militia companies to demand the participation of all males between the ages of 16 and 60.[2] After the American Revolution, citizens and state, and federal officials, considered the issue of military service and found what were, at best, imperfect solutions. Memories proved short, especially once the immediate frontier was settled and the prospect of European war receded beyond the Atlantic Ocean. The absence of immediate threats discouraged hard solutions regarding who should serve. Crisis lent little clarity. Even during the Civil War, both sides initially relied on manpower policies that dated back to the late eighteenth century.[3] Attempts to invoke national conscription were ineffective at best or, in the case of the New York draft riots of 1863, disastrous.

In October 1940, with the United States perched between neutrality and mobilization for World War II, Franklin Roosevelt invoked US history as he tried to rally the country behind national military service. Speaking at the start of America's first peacetime draft, the president claimed: "On this day more than sixteen million young Americans are reviving the three hundred year-old American custom of the muster. They are obeying that first duty of free citizenship by which, from the earliest colonial times, every able-bodied citizen was subject to the call for service in the national defense."[4] Not surprisingly, Roosevelt was selective about both the past and the present. On the brink of World War II, as the United States considered the largest military mobilization in its history, a number of factors qualified what "universal" service entailed for most Americans.

Simple practical concerns would determine military numbers. If the United States wanted to turn its formidable industrial economy toward war, more workers needed to remain at their machines. The same was true of farm labor necessary to feed the country and the military. The concept of what was essential to the American war effort, defined by vocation, education, or potential contribution, remained malleable and subject to considerable debate during World War II and long afterward.

Similarly, as a matter of practicality, not every American was allowed to serve. Physical and mental disabilities disqualified millions from service. Other restrictions reflected the biases of the time. Prior to the Korean War, the American military adhered to a policy of strict segregation. Gender also restricted military service. When the draft began in 1940, subsequent amendments to include unmarried, unemployed women appeared throughout the war. Generally, the idea of conscripting a narrow section of American women enjoyed considerable public support. However, although a 1944 Gallup Poll noted that 75% of respondents approved of the measure for noncombat jobs, these proposals went nowhere.[5]

Additional subjective factors also played a part. Simply put, not every American wanted to serve in the military. Individual industries, organized labor, and advocates for preserving the American family all formed lobbies to deflect or defer military service. Individuals challenged the idea of time in uniform as a matter of personal moral convictions. Religious organizations agreed and cited legal precedents extending all the way to the First Amendment of the Constitution. This final feature is important, particularly with respect to the relationship between American citizens and the military. The people who served during World War II, Korea, and Vietnam were not simply bodies occupying uniforms. Their roles were defined by a long-standing tradition that placed the armed forces at the behest of civil society. Historically, most Americans tended to tolerate military service as a necessary evil in times of crisis rather than a persistent, lifelong obligation. These expectations defined both the volunteer and the draftee. Collective and individual motivation essentially determined whether or not the military could accomplish its mission in a time of war.

While history and tradition shaped the relationship between citizens and the military, the subjective public perceptions of World War II, Korea, and Vietnam provide a final piece of critical social context. Recent scholarship on US conflicts in Iraq and Afghanistan has spent considerable time examining a host of factors that influence public support for military operations abroad. The clarity of military objectives, the duration of the conflict, the stance of "elite" opinion makers, and the number of casualties all play a part in validating or diminishing military service.[6] In essence, it is not possible to be "for the troops, but against the war" without consequences.

Veterans are a key element missing from this discussion. It is possible that the axiom that "the lessons of the last war apply to the next" pertains to veterans. As a group, they carry the legacies of their wars into any public discussion regarding conflict and service. Historian Stephen Ortiz rightly claims that years of lobbying for their World War I bonus placed veterans at the center of Depression-era politics and the New Deal.[7] However, individually and as a collective whole, veterans are also the members of society closest to the wartime experience. Whether lobbying for public policy as members of the Veterans of Foreign Wars or rehashing old exploits around the dinner table, they potentially had the strongest influence on the social acceptability of military service.[8]

Collectively, the decision to join up involved a series of complex and interrelated factors. It was at once an intensely personal decision about citizenship and the subjective understandings of the burdens and benefits that accompanied it. Joining up was also a product of social context. As much as individuals considered the potential life-and-death risks of military service, it was the outside world that invested it with legitimacy or took it away. Understanding the interplay between the personal and the contextual is key to unspooling the myths and realities that started a person on the path to becoming a veteran.

The Past, "Popular" Wars, and Volunteering for Military Service

When we think about the acceptability of military service, World War II and Vietnam tend to define opposite ends of the spectrum. In *Flags of Our Fathers* (2000) James Bradley wrote that "America's boys were spoiling for vengeance" in the aftermath of Pearl Harbor.[9] It was a familiar characterization of a country ready to defend the free world against German and Japanese fascism. To be sure, World War II enjoyed clearly defined enemies and the finite, if daunting, goal of "unconditional surrender" after the capture of Berlin and Tokyo. Tom Brokaw described the atmosphere of the time: "In America, young men were enlisting in the military by the hundreds of thousands. Farm kids from the Great Plains who never expected to see the ocean in their lifetimes signed up for the Navy; brothers followed brothers into the Marines; young daredevils who were fascinated by the new frontiers of flight volunteered for pilot training."[10] All appeared ready to participate when the government "asked of them extraordinary service, sacrifice, and heroics."[11]

The conventional wisdom surrounding Korea and Vietnam offers a stark contrast to these heroics. Although the array of books written on these wars is truly staggering, they tend to agree on a number of common denominators. Both Korea and Vietnam lacked the clear objectives that defined World War II. Terms like "deterrence" and "containment" lacked the hard edges of the so-called good war against fascism. Inconclusively applied against a resilient enemy thousands of miles away in Asia, military stalemate corroded public support for both wars and their veterans. According to a 1971 Harris Poll, most Americans characterized Vietnam veterans as "suckers, having to risk their lives in the wrong war, in the wrong place, at the wrong time," a judgment that seems equally applicable to the Korean conflict.[12]

However, the events surrounding these wars and Americans' approach to military service do not fit into such neatly crafted boxes. Prior to World War II, the prospect of conflict and the concurrent obligations of American citizens were bound up in contemporary debates over isolationism. For the generation of men reaching adulthood in the thirties, the enthusiasm with which Americans entered the Great War in 1917 had largely curdled into outright skepticism. In contrast to the sacrifices made for Woodrow Wilson's promise of a world made "safe for democracy," many Americans struggling through the Great Depression were ready to believe that the best of a generation had died for big business and war profiteers, the "merchants of death." A 1934 book of the same title claimed that the armaments industry was part of a "well-organized, ruthless conspiracy to block world peace and to promote war."[13] Such sentiments gained easy traction on the fifth anniversary of Wall Street's collapse. As Paul Fussell notes, the generation coming of age before World War II was far more jaded with the prospect of war than the men of 1917. Many were familiar with, if not well versed in, the literature of Ernest Hemingway, Siegfried Sassoon, and Erich Maria Remarque as well as the backdrop of the neutrality debates that raged in the years before Pearl Harbor. For these individuals, the Great War offered a stark contrast between naïve romanticism and systematized horror that they had no intention of repeating.[14]

The growing threat of military aggression abroad did little to change this perspective. Faced with the Japanese occupation of China, the Italian invasion of Abyssinia (present-day Ethiopia), and an increasingly belligerent Nazi Germany, Pennsylvania governor George Earle proclaimed in 1935, "If the world is to become a wilderness of waste, hatred, and bitterness, let us all the more earnestly protect and preserve our own oasis of liberty."[15] Entrenched isolationism persisted as late as the summer of 1940. Speaking for the America First Committee only days after the fall of France, Charles Lindbergh argued against any involvement in what he considered a European conflict. "Lucky Lindy," an international hero after his famous 1927 transatlantic flight, lent his name and reputation to avoiding the war in Europe. He warned that the Roosevelt administration and like-minded interventionists had "baited the trap of war with requests for modest assistance." More important, Lindbergh argued that military mobilization would cost more than money. To properly prepare for war, he maintained, "we must turn to a dictatorial government, for there is no military efficiency to be lost."[16]

Interestingly, the World War I veteran's experience appeared to have little impact on swaying this discussion of the late thirties and early forties. Prior to the war, the American Legion conducted a campaign for universal military service.[17] Year after year, the Legion forthrightly argued for readiness against an accumulating global danger anyone could read about almost daily in newspaper headlines. Also couched in demands for preparedness was the question of fairness. As late as 1942, the Legion demanded an end to the "double standard of wartime patriotism" that had tainted service in World War I. One bluntly worded press release noted that while millions of men served and "fought and bled, to win the war, influential slackers had spent their evenings on porch swings, fanning our girls with their exemption certificates."[18] In the end, the Legion's effort for a total mobilization of manpower largely failed. When Germany invaded Poland in September 1939, the US armed forces were pitifully inadequate.[19] Moreover, while the United States eventually overcame its deficiency in numbers, political, economic, and other considerations proved formidable obstacles to universal military service.

Overcoming these entrenched sentiments was a difficult task under the best of circumstances. Unfortunately, the Roosevelt administration struggled with articulating American war goals almost from the outset. Fussell writes that during the early days of World War II, Americans better understood what they were fighting against rather than the positive objectives the country was attempting to advance.[20] The Four Freedoms—freedom of speech, freedom of religion, freedom from want, freedom from fear—first introduced by Roosevelt in a January 1941 speech and later restated in the Atlantic Charter, proved to be too abstract to serve as a public rallying point.[21] In an attempt to counter this problem, in 1942 the War Department commissioned Hollywood director Frank Capra to produce his Why We Fight series. The films were designed to explain American goals to incoming recruits. After some initial resistance from the Pentagon, the series appeared in public theaters a year later to mixed reviews.[22]

The combination of public skepticism and official missteps hurt mobilization efforts at the start of the war. As the American public contemplated placing millions of men in uniform, the overall mood was decidedly ambivalent. When the topic of selective service began to circulate in early 1940, polls recorded that, in July 1940, 87% of newspaper editors were in favor of conscription. However, at the same time, mail to the White House ran two to one against the idea of only one year's mandatory service for 20-year-olds.[23] When official mobilization began, Americans joined up with a marked sense of sobriety. An October 1940 *New York Times* story reflected on the "philosophical resignation" of many men who first registered for the draft.[24]

Selective service rather than universal service was an important result of widespread public hesitancy toward war. As he pressed forward with his case for intervention, Roosevelt was forced to do so incrementally. The 1940 Selective Service and Training Act limited recruits to one year on active duty with an additional 10 years in the reserves. The law also explicitly restricted this new manpower to the Western Hemisphere and US territories abroad.[25] Extending these limited commitments proved difficult. Troops training in the field openly challenged the idea, promising to "go over the hill in October" when the War Department proposed extending the one-year term of service during the summer of 1941.[26] Public support evenly split over the idea. According to one Gallup Poll, 51% of respondents favored extending the term of service, while 45% were against the idea. Some 50% opposed the idea of sending draftees overseas.[27]

Pearl Harbor settled the question of whether or not America needed mobilization. It did not, however, settle the question of public support for military service or resolve personal questions about volunteering. It is somewhat ironic that of the three wars, World War II contained the largest percentage of draftees, while Vietnam had the smallest.[28] Although it is clear that Americans understood the necessity for war in 1941, it is equally clear that the greatest generation lacked the uniformity of purpose retroactively applied by revisionist histories written decades after the war. In *Flags of Our Fathers*, James Bradley discusses a variety of motives that accompanied, and competed with, the decision to join up. Some concerns were economic. Wartime industrial mobilization effectively erased the Depression and opened up career opportunities for the first time in more than a decade. Many waited to see how Washington might eventually sort out an often-chaotic national mobilization. Still other Americans approached service in a manner influenced by their moral upbringing and personal preference. Despite the shrill propaganda that engulfed the country, they were reluctant to abandon their individual convictions. It is interesting that James Bradley, who praises the six flag raisers at Iwo Jima, one of whom was Bradley's father, as "All-American Boys," also records the fact that only two were in uniform at the start of 1943.[29]

While World War II ground on, the home front stabilized as the country unraveled the enormous complexities involved with fighting a global conflict. During the war, inductions averaged approximately 200,000 men per month.[30] At the same time, casualty rates also steadily increased. By 1945, more than one million Americans had died or been wounded in the war.[31]

Public tolerance for such sacrifices was governed by the expectation that the war would end. Encroaching war weariness was tempered by a sense that peace, a finite goal, was within reach. Indicative of this atmosphere was the seventh and largest war bond drive, the "Mighty 7th," which set records for fund-raising by combining "the old-fashioned elements of vaudeville, the country fair, the Fourth of July parade."[32] When the Mighty 7th began in May 1945, the war in Europe was largely over. The war in the Pacific was only approaching its crescendo. The US invasion of Iwo Jima cost 24,000 American casualties, with an additional 12,410 dead and 44,613 wounded while reducing Japanese defenses on Okinawa.[33] The potential cost of the final step in the Pacific "island-hopping" campaign dwarfed these figures. Conservative War Department estimates for the planned invasion of Japan placed the casualty rate as high as 250,000.[34]

World War II Legacies

How far did World War II's legacy extend to subsequent generations who considered joining up? One recent history of the Korean War notes the powerful impact of the Great Depression and World War II on the decision to enter the military. The dual influences of poverty and public acclimation to contribute to national defense left a deep mark on Americans in 1950.[35] Arguably, these same two features formed the cornerstones for baby boomers who contemplated the question of service in the sixties. If many of the soldiers bound for Vietnam lacked the same economic adversity of their parents, history still lay heavily on their worldview. Speaking of his generation, James Webb captured this sense beautifully in *Fields of Fire* (1978): "They would stand shyly at the outer fringes of the gathered farmers who had come to spend their Saturdays in the courthouse square. The men would sit in gaggles, chewing slowly on cuds of tobacco or rolling their own cigarettes, talking of their wars and scratching faded scars."[36] While there are some collective external influences shared by the veterans of all three wars, individual choices regarding military service also appear to one degree or another. Many of the memoirs written throughout the post-1945 period mention a sense of boredom and impatience common to young men of any time period. Philip Caputo recalled life in a new Illinois suburban subdivision in the fifties: "I can still see myself roaming around out there, scaring rabbits from the brambles, the tract houses a few miles behind me, the vast, vacant prairies in the front, a restless boy caught between boredom and rural desolation."[37] Throughout Caputo's and many other recollections is an almost palpable sense that peacetime represented a missed opportunity.

Many of the boys growing up in the wake of World War II wanted to be heroes. To a degree, sports offered one outlet. Millions joined in the rite of passage and played American Legion and Little League baseball along with Pop Warner and "midget" football. A whole generation of boys followed the on-field exploits of Joe DiMaggio and Mickey Mantle as their careers peaked in the forties and fifties.

Heroism on the field of play had its limits, however. Athletes had a difficult time competing with the decorated military heroes who returned home after World War II. Perhaps the most famous of these was Audie Murphy, who rose from his humble Texas origins to win the Medal of Honor and become a nationally recognized celebrity. Philip Caputo, Ron Kovic, and a host of Vietnam veterans make mention of worshipping Murphy for his larger-than-life exploits in *To Hell and Back* when it reached theaters in 1955.[38]

Interestingly, in depicting wartime heroism, fiction outshone fact for many boys. John Wayne, who never served a day on active duty, achieved iconic status in movies like *The Flying Tigers* (1942), *The Fighting Seabees* (1944), *Back to Bataan* (1945), *They Were Expendable* (1945), and *The Sands of Iwo Jima* (1949). By the sixties, truly epic war movies became box-office staples, from *The Great Escape* (1963) to *The Dirty Dozen* (1967) and *Patton* (1970). On television, *Combat!* (1962–67), and *Rat Patrol* (1966–68) were recurring popular dramas.[39] In the meantime, lacking the filter of wisdom or experience, boys constantly reenacted what they saw as the drama of combat. The backyards, woods, and empty lots across postwar America became places to endlessly explore the game of war.[40]

The Influence of Korea

In contrast to the consistently positive influences on young men considering military service, there were also elements of the Korean and Vietnam Wars that eroded attitudes about joining up. The June 1950 invasion of Korea was certainly a shock on par with Pearl Harbor that most Americans could understand. But the Communist forces crossing the 38th parallel were better defined by a Cold War context that made the Korean War far more alien and distant than the crisis that shook Americans in 1941.

As South Korean and US forces reeled under the Communist onslaught, the United States was no longer a bystander in world affairs. It was, by virtue of rhetoric and policy, responsible for the security and prosperity of the "free world" against Moscow and Beijing. The policy of choice at the time was an adaptation of George Kennan's "containment," the product of State Department strategists rather than public consensus. Although it promised a framework for the use of armed force, prompting the creation of the North Atlantic Treaty Organization (NATO) and other military alliances, it was an abstract concept at best. Gaps in this understanding are the likely cause of the Korean War, an outcome that historians still debate to this day.[41] If policy makers lacked clarity of purpose, there is little doubt that this confusion trickled down to the public at large.

The Cold War in 1950 was at once more dangerous, more pervasive, and more difficult to understand and rally around than any other previous American conflict. The invasion of South Korea was another move in an ongoing series of superpower confrontations that appeared far away but were constantly within reach of home, either through atomic escalation or domestic subversion, the latter a constant refrain in the bitter congressional debates of the moment.

Consequently, Korean War military service lacked the clear sense of risk and reward apparent during World War II. Chinese intervention in 1950 eliminated the possibility of liberating North Korea. What followed was a stalemate, whereupon constant fighting provided a suitably Orwellian backdrop for years of peace talks at Panmunjom. Americans largely rejected this new Cold War model. A *New York Times* article from April 1951 focused on public disenchantment rooted in seemingly contradictory goals: "They can 'take' casualties when there is a clear and stated objective, but if no such objective is apparent their national patience is certain to manifest itself."[42]

On a deeper, more personal level, there was also considerable resentment about the lack of shared sacrifice between the home front and the US military in South Korea. Journalist Eric Sevareid commented in 1952 that "American wars of this century have meant that some men have lived the worst life they had ever known, and nearly all the rest lived the best that *they* had ever known, and from the same cause."[43] One marine who came home from Korea in 1952 put it this way: "In the vernacular, nearly everyone here is fat." He also noted, "A badge of honor no longer goes with sacrifice. The temper of the times bid otherwise."[44]

Within the military, policies designed to ease the burdens of Korean service inadvertently caused additional dissent among the troops. In 1951, the Defense Department started a rotation policy designed to limit exposure to the war. Combat troops could earn 4 points for each month in the line and rotate home after accumulating 36 points.[45] Overall, the rotation system was an attempt to compensate for the hectic, often chaotic, system of mobilization that had called up draftees, reservists, and National Guard troops for deployment at the outset of the war. In October 1951, the Joint Chiefs of Staff reported that they had "plans in operation to bring veterans back as fast as replacements could be found," relying on a "first in, first out" system that gave priority to World War II veterans recalled to active duty.[46] As the war continued, the purpose of the draft was not only to sustain a military force necessary for operations in Korea but also to replace the constant stream of men being rotated home.

As was the case in Vietnam, the rotation policy heavily influenced the nature of military service in Korea. A May 1951 newspaper article claimed that military morale had essentially become a function of the rotation system: "To the G.I., the most important aspect of this war is his ability to keep alive until he is rotated."[47] While other factors clearly played a part in defining the relationship between soldiers and the war, there is a kernel of truth in this broad conclusion. The importance of the rotation system pointed to the absence of a nobler, overarching purpose to the Korean War. In "College Men at War," a lengthy study published in 1957 that examined veterans of World War II, John Monks revealed that 76.8% found the prospect of service in Korea "definitely distasteful," while 18.3% were "indifferent." Only 1.1% said they would be glad to return to active duty.[48] Monks's research, like the *New York Times* piece, illustrates the fact that personal, subjective qualities were more important in defining Korean War military service than any universal concept of national duty. Lacking other finite goals like capturing an enemy capital or awaiting unconditional surrender, two staples of older, more conventional wars, men applied their own standards. They served and waited for their obligations to expire. Career professionals at the core of the military faced their own challenges. A 1953 Defense Department report noted "instability and abnormal hardship" in maintaining combat effectiveness. Moreover, "disruptions of family life have increased living costs, multiplied personal problems, strained marital relations, and, in many instances, destroyed families."[49] In the end, Korea produced a strange hybrid regarding military service. Although a "hot war" in practice, its veterans treated participation more as a temporary, peacetime interruption of civilian normalcy. Many appeared as vested as the public back home in making Korea a "forgotten" war.

Joining Up during Vietnam

Service during the Vietnam War rested on a foundation similar to that of Korea, although it produced much different outcomes. The abstract concept of containment persisted from the fifties into the sixties, creating a box that trapped each president as he took his turn in office. Discussing the need to maintain American credibility in the Cold War against priorities at home, Lyndon Johnson told Doris Kearns Goodwin in 1970: "I was bound to be crucified either way I moved. If I left the woman I really loved—the Great Society—in order to get involved with that bitch of a war on the other side of the world, then I would lose everything at home."[50] However, as Kearns later wrote, the former president's bitterness failed to take into account his own hubris. Johnson believed for a time that he could simultaneously control events in Vietnam as he built the Great Society. His failure is a testament to his arrogance.

As much as Johnson deserved blame for Vietnam during and after his presidency, the onus was not all on him. When his administration escalated the war without a mass mobilization, it did so for the same reasons Truman and Eisenhower avoided the decision. A full-scale commitment of American power to Vietnam would have meant a severe disruption of the postwar economic boom at home, a decision tantamount to political suicide. Leslie Gelb points out that the public and, consequently, American political leaders pursued a muddled contradiction with respect to the war in Southeast Asia. On the one hand, they bought into the imperative that South Vietnam could not fall to communism, but with a series of constraints regarding the cost of this effort. Interestingly, the Korean experience figured into this calculation. Very few people had any illusions about victory from an early point. In the fall of 1965, 30% of those polled believed that Vietnam would end in a stalemate like Korea, 29% believed the United States would be victorious, while 26% made no prediction.[51] Between 1965 and 1968, the public generally supported escalation, while it expressed concerns over cost. During the US buildup, polls consistently reflected support for Operation Rolling Thunder, the strategic bombing offensive against North Vietnam. In contrast, when asked if the United States should take a more direct role in the war effort, without South Vietnam as an ally, the response was consistently negative.[52]

The year prior to the Tet Offensive perhaps best illustrates the tension between support for the war and resistance to its costs. In August 1967, the Johnson administration announced a 10% surcharge on corporate and individual income taxes, a measure intended to compensate for the rapidly increasing cost of the Vietnam War. The tax increase took away the cushion enjoyed by most households that had not contributed a father or son through the draft or by volunteering. Consequently, almost immediately after the announcement, polling reacted strongly against the war. Both Gallup and Harris noted for the first time those who believed the war was a "mistake" (47%) outnumbered those who thought it was not (44%).[53] However, throughout 1967, more than half of those polled still favored increasing air attacks on North Vietnam.[54]

This particular "box" dictated manpower policy to an important degree during the Vietnam War. At the start of the US buildup, Johnson explored and rejected the option of mobilizing 235,000 reservists for active duty.[55] As many historians have subsequently noted, the decision was almost entirely political. Johnson was a junior senator from Texas during the pell-mell 1950 preparations for Korea. He had no intention of repeating Truman's mistake by provoking the well-organized and influential constituency that comprised the National Guard and reserves.

His decision seriously warped the standards for who joined up during Vietnam. The US military met part of the increasing demand for manpower by cannibalizing active-duty units in other US responsibilities, particularly NATO. The draft provided a portion of the remainder. As the United States ramped up its involvement in South Vietnam, the Selective Service System followed suit. In 1964, there were 21,000 American military personnel involved in the war. By the end of 1965, more than 180,000 had been deployed to Southeast Asia; a year later, the number stood at 235,000. At the war's peak in January 1969, a total of 543,000 Americans were serving in and around South Vietnam.[56] Draft calls rose in concert with troop deployments: from 103,328 in 1965, to 343,481 in 1966, to 298,559 in 1967, and 383,000 in 1968. However, averaging just 40,000 inductees a month, the tempo of Vietnam conscription never reached the levels of World War II (200,000/month) or Korea (80,000/month).[57]

Volunteers are what sustained force levels throughout the Vietnam War. From August 1964 to February 1973, approximately 25% of those who served were draftees.[58] The remainder joined up willingly, in contrast to the 38% of enlisted strength drafted for Korea and the 10.1 million men inducted for World War II service.[59]

It is important to understand two characteristics of volunteers during the Vietnam War. The first was that they originated from a fairly representative cross section of America. In 1964, for example, approximately 17% of the men joining the army had some college education. Between 1965 and 1968, the number of men with some college training volunteering for service tripled and remained consistently higher than those without any higher education.[60] A 1981 survey of 1,380 Vietnam veterans indicated that college graduates (15%) and men with graduate school training (7%) outnumbered those without high school diplomas by more than three to one.[61] Military racial

Table 1.1. The principal occupations of fathers of veterans and nonveterans in the study population (percentage)

Father's occupation	*Vietnam veterans*	*Vietnam-era veterans*	*Nonveteran*
Professional-technical	8	7	17
Managerial	15	15	19
White collar	8	10	10
Crafts	21	24	20
Blue collar	47	43	33

Source: Arthur Egendorf, Charles Kadushin, Robert S. Laufer, eds., *Legacies of Vietnam: Comparative Adjustment of Veterans and Their Peers: A Study Conducted for the Veterans Administration* (New York: Center for Policy Research, March 1981), 105.

demographics also generally paralleled civilian society. At the outset of the Vietnam War, African Americans represented approximately 10% of the US armed forces, a number similar to their proportion of the general population.[62] Some disparities do appear with respect to class and occupations. When examining the principal occupations of veteran's fathers, the 1981 survey found that 8% of those who served in Vietnam and 17% of nonveterans had fathers in the "professional-technical" field. However, the "managerial," "white-collar," and "crafts" fields were roughly similar.

A second characteristic is also important to consider when evaluating volunteers, draftees, and military service. In *The Draft*, George Q. Flynn points out the often misunderstood distinction between military *entrance* standards and military *assignment* policy during Vietnam. When men entered the military, the Defense Department assignment process attempted to make cost-effective decisions that most benefited the military. Inductees with high aptitude scores and longer enlistments justified an investment of more expensive training. These individuals were important to a military institution that, by the mid-sixties, was increasingly reliant on logistical support and modern technology. By 1968, only 29% of total US military personnel were actually assigned to the combat arms, down from approximately 60% during World War II.[63] Generally, better-educated volunteers and conscripts gravitated toward support specialties. Draftees with a legal commitment of only two years' active-duty service and men with lower aptitude scores tended to be placed in the combat arms, where training standards were lower and less expensive for the military in the long run. On the surface, this system appeared patently unfair to the layperson as it placed disproportionate numbers of poorly educated, minority, and blue-collar men in harm's way. For the Pentagon at the height of the Robert McNamara years, it represented a logical, albeit ruthless, means to maximize efficiency.

As the emerging public debate turned against the Vietnam War, it generally failed to make these, or other, subtler distinctions. Hawks and doves conflated the expansion of the conflict into Laos and Cambodia, the fairness of the draft, and the culpability of individual soldiers for a larger institutional failure. The number of Americans who considered the war to be a "mistake" more than doubled between August 1965 (24%) and May 1971 (61%).[64] The emerging condemnation of the war carried over to a general condemnation of the military institution and its membership. According to a March 1971 Harris Poll, 82% of respondents believed that the draft had produced soldiers who did not want to fight, 61% responded that drugs had broken down military discipline, and only 59% believed that the American Army could "outfight any other army in the world."[65]

For the men and women who joined up between World War II and Korea, the decision reflected a complex combination of motives, some the product of personal preference and others likely subject to a larger social context surrounding all three wars. Patriotism and the desire to answer a call to arms in defense of the country clearly motivated many to put on the uniform. World War II offered a degree of clarity and a sense of purpose, although periodically exaggerated, for Americans who wanted to join up. During the next two wars, this quality diminished along with public support for conflict abroad. Service in Korea and Vietnam in some respects reflected a trajectory formed by the legacy of the good war that slowly bogged down as grudging skepticism matured into outright criticism. Military service, endured in 1945 despite horrific casualties as a necessary expedient, became a lightning rod inviting stigma and accusations of race and class bias by the early seventies.

Joining up was clearly a decision shaped by both personal preference and social context. Yet a significant portion of Americans who served in World War II, Korea, and Vietnam were, as one veteran's organization described them, "involuntary volunteers."[66] Tens of millions of Americans served as draftees, fulfilling a statutory requirement that extended almost unbroken from 1940 to 1973. As noted previously, World War II utilized the largest percentage of conscripts, with Korea and Vietnam relying on them in diminishing numbers.

However, the importance of the draft extends far beyond the statistics. Over the course of more than 30 years, the threat of conscription was a powerful motive to volunteer. Bradley notes that many of the Iwo Jima flag raisers, facing the prospect of having a military branch imposed on them, volunteered for the Marine Corps to at least be in charge of that part of their service.[67] After World War II, the Truman administration used the mere threat of the draft as a cheap means to bolster recruitment, a policy that proved successful prior to the Korean War.[68]

Perhaps the most important feature of American conscription between 1940 and 1973 was its impact on the terms and conditions of military service. "Selective service," by definition, came with a large array of conditions that were picked over and contested for more than three decades. The resulting Selective Service laws represented a constant struggle between military need and domestic politics. More often than not, the latter dominated the former.

In terms of raw numbers, the men available for conscription always appeared formidable. The original Burke-Wadsworth Act that initiated conscription in October 1940 required men 21 to 36 to register. Over the next five years, 49 million Americans eventually submitted their names for the draft.[69] When the War Department first considered conscription, planners saw a need to induct 1.5 million men in its first year.[70] However, as the war progressed, it became apparent that millions more were necessary to simply match the respective Axis militaries and effectively deploy adequate forces to fight overseas. Overall, more than 16 million Americans served during World War II. Yet this number did not come close to the available manpower pool. Finite national resources account for part of this disparity. Even with a massively expanded industrial base, there were practical limits to how many military personnel the United States could feed, clothe, arm, and transport during the war.

Economic limits aside, a series of deliberate decisions, contained specifically in American deferment policy, dictated manpower use during World War II, Korea, and Vietnam. Again, practical considerations were unavoidable. In times of war and peace, the country needed to feed itself and provide enough labor for its massive industrial base. Although policy makers could periodically tap new pools of labor—particularly women and minorities during World War II—coordinating economic and national security priorities was essential. This effort, while initially clumsy and difficult between 1941 and 1945, was ultimately successful. Neither Korea nor Vietnam involved the full-scale national mobilization of World War II, although both wars affected employment, inflation, and the overall national economy.

Once the issue of deferments moved beyond strategy and statistics, it became far more subjective and controversial. Local draft boards were perhaps one of the best illustrations of this problem. In terms of bureaucracy, they were a stroke of genius, allowing community leaders to implement a difficult national policy at the individual level. Unfortunately, local draft boards also invited parochialism and prejudice in their proceedings. Women were effectively banned from membership for years, as were minorities in most parts of the country. Draft boards in World War II initially proved reluctant to induct African Americans. Twenty years later, with incrementally larger minority membership they inducted significant numbers of African Americans, many of whom lacked educational and medical deferments. Charles Moskos's well-known study of race in the military noted that between 1960 and 1970, African Americans represented 16% of army draftees, although by 1971 they were 11.1% of the total armed forces. Draft boards in the sixties also experienced the same "generation gap" prevalent in America at the time. A 1966 Presidential Commission on Selective Service reported that the majority of active draft board members were white men over the age of 50.[71]

When draft boards examined potential inductees, the types and legitimacy of different deferments made their decisions even more complex. World War II started an extensive and sometimes bitter national debate about what constituted a valid reason to stay out of the service. Some questions were resolved relatively quickly. In 1941, the courts ruled that the potential loss of a college athletic scholarship did not constitute a convincing burden to a potential draftee. Professional teams also abandoned their objections to the draft early in the war.[72]

A man's age and family standing proved to be a pricklier dilemma for the Selective Service System. Taken as a whole, policy makers wanted to protect the youngest eligible for service from war. Their arguments ranged from a sincere desire to shield young men from the horrors of combat to a more practical belief that teenagers lacked the required maturity for military service. Over the course of three wars, Selective Service often followed contradictory policies. In Korea, local draft boards were under orders to draft older men, aged 21 and over, to replace recalled World War II veterans. However, by 1952, US officials increasingly called up 19-year-olds to fill gaps left by discharged veterans and deferred older married men. The average age of an army enlisted man during World War II was 26 but only 23 during the Korean War.[73] This same trend continued into the sixties when young, unmarried, undeferred males became the inductees of choice during Vietnam.[74]

Fathers enjoyed a fluctuating status in all three wars. During World War II and Korea, manpower needs often overrode the protections enjoyed by married men. At the start of World War II, they were routinely deferred until it became apparent that thousands were entering into wedlock to avoid military service.[75] As the war progressed, Selective Service redefined deferments with "dependents" to include a wife and one or more children.[76] A year into the Korean War, husbands supporting only their wives again lost their deferments and became eligible for the draft.[77] By the time the United States began escalating troop deployments to South Vietnam, Selective Service generally did not reach men with children, in part because of the relatively smaller numbers of monthly call-ups, but largely because of the vastly expanded reservoir of individuals eligible for induction. The arrival of the baby boom, which increased the draft age cohort of 19- to 25-year-olds from 8 million in 1958 to 13 million by 1974, spared fathers from their military obligations.[78]

A man's work also constituted a hotly contested qualification on military service. As noted earlier, World War II required a massive increase in skilled and unskilled labor to support mobilization. Yet, even as the demand for both types of worked boomed, it became clear that the latter was far more vulnerable to the draft. For example, men classified as "operators" and "laborers" made up only 2.5% of 18- to 44-year-old workers but provided 41% of all men drafted in June 1945.[79] During the war, separate federal agencies, labor unions, and industries battled each other to determine which jobs were essential to mobilization. Specific sectors from shipbuilding to ammunition and aircraft production all argued that their work was essential to the war effort, a claim that extended into virtually every other sector of the economy. In 1944, the draft board of Clark County, Wisconsin, refused to induct 20 cheese makers, deeming their work essential to the war.[80]

Organized labor's role in the draft proved problematic throughout World War II. At first, the Selective Service System deferred to union leaders on the premise that it would improve industrial efficiency. Unfortunately, this honeymoon soon soured as individual plants and a number of powerful unions, most notably the United Mine Workers, broke the informal "no strike" pledge to pursue better wages and shut down key sections of the wartime economy.[81]

Industrial owners were also responsible for disrupting and manipulating the Selective Service process. Managers commonly threatened to remove essential status from individuals known to be union organizers. This particular measure was an often-used tool by the federal government as well. In 1943, Selective Service advised local draft boards to reclassify strikers as eligible for the draft.[82] During a 1943 coal strike, Roosevelt himself threatened to draft 250,000 miners between the ages of 38 and 45.[83]

The post-1945 boom and absence of full-scale economic mobilization for Korea and Vietnam almost entirely negated the issue of work deferments. For all appearances, American prosperity was adequate to support the increased military buildups necessary for the two wars. Moreover, each American president, from Truman to Nixon, was keenly interested in compartmentalizing the domestic economy from the disruptions of "hot" wars abroad. Although they largely failed to protect domestic prosperity from the costs created by the Cold War, most American men who were out of their early 20s and employed were generally safe from military service.[84]

Education proved to be one of most enduring obstacles constructed against the draft. From the outset, colleges and universities challenged the prospect of students leaving their campuses for the military under the 1940 Selective Service Act. When the Roosevelt administration introduced a revision to the law, reducing eligibility for conscription to 18, higher education immediately protested the potential demise of undergraduate programs and school closings. Reverend Robert I. Gannon, president of Fordham University, claimed, "The drafting of eighteen and nineteen year-olds, without the careful planning that we are sure is being made by Washington, would effectively cripple the colleges of the country."[85] Roosevelt was able to assuage fears to a degree by increasing War Department training programs within American universities. The army Specialized Training Program and the navy V-12 Program sent thousands of military personnel to college campuses around the country and offset draft call-ups in higher education to a degree.[86]

During the fifties, the increasing emphasis on educational standards throughout America had a corresponding ripple effect on deferments. As more Americans enrolled in college, the public developed a greater expectation that school was an appropriate reason to delay military service. By 1955, 300,000 students had been deferred to finish their studies.[87] Two years later, amid the panic over *Sputnik I* and the resulting space race with the Soviet Union, intellectual pursuits took even greater precedence.[88] Consequently, for millions of young men and baby boomers, completing the Selective Service College Qualification Test (SSCQT) to justify reclassification to 2-S (deferred for college) became a regular rite of passage.

The struggle to refine educational deferments created an interesting paradox within the US military. By the end of the fifties, 4.4% of the enlisted men in the army were college graduates.[89] However, as the Selective Service System exempted college-bound men in increasing numbers, the US military also resorted to accepting those with much lower mental abilities. In 1957, for example, 40% of those drafted scored between 10 and 30 on the Armed Forces Qualifications Test (AFQT), results placing their IQ scores between 70 and 90.[90] This situation presented a significant problem for the armed forces, particularly the branches increasingly dependent on sophisticated weapons systems. Despite this, educational deferments increased during the sixties by a factor of 10. In 1970, Selective Service deferred 2.3 million men to pursue school.[91]

By the mid-sixties, the Defense Department took a new tack with respect to education, portraying military service as a means to promote individual advancement rather than allow Selective Service to automatically disqualify men who failed to meet minimum mental standards. When Robert McNamara launched Project 100,000 in 1966, it appeared to combine the altruistic elements of the Great Society—depicting the Defense Department as "the world's largest educator of men"—with the concurrent need for additional manpower in South Vietnam.[92] In principle, Project 100,000 was an opportunity for disadvantaged draft-aged men who had been previously rejected for low scores on the AFQT that placed them in Category IV (between 10% and 30% on the test). Under the stated conditions of Project 100,000, Selective Service would now accept these individuals with the caveat that they would receive additional remedial training in the service. During World War II, military "special training units" provided education to the fourth-grade level for those who were illiterate, non-English-speaking personnel, and individuals in the lowest intelligence group, according to military intelligence tests. By 1945, 1 in 10 inductees received such training.[93]

McNamara praised the program for giving these generally poor and uneducated inductees "an opportunity to return to civilian life with skills and aptitudes which for them and their families will reverse the downward spiral of decay."[94] Between 1966 and 1968, Project 100,000 added approximately 250,000 men to the US military through the Selective Service System. In 1966, 25% of the army's recruits came from Category IV inductees. That same year, a full third of Project 100,000 men were African American.[95]

Beyond providing a new pool of poorly prepared recruits for the Pentagon, Project 100,000 was an abject failure that became a magnet for critics of the Vietnam War. Despite McNamara's optimism regarding the military education system, the individual service branches made practically no changes to their training standards to accommodate increasing numbers of Category IV draftees. Voluntary educational programs were eventually made available, but these affected only 7.5% of all Project 100,000 personnel.[96] Lacking skill levels adequate for most occupational specialties, approximately 37% of the so-called New Standards Men were assigned to the combat arms, a rate more than a third higher than that of other recruits.[97] Civil rights leaders almost immediately attacked the initiative for the disproportionate burden it placed on the black community. Floyd McKissick, national director of the Congress of Racial Equality, called the program "a cynical method to punish black youths for the social ills imposed on them by the major society."[98]

For most of its tenure, the draft generated controversy that inspired both individual and collective resistance. The sources of this dissent were complex, shaped by biases within each amended version of the Selective Service law and, often more subtly, prejudices rooted in contemporary American society. As occurred during most American wars, resistance to military service was a constant during World War II, Korea, and Vietnam. However, as it continued, the dissent evolved and became both broader and more systemic by the time the Vietnam War began to escalate.

At the start of World War II, legislators understood that a small contingent of American men might reject military service for religious reasons protected by the law. The original 1940 Selective Service Act defined conscientious objectors (COs) beyond traditional churches like the Quakers and Mennonites, as in World War I, to include anyone "who, by reason of religious training and belief, is conscientiously opposed to participation in war in any form."[99] The decision was controversial, yet few took advantage of the new option. Throughout the war, only 42,973 American men claimed CO status. More than half sought service as medics or other noncombatants. Another 12,000 worked for the federal government in the United States. Approximately 6,000 went to prison for their moral convictions.[100] In Korea, COs increased to a degree, with approximately 25,000 declaring CO status in a far smaller number of troops mobilized for the conflict.[101] During the Vietnam War, however, the number of COs rapidly increased along with growing troop deployments to Southeast Asia. In 1964, 7,900 declared CO status; by 1970 this had increased to 61,000.[102]

In each of the three wars, American men had the right to appeal their conscription through official channels within the Selective Service System. During World War II, a relatively insignificant three per thousand took this option. By the time the United States was fighting in Korea, it had increased to 47 per thousand inductees. At the peak of the Vietnam War in 1969, appeals had more than doubled to 98 per thousand.[103]

Enormous numbers of men also avoided military service because of medical deferments. Between 1940 and 1945, Selective Service disqualified approximately five million men for physical and mental disabilities. The sheer scale of the problem provoked a larger discussion on the impact of the Great Depression on national health and national policies necessary to fix it.[104] Few answers were forthcoming. At the outset of the Korean War, identical health concerns reappeared within the available manpower pool. Almost a third of examined personnel were disqualified for mental and physical reasons. Lacking viable alternatives, the military reduced standards to replenish the ranks of draftees for Korea deployments.[105]

During the Vietnam War overall medical deferments remained significant but increasingly took on a character that set them apart from the earlier wars. In 1966, 24.2% of men failed their draft physicals; by 1969 that number had increased to 32.5%. The largest increases appeared to be in northern states. Massachusetts had a 45.7% failure rate in 1969; New York's was 42.3%.[106] Poor men, who lacked the benefits of the modern American health-care system and who were still beyond the reach of Great Society programs like Medicaid, were disqualified for military service at consistent, historical rates. However, accompanying traditional medical obstacles—malnutrition, the absence of early preventive health care—were more deliberate actions taken to manipulate the medical system. A 1970 *New York Times* article reflected on the increasingly common practice for family doctors to support Selective Service appeals based on preexisting conditions such as asthma. Well-to-do families with sympathetic medical professionals could often produce extensively documented maladies to go with their appeals. The author cited one faculty member at Dartmouth, who estimated that as much as 60% of the school's senior class was permanently disqualified from military service for medical reasons.[107]

The story of medical deferments in 1969 points to two important trends regarding Selective Service and draft resistance during the three wars. For the most part, public support for conscription paralleled a larger public consensus that tended to support social, political, and economic institutions after 1945. When Selective Service began in 1940, the majority of people tolerated it because they believed that the system was generally equitable. Although constantly contested during World War II, the sheer size of mobilization and the burdens it placed on a broad cross section of American society reinforced an overall sense of fairness.

By the sixties, this consensus was badly eroded. As mentioned previously, civil rights leaders constantly challenged the nature of African

American sacrifices on the battlefield, letting their disproportionate casualty rates serve as a referendum on the draft. Others raised the increasing influence of class distinctions on service. Numerous studies conducted during the Vietnam War indicated working-class and poor families were far more likely candidates for the draft and the combat arms.[108] The perceived higher likelihood of death by virtue of exposure to combat naturally sharpened this debate.[109] A study of Chicago residents who served in Vietnam revealed that men from poor neighborhoods were three times as likely to die than residents of wealthy neighborhoods.[110]

Unfortunately, the highly charged issues of class and race did not provide a complete picture of the draft or its application. A great deal of the crisis of faith in Selective Service was defined by ignorance. It is important to note how few Americans understood even the basic terms of military service under the draft. A study commissioned in 1970, for example, noted that 50% of people surveyed did not know that draftees had a two-year service obligation.[111] Other facts about combat in Vietnam were far more arcane but important to the issue of risk and death. The Vietnam War reversed trends prevalent in World War II regarding the geographic origins, race, and education of combatants. In the earlier conflict, the burden of combat was more evenly spread across the service branches. Bomber crews, infantry, and marine units were among the hardest hit in terms of casualty rates. The US force structure during Vietnam skewed this shared burden. Ground units carried the brunt of the war. During World War II the Army Air Corps suffered 17.9% of total casualties, while in Vietnam the US Air Force incurred 2.8% of deaths and wounds suffered by American forces.[112] Consequently, draftees, who made up a large portion of ground combat assignments in Vietnam, suffered disproportionate casualties by virtue of factors that went beyond class and race.

A second trend that emerged with respect to draft resistance was its growing sophistication. In *The Nightingale's Song*, Robert Timberg makes note of the extensive "draft counseling" infrastructure that existed throughout the Vietnam War.[113] It is a common assumption that the war brought about the creation of a network designed to support draft evasion in the sixties. This is historically untrue. During the Civil War and World War I, religious groups represented the core constituencies raising objections to compulsory military service. As noted earlier, during World War II, they were joined by a number of secular organizations intent on defining the terms of Selective Service.

The postwar peacetime draft introduced a type of military service that was unprecedented in American history and one that transformed draft resistance in the modern era. When Congress debated the renewal of Selective Service in 1948, it did so without the imminent threat of war. At the time, defense cuts drove much of the conventional wisdom regarding military preparedness. American foreign policy was largely defined by trade and aid, the crux of both the Truman Doctrine and the Marshall Plan. The absence of a clearly defined threat fueled opposition to the draft. During the 1948 presidential election, the Progressive Party made opposition to the peacetime draft one of its central tenets. National organizations, such as the Central Committee on Conscientious Objection, formed to offer overt guidance on draft resistance. The hardening Cold War, punctuated by the collapse of Nationalist China, Soviet acquisition of the atomic bomb, and the Korean War, seriously contested this dissent but did not eliminate it.[114]

If the 1948 draft law triggered challenges to Selective Service's goals, the Korean War placed its methods into serious doubt. The hectic mobilization following the North Korean invasion eventually met the needs of the US armed forces but at the cost of considerable domestic political capital.[115] As the fifties proceeded, the premium placed on student deferments blossomed into a rift that divided increasingly large segments of American society. Ironically, when the Selective Service System attempted to broaden participation to compensate for Vietnam deployments, extending the draft into the existing college population, it produced a proportional backlash. Proposals from Selective Service and Congress to reclassify student draft protesters for induction as punishment precipitated an open break with the Justice Department and the courts and made matters far worse. In the end, the draft achieved neither efficiency nor fairness, accumulating along the way multiple layers of controversy that redefined military service in largely negative ways.

Hindsight indicates that, years before the Vietnam War began winding down, the draft was already on its last legs. The crisis of faith that eventually plagued American military and political institutions had already reached the Selective Service System. In November 1966, a Harris Poll indicated that 49% of respondents believed the draft was fair.[116] In contrast, at the end of World War II, 79% of the public agreed that draft boards were fair.[117]

Function followed public intent. A series of draft reforms paralleled the Vietnam War. Student deferments continued unchecked even as deployments to South Vietnam demanded ever-greater numbers of men. Selective Service experimented with a draft lottery. After 1969, the number of men drafted steadily declined in concert with American troop withdrawals. By 1973, Selective Service inducted only 50,000 men, a fraction of manpower mobilization at the height of the Vietnam War.[118] That same year, conscription ended, and with it one of the primary systems defining military service in modern America.

The "Onerous Obligation" of Cold War Military Service

America spent most of the period under consideration in a technical state of peace. The half decade after World War II and the 12 years that passed between Korea and deployment of major ground forces to Vietnam were filled with constant tension but not open conflict. Even during the two "hot" wars in Asia, most Americans in uniform served elsewhere, on posts scattered across the United States or bases surrounding Communist bloc countries throughout the world. The maintenance of these forces over the course of two generations determined a significant part of the modern veteran's experience.

The intent at the start of the Cold War was to apply the hard-won lessons of World War II to the issue of military service. Advocates for readiness argued that the Unites States could not subsist on the tradition of a small peacetime military and geographic distance from threats to American security. The nature of modern warfare, particularly with its refinement of long-range air power equipped with atomic weapons, exposed this embedded historical practice as obsolete.

One proposed alternative was universal military training (UMT). This option offered the advantage of creating a large mass of consistently trained men who could be quickly mobilized in the event of a national crisis. Supporters also argued that the universal nature of service, in contrast to the existing Selective Service law, would make the burdens of postwar American security more equitable. Veterans groups such as the American Legion wholeheartedly endorsed the idea of universal military service from the outset. In 1942, it recommended one year of training for all males before their twenty-second birthdays as well as "pre-induction training and education" in colleges and high schools.[119]

Despite these apparent advantages, the UMT proposal failed badly after World War II. Many critics repeated arguments that were familiar during the neutrality debates before Pearl Harbor: mandatory service was inherently undemocratic; it would foster militarism in the country and subvert existing political institutions. Congress rejected UMT for reasons cited during World War II. Lawmakers believed that universal training placed an undue burden on the country and would not serve the "national interest" criterion contained in existing Selective Service law.[120]

Apart from UMT, the Truman and Eisenhower administrations' overall approach to readiness after 1945 seems almost counterintuitive to an observer today. With the brief exception of the Korean War surge, the US military experienced years of continuous retrenchment after World War II. This decline is made all the more interesting since, at the time, the country, as well as the Congress, contained a gigantic mass of veterans from wars extending back to the nineteenth century.[121] When Omar Bradley took over the Veterans Administration (VA) in 1945, eight Civil War veterans were still under its care. The 80th Congress that entered office in 1947 counted more than half of its members as veterans.

Yet this constituency did not arrest substantial budget cuts. Presented with a $15 billion defense budget the armed forces considered minimal for "austerity" operations, Truman slashed spending an additional 30% and sought even more savings from the military.[122] Consequently, at the start of the Korean War, the US armed forces were more than 500,000 personnel below their authorized strength. When hostilities broke out, the army could count on the 82nd Airborne as its only combat-ready division.[123] After Korea, manpower cuts returned, driven by Eisenhower's fiscal conservatism. His nuclear-dependent "New Look" emerged as a cost-saving substitute of technology for large standing forces. During the fifties, American ground forces took the brunt of the military economy campaign.[124]

Nor did the mass of veterans in American society counterbalance the declining prestige of active-duty military service. A 1948 survey of the military profession expressed numerous public doubts regarding the armed forces. Many considered the military to comprise the dregs of society that would expose new recruits to "loose morals and evil companions."[125] A similar stigma persisted after the Korean War. An October 1953 Department of Defense manpower study complained: "There exists an unwholesome amount of irresponsible criticism of the implementation of our national military policies. The more vociferous critics aim their slanderous attacks at our military leaders whom they refer to derogatorily, collectively and repeatedly, as 'the brass.' More recently 'the brass' has been extended to connote all career military officers as a class."[126] According to a 1955 poll, those surveyed rated a mail carrier, plumber, and garage mechanic over enlisted members of the military as career options. The same survey rated a public school teacher over a military officer.[127] The key target audience for recruiters, American youth between 16 and 20, saw military service as an "onerous obligation."[128]

A number of factors may explain this decline. Historically, Americans treated military service as an unwelcome expedient necessary to restore the peacetime status quo. In peacetime, the once-celebrated soldier saw his prestige diminish as civilian priorities reasserted themselves. Truman and Eisenhower could pursue their respective economy drives because they were popular. Despite his lifelong military record, as president, Eisenhower was fixated on balanced budgets; he was unwilling to let military spending "bankrupt" the postwar boom.[129] In his 1953 "Peace in the World" speech, he presented a stark picture of the zero-sum calculation regarding American security policy: "We pay for a single fighter plane with a half million bushels of wheat. We pay for a single destroyer with homes that could have housed more than eight thousand people. This is—I repeat—the best way of life to be found on the road the world has been taking. This is not a way of life at all, in any true sense. Under the cloud of threatening war, it is humanity hanging from an iron cross."[130] Large electoral majorities agreed with his priorities.

A more proximate reason for declining attitudes toward the military was the general unpopularity of the Korean War. Americans did not openly protest its confusing objectives and controversial methods. However, they did exit the conflict with a clearly established sense of skepticism regarding the Cold War conflicts. When Eisenhower proposed replacing ground forces with a muscular nuclear deterrence, he shrewdly cultivated a domestic backlash against Korea. Many contemporary writers even claimed that the foot soldier was obsolete in the new age of push-button war.[131]

Continuing reservations about the military percolated into popular culture, where it touched many potential recruits. Although men like Philip Caputo and Ron Kovic would be inspired by the glory of war from the *Sands of Iwo Jima*, films produced after Korea conveyed a much darker perspective. *Attack* (1956), *Paths of Glory* (1957), *Pork Chop Hill* (1959), and *Hell Is for Heroes* (1962) all represent a pervasive sense of principles gone badly wrong. A *New York Times* film critic applauded *Paths of Glory*, Stanley Kubrick's first major release, for its depiction of "agonizing, uncompensated injustice."[132] *Pork Chop Hill* was notable for juxtapositioning the absurdity of enormous casualties and individual bravery against the Panmunjom peace talks, which treated the sacrifices of both sides as a political bargaining chip.[133]

The American military inadvertently diminished its own image during the course of the Cold War. The armed forces of the fifties and sixties were distinctly different from the small, cloistered institution that predated World War II. They were, despite budget cuts, far larger than the tiny pre-1939 military. In 1961, the US Army alone maintained more than a million men and women under arms, a number far larger than the force of 227,000 in place when Germany invaded Poland.[134] The size of the military in the fifties, populated by an endless stream of short-term draftees, fostered an increasingly anonymous culture. A 1960 publication described military service as "marginal and ambiguous."[135] David Hackworth, who enlisted after World War II and served in Korea, captured the spirit of the New Look military in the decision to add individual name tags to uniforms:

> *Name tags were all very well for the new-style officer who stayed in a peacetime command only long enough to jockey his way into a better, career-furthering slot: why bother memorizing names, went his thinking, he'd never use again? But for the trooper, personalized uniforms were just another gimmicky example of an increasingly impersonal, almost corporate Army—one difficult to love, let alone have the allegiance to that would serve him and the country well in the event of war.*[136]

Military culture shifted further when manpower policy between the wars attempted to make a career in the armed forces more competitive with those in the civilian sector. Defense officials placed increasing emphasis on pay, medical benefits, and housing. Overall, between 1945 and 1955, gross compensation for all military personnel increased by 19%, bringing them closer to compensation in the civilian sector.[137] Individuals with special skills could earn even more. An airman on flight status in 1949 made more ($3,135) than the median annual income after taxes ($2,998) of an American family with a head of household under 35. The armed forces offered better pension plans to the extent that they did not require employee contributions and, by law, became available after 20 years of service.[138] A young man right out of high school could "retire" at 38 or start a whole new career. Better compensation also allowed service members to support families to an unprecedented extent. The Cold War witnessed an enormous increase in "dependents" in military families, from only 67,000 in 1940 to 500,000 by 1971.[139]

The peacetime Cold War military reinforced priorities that had little to do with its mission. To make the "onerous obligation" more palatable, the defense establishment improved working conditions often at the expense of military readiness. Aside from a small core of career professionals, the constant turnover of personnel significantly reduced the cohesiveness of "primary groups," the squad- and platoon-level units absolutely critical to survival in combat.[140] One author commented in 1960 that "for most draftees the army becomes an eight hour job."[141]

Maintenance of the peacetime armed forces also produced a distinctly different set of expectations for men and women entering the military at the outset of the Vietnam War. Manpower policy compromises, in addition to alterations to Selective Service deferments, produced a system in which institutional priorities became increasingly vulnerable to individual prerogatives. Writing about baby boomers in the fifties, sociologist Doug McAdam noted, "Instead of waiting to grow to adulthood to occupy center stage, as most generations have to do, the postwar generation had the stage turned over to them at an early age. Or perhaps more accurately, they had a stage constructed especially for them."[142] McAdam's research addressed the impact of affluence on white members of the emerging civil rights movement, but it is clear that similar trends were finding their way from civilian society into the American military. The sense of individualism that would become a touchstone of the sixties clearly influenced service in the armed forces. For all outward appearances, the military institution of the sixties may have resembled that of World War II, but internally, it was the product of a new generation with markedly altered individual and collective priorities.

The Nature of Minority Volunteers and Draftees

Minorities served in large numbers and with distinction in World War II, Korea, and Vietnam. Approximately one million African Americans participated in the US military during World War II, making up 16% of all American enlisted personnel.[143] However, when the Truman administration officially desegregated the military in 1948, African American participation had shrunk to 5.9% of the total armed forces, about half their total portion of the civilian population.[144] When the Vietnam War started, African Americans composed approximately 10% of the US armed forces.[145] Accurate estimates of Hispanic military service are more difficult to ascertain given their relatively smaller numbers and absence of consistent statistics. During World War II, approximately 375,000–500,000 Mexican Americans and 119,000 Puerto Ricans served, approximately 2.5% of the total. In Korea, this number increased to 4.0%, and in Vietnam, 4.2%.[146]

A complex set of expectations motivated minority service, many of which transcended the controversies surrounding race in America. As was the case for many citizens, patriotism clearly played a part in the decision to join up. Reflecting on his decision to enlist in the US Marines in 1963, an African American veteran recalled, "I grew up in a family that was fair. I was brought up on the Robin Hood ethic, and John Wayne came to save people."[147] When Joseph Lopez joined the army in 1955, his father encouraged him to serve as part of his obligation as the first generation to be born in America.[148]

Other motives were more tangible. The existing data suggest that minority recruits joined for the opportunities—pay, benefits, and the prospect of training—offered by the armed forces. According to a 1964 National Opinion Research Center survey, African Americans cited "self-advancement" as the primary reason for joining the military.[149] These figures are consistent with a 1981 VA study in which black Vietnam veterans considered service-related benefits (education, health care) more important (58.2% to 37.6%) to their decision than white Vietnam veterans did.[150] These attitudes corresponded to a greater desire among African Americans to make the military a career. Charles Moskos's study reported that African Americans reenlisted at twice the rate of white servicemen before 1968. Individuals interested in a military career were also more prone to seek out and accept high-risk assignments, such as airborne and combat units, for the sake of additional pay and promotion. By the conclusion of the Vietnam War, this produced a growing prevalence of African Americans in leadership roles, particularly senior noncommissioned officers in the combat arms.[151]

Intangible factors also played an equal if not more important role in motivating minorities to join up. African American and Hispanic men took political rhetoric linking war with social progress to heart. When Franklin Roosevelt spoke of the universal rights embodied in the Four Freedoms in 1941, the National Association for the Advancement of Colored People (NAACP) echoed these concepts in its famous "Double V" campaign. During the Cold War, the contest between the free world and the Communist bloc spurred inevitable pressures to redefine civil rights in America. When Héctor García founded the American G.I. Forum for Hispanic veterans in 1948, it was with the expectation that citizenship extended to all Americans regardless of race.[152]

Consequently, as William Arce, a scholar of Latino service in Korea and Vietnam observes, war and military service promoted the possibility of renegotiating the value of American citizenship. In a period marked by recurrent war and superpower tension, circumstances made military service a valued common denominator in American society. Consequently, minorities who were willing and able to participate in the armed forces could occupy a place in the social mainstream by virtue of their sacrifice for the common good. Arce points out that success or failure in this process was more complex than simply assimilating into the majority culture or rejecting it (or being rejected by it). Instead, what military service did was provide a means for advancement (training, education, prestige) that fostered higher expectations and the ability to transfer racial and ethnic identity into the core of society.[153]

Many of these expectations started in the military itself. Although clearly not free of the racism existing in mainstream American society, the armed forces by virtue of their emphasis on merit, offered opportunities that often placed them far ahead of the rest of the country after World War II. National polls in 1965 and 1966 illustrated the belief among African Americans that they would receive fairer treatment in the military.[154] Thomas A. Johnson, writing in July 1968, remarked that African American veterans frequently left the service with the understanding "that the dramatic racial changes in military service, especially in Vietnam, would be reflected in civilian life."[155]

In more than a few cases, hope prevailed over the past and personal experience. While some fathers imparted to their sons the sense of patriotism that led them to enlist, other men exposed to the racism of the segregated military in World War II were far less supportive. Harold Bryant's father drove supply trucks as part of the "Red Ball Express" during Patton's drive across France and counseled his son against enlisting in 1965.[156] Pinkie Houser joined the army in 1964 despite opposition from her brother and a sister, air force veterans who had served in the fifties.[157] Similarly, many Hispanics deliberately set aside racism produced by personal experience and official policy (e.g., mass deportations in the thirties and fifties) and decided to enlist anyway.[158]

Hope also prevailed against more direct threats. Minorities faced disproportionate danger in wartime, particularly during the Vietnam War. As discussed, casualty rates reflected a Selective Service System that exposed minority draftees to combat at a higher rate than the general population. Because minorities with low AFQT scores lacked college deferments and were at a disadvantage because of poor public schooling, the Pentagon disproportionately assigned them to the combat arms. Many minorities who were military careerists also sought out combat for better pay and promotions. The cumulative effect of both proved devastating. When major combat operations commenced in Vietnam in 1965, African Americans composed approximately 10% of the US armed forces. However, that same year, they made up 20% of combat troops. Between 1966 and 1967, African Americans suffered 25% of US battlefield deaths in South Vietnam.[159]

If Arce's argument that minorities could renegotiate their standing in America was true, Vietnam proved that the cost might ultimately be too great for individuals and the country. The prospect of death and injury far out of proportion to their numbers must have given many men reason to pause before volunteering or submitting to the draft. Muhammad Ali's refusal to submit to the draft in 1967 highlighted the early stages of a national debate that raged for years regarding military service, equity, and race. By the early seventies, as US forces began to pull out of South Vietnam, they were crippled by racial tensions that periodically exploded into full-scale rioting.[160] Stories illustrating the disillusionment of returning African Americans or Hispanics were commonplace in the American media.[161]

It appeared that, given a free choice with the end of Selective Service in 1973, minorities would abandon the armed forces. Yet the opposite happened. When the American military replaced the draft with an all-volunteer force, minorities enlisted in droves. By 1980, African American men made up 22.4% of the military and 32.9% of the army. Although according to official statistics, Hispanics lagged behind, making up approximately 4% of the US armed forces, time and shifting immigration trends soon altered that percentage. By 2000, Hispanics made up 9% of all enlisted personnel in the US military.[162] Clearly, difficult economic times and the absence of opportunities in the civilian job market drew minorities to the armed forces. However, these elements were present throughout the twentieth century.[163] It is equally likely that continued patriotism and a sense of hope for the future accompanied hard economic reality.

The Women Who Volunteered

All of the women who served during World War II, Korea, Vietnam, and peacetime were volunteers. The public mood regarding the prospect of drafting women was dictated by ambivalence throughout the period. During World War II, people generally appeared willing to contemplate inducting single women into uniform.[164] When the Korean War broke out, a large plurality (48%) of those surveyed supported drafting women for clerical duties.[165] During the sixties, national opinion took the opposite tack. In 1969, a similar plurality (49%) opposed including women in the Selective Service System. Two years earlier, a strong majority (58%) disapproved even drafting women for civilian medical service in the United States.[166] When Congress periodically renewed the Selective Service Act, it never seriously considered including women. This prompted one inventive challenge to the draft in 1970, when four men appealed their induction, claiming sexual discrimination.[167]

Table 1.2. Women in the US military

World War II	400,000
Korean War	120,000
Vietnam War	7,000

Source: US Department of Veterans Affairs, National Center for Veterans Analysis and Statistics, *America's Women Veterans: Military Service History and VA Benefit Utilization Statistics* (Washington, DC: Department of Veterans Affairs, November, 2011), 1.

Women's service during this period is remarkably small in terms of overall numbers. The mass mobilization of personnel for World War II prompted the largest inclusion of women in the military in the twentieth century. Approximately 400,000 eventually served during the course of the war. After 1945, however, the total number of women in the military dropped significantly over time.

Part of this decline can be explained by changes in the law and defense policy. The Women's Armed Services Integration Act of 1948 officially capped female enlisted strength in the US military at 2% of the total force structure. The statute reflected prevailing congressional and military attitudes that World War II was essentially an aberration with respect to personnel shortages. This standard did not undergo significant revision for another 20 years.[168] Manpower policy followed a similar track. In 1941, the Pentagon restricted the number of military occupations open to women to four. However, by war's end, through a combination of demonstrated ability and practical need, the list had expanded to include 239 separate specialties.[169] Retrenchment followed in the postwar period as the military rapidly shed personnel, particularly women, to keep pace with defense cuts. By 1958, the US Army offered 125 military occupational specialties to women, 32% of its total available. In the US Navy, women were allowed to serve in only 21 "ratings" (jobs).[170]

Contemporary American social norms also proved to be a substantial barrier to women's military service. When World War II concluded, the conventional wisdom after 1945 focused on reconstructing domestic stability in the country. Most Americans considered women to be an intrinsic part of this transition, both for returning veterans and their families. In November 1950, for example, Howard A. Rusk, chairman of the Selective Service Medical Advisory Committee, opposed even using women in war industries: "It would be a tragedy to take women out of their homes. Those who worked during the last war are now paying the price with the problems arising with their children."[171] Although feminists like Betty Friedan would begin a discussion regarding priorities other than husbands, family, and home, it would take another generation before this standard underwent serious change.

Legislative and social obstacles severely diminished the number of women in uniform after 1945. When the Korean War began, women constituted only 22,000 active duty personnel, approximately a third of whom were in medical services.[172] The frantic mobilization that followed quickly exposed the flaws in the 1948 law. New contingencies required additional women in logistical and health-care specialties. American military mobilization eventually included 120,000 women during the war.[173] Vietnam proved to be a different story. When the first American advisers deployed to assist the Saigon government, only a handful of women went with them.[174] As division-sized units began arriving in country, the number of women increased but was largely limited to essential medical support, particularly trauma care, and other logistical functions.[175]

Despite these many obstacles, women joined up for a variety of motives that remained consistent from World War II into the Vietnam era. Like their male counterparts, women volunteered out of a sense of sincere patriotism. Family tradition shaped much of what they saw as duty to the country. Georgia Jane Ford joined the air force in 1951 after her father expressed concern that Korea would be the first war since the American Revolution in which a Ford had not fought.[176] Becky Pietz's father claimed a lineage that took him back to Robert E. Lee. She was attracted to the idea of military service through family members and friends at Virginia Tech. Period cultural icons that attracted young men did not escape her notice: "You grow up with Audie Murphy and John Wayne movies, and—even if you're a girl—you know you're going to go and be a hero somewhere."[177] Like many young men, women thought that the military might provide an outlet for their restlessness and dissatisfaction with civilian life. After her friends enlisted, Constance Anderson, who served as an army nurse during the Korean War, was "determined to catch up with them and find them." She recalled that service offered exciting possibilities: "I was always looking over the hill for a greener pasture. . . . I felt maybe there was something out there that I haven't seen or needed to see."[178] Some had no idea why they chose the military or where it might take them. Mary Chatfield literally flipped a coin during the Vietnam War: "heads" took her into the air force as a nurse; "tails" would have taken her to Trans World Airlines as a stewardess.[179]

Superior pay and benefits clearly attracted many women to the military. In 1970, the pay and benefits for an E-1, the entry-level rank in the military, made $5,419.17 a year. This compared very favorably with professional ($5,099), clerical ($4,451), crafts ($4,557), and "operatives" ($4,309) positions available at the time for women between the ages of 18 and 24. Reenlistment rates reflected the attractiveness of military service for women at the end of the Vietnam War. By 1972, first-term reenlistments for women (40%) ran at almost twice the rate for men (23%).[180]

The type of woman who joined the military remained remarkably consistent over the course of three decades. As a group, they tended to be better educated than men, the product of their service in professional services like nursing. In one surveyed group of World War II servicewomen, 54% had various degrees of college training. The study recorded similarly high participation for women with service during Korea (44%) and the Vietnam era (53%).[181] Educational proficiency translated into higher mental classification than men. According to standardized testing, in 1972, there were more than twice as many women in Categories I and II than men.[182] Other social distinctions also stand out. Most women in the military were white and the products of middle-class families. In terms of age, female volunteers tended to parallel men. During World War II, a third were 25 or older when they entered the armed forces. During the Vietnam era, only 8% fit that category. However, in some occupations, the gap between men and women actually widened. A surveyed group of army nurses stationed in Vietnam had an average age of 23.6 years. Air force and navy nurses averaged 28.2 years old.[183]

The motives that drove women to volunteer may have mirrored those of the young men of the time in some ways, but many of the double standards that they endured did not.[184] A general ignorance regarding women's military duties persisted throughout the era. During World War II, few people could correctly identify the new military organizations created to organize female service. A 1943 *New York Times* story reported that a woman, spotting Lt. Cmdr. Dorothy C. Stratton on a train, asked: "Are you a Wac, a Wave, or a Spam?"[185]

A clear social stigma clung to women's military service during all three wars. Most American families reflexively rejected the idea that a young lady might be exposed to the harsh, vulgar, and corrupting influences of the active-duty military. One poll conducted during World War II noted that 41% of women who enlisted did so despite resistance from their relatives.[186] At the peak of the Vietnam War, as the sexual revolution began emerging in America, very little had changed. When she asked her parents to sign for her enlistment in 1969, Ann Powlas met with resistance: "In my mom and dad's day, during World War II, women in the service were considered to be bad people. They just knew I was going to come out a whore."[187]

Homosexuality was a constant source of concern. Speaking to a group of women in 1943, Lieutenant Commander Stratton assured them that "we're not amazons or something queer, but women trained to do a job."[188] By 1971, military recruiters seeking out female enlistees were well versed with the issue. Capt. Maureen Fullerton, a marine, assured parents that if their daughters "might encounter Lesbianism," the perpetrators would be immediately discharged from the military.[189]

Despite these formidable obstacles, women's volunteerism persisted and eventually broke down the barriers confronting it. Policy eventually changed to reflect this ongoing interest, women's proven utility to the armed forces, and the changing times. In 1967, Congress officially rolled back the 2% cap on service as well as the limitation on women holding senior rank. However, the declining popularity of the draft proved to be the decisive element in the defense establishment's "rediscovery" of women in the late sixties. Anticipating a significant shortage of men willing to accept voluntary enlistments, military officials addressed entry testing standards, training, and military occupations open to women.[190] One particular concern was the low retention rate for female recruits. Between 1966 and 1971, the navy had the highest retention rate (46.2%) for women with 30 months of service, while the Marine Corps had the lowest at only 27.6%.[191] The anticipated influx of women volunteers coincided with the end of the Vietnam War and the start of the all-volunteer military in 1973. Personnel shortages appeared almost immediately after the conclusion of the draft, and women rapidly filled them. By 1980, women made up a total of 171,000 personnel, or 8% of total active-duty forces.[192]

This late victory left two important legacies for the military and women veterans. The first regarded military assignment policies for women, specifically in combat roles. While the question of support and logistical duties had long been settled by actual experience, the debate over women in combat continued within as well as outside the military. What was the best course with respect to reconciling doctrine, mission effectiveness, and sex? The dissonance created by these questions directly affected perceptions regarding women's service for decades to come.[193]

A second important factor was the relatively small size of the female veteran contingent between World War II and Vietnam. According to the VA, by 1972, women made up only 1.9% of all living veterans.[194] Despite periodically increased mobilization in each of the three wars, the number complies almost exactly with the 1948 Women's Armed Services Integration Act. The past would have a clear impact on the future. Even as increasingly large numbers of women began to be incorporated into the military, institutions designed to support them lagged badly behind. This was particularly the case within the VA, which lacked appropriate internal protocols and staff to address the physical and mental disabilities incurred by women in military service.[195] Arguably, it would not be until the First Gulf War and deployments after September 11 that many of these veterans would receive long-awaited attention.

Conclusion

The volunteer spirit clearly motivated millions of Americans to defend the country in World War II, Korea, and Vietnam. Millions joined the armed forces for patriotism, for their belief in American democracy, or simply because they felt a sense of duty to their peers and fellow citizens. Others saw opportunities in the military: advancing themselves with new training or enjoying the possibility of adventure. However, volunteerism was a heavily qualified commitment for most Americans. The evolution of the Selective Service System illustrates just how many qualifications on military service—work, family status, education, race, and gender—accumulated over the course of 30 years. While most Americans considered military service a legitimate obligation, they clearly wanted to accomplish it on their own terms.

Volunteerism progressively involved incentives to service that took on a permanent, institutional form over time. For the individuals who served in World War II, the GI Bill came as an unprecedented collective reward for individual sacrifice that set a precedent for veterans' expectations afterward. Although it was not quite as expansive, the 1952 version of the GI Bill (the Korean Veterans' Assistance Act) reinforced the same expectations.[196] When the Bradley Commission published its report in 1956, it warned that "military service must be regarded as part of the responsibilities of a citizen."[197] This was only partly true at the time. To make military service more attractive, the defense establishment came to rely on a combination of appeals to patriotism but also pay, benefits, and other attributes that would make a military career competitive in the civilian marketplace. Ironically, Omar Bradley was arguing for temperance barely 10 years after he successfully secured these benefits as head of the VA. In 1956, it was too late to change course. The progressive commodification of military service was an entrenched reality.[198]

An author writing in 1971 drew the contrast between contemporary "veteranized" American society, containing millions of men and women with military experience, and an increasingly "civilianized" military.[199] Veterans permeated nearly every corner of life, reflecting the reality that military service had become a normal, expected rite of passage. However, this particular rite encompassed an accumulating number of qualifications and compromises that also reflected civilian standards and expectations.

Each war witnessed the influence of these "civilianized" standards on military service. At first glance, the standards governing expectations seem relatively straightforward. The pool of potential volunteers and draftees, along with the public as a whole, approached service with the expectation that the overall purpose of war would, in the end, justify their sacrifices. A "just war" was, in effect, a reward in and of itself. Additional, more substantive rewards—job training, housing, college tuition—translated the social consensus on war into a very tangible, personal form of recognition. World War II saw the strongest and most cohesive combination of these qualities. Once the country overcame doubts regarding neutrality, public opinion rallied behind the idea of service and mobilization moved forward. As the war neared its end, the focus shifted toward recognizing veterans' service. The GI Bill bypassed distinctions between draftee and volunteer by establishing a universal standard for individual recognition. The process was not without problems or conflicts, but, as Michael Shafer observes, the unprecedented scale of mobilization in World War II masked the numerous root compromises present in the Selective Service System.[200]

Korea saw many stress cracks form when the country attempted to resurrect military mobilization. A "hot" war in distant northeast Asia seemed difficult to comprehend much less serve as a public rallying point. Although most Americans retained a broadly held belief in service, by 1950 it was counterbalanced by the competing desire to enjoy a rapidly emerging postwar prosperity. Consequently, there was no massive mobilization to paper over the inequities of military service. To make matters worse, the public discussion regarding veterans' benefits took an alarming change of direction in the fifties. Rather than adopt an expansive, universal approach to rewarding veterans' service, "economy" was the watchword of the day. Retrenchment challenged recognition.

By the sixties, these stress cracks had widened into a chasm. Vietnam, in contrast to World War II or even Korea, was a limited conflict governed by deliberate, gradual escalation.[201] There was no shared burden to link the public with its military effort. Military service reflected its own form of escalation. Volunteers and draftees filled out American ranks but were subject to accumulating qualifications on service. During Vietnam, the reserves and National Guard stayed home. While significant numbers of college men and women were in uniform during Vietnam, education, income, and race became important cleavage points with respect to service, sacrifice, and recognition.

CHAPTER 2
The Warrior and the Veteran
The Combat Experience and Its Aftermath

We were all animals, really, torn between fear—I was mostly frightened—and a murderous rage at events. One strange feeling, which I remember clearly, was a powerful link with the slain, particularly those who had fallen within the past hour or two. There was so much death around that life seemed almost indecent.

—William Manchester, writing about his service in the Marine Corps during World War II[1]

Don't let the news media fool you. These kids may be eighteen or nineteen, but they're beautiful killers—just beautiful.

—US Army major assigned to the 25th Infantry Division in South Vietnam[2]

Introduction

Throughout modern history, there is a clear link between war and trauma to veterans. As far back as the American Civil War, military medicine referred to the physical signs of combat stress as "cardiac muscular exhaustion."[3] In the twentieth century, doctors found new labels for the same old problem. During World War I, it was "shell shock." In World War II and Korea, "combat exhaustion" collectively described the process by which soldiers deteriorated under the constant stress of battle. In the latter stages of the Vietnam War, the term "post-Vietnam syndrome" began to appear within a medical community attempting to ease veterans' successful reassimilation to civilian life.[4]

Labels touch only the surface of the combat experience and its impact on veterans of World War II, Korea, and Vietnam. Some distinctions were obvious to contemporary doctors. When mental health professionals like Robert Jay Lifton, Chaim F. Shatan, and Sarah A. Haley discussed the impact of combat on Vietnam veterans in the early seventies, their starting point was the unique features of an undeclared, guerrilla conflict on its participants.[5] Later scholarship picked up this same thread. "War Stress and Trauma," a 1984 article in the *Journal of Health and Social Behavior*, continued the theme that Vietnam was "new to the American experience" as it attempted to decipher the specific damage inflicted by unconventional war on its veterans.[6] Over time, this assumption broadened and hardened into an accepted fact within the mental health community, the media, and the general public. When Christopher Walken won an Oscar in *The Deer Hunter* (1978) for his portrayal of a mentally scarred Vietnam veteran, the label applied to one generation was already part of the mainstream. Sylvester Stallone embedded the cultural image further in *First Blood* (1982). However, the assumption begs a number of questions: Was it true? Was it limited to Vietnam? In reality, how much distance separated combat trauma in World War II from that in Korea and Vietnam? What other factors contributed to damage from combat and its aftermath?

The warrior has been and remains a powerful figure in society. Writing in 1973, Robert Lifton explained his value: "The warrior has always laid claim on our emotions. He has been celebrated by virtually all known cultures for his individual courage, and for the collective glory he makes possible. The quest for such glory is, in turn, part of man's general struggle, in the face of inevitable biological death, for a sense of immortality."[7] In their actions, warriors present an image that creates a sense of legitimacy to both individuals committed to combat and the societies they defend. As a reward for their sacrifices, warriors and their wars are remembered and commemorated through an ongoing series of social rituals that go back to time immemorial.

Yet, as an actor or a symbol, the warrior does not represent a fixed, immobile point in society. His definition is subject to the nature of the war in which he fights. Western society has debated the meaning of a "just war" for centuries, from medieval times to the aftermath of the September 11 attacks.[8] Presently, a great deal of time and effort has gone into understanding the contemporary public tolerance for war. Scholars and pollsters examine the clarity of war aims, casualties, the duration of conflict, and elite influence on opinion.[9] These issues are hardly new, but they do point to a significant reality. In a very important sense, the warrior's value is ultimately the product of the social consensus that defines his war.

Armies cannot escape the societies from which they are drawn. Basic cultural standards have a direct impact on the success or failure of military doctrine and operations. Harvesting and planting seasons dictated the cycles of military campaigns in colonial America. In the more recent past, racial segregation defined the limits of manpower policy in the United States. As Walter Millis noted in his landmark 1956 book *Arms and Men*, the American "way of war" was the product of the imperative of collective defense on the frontier as much as the growing tradition of consensual decision making in a colonial outpost far from England.[10]

It is also important to consider that, as much as warriors are derived from general society, the military is a unique culture. The standards and practices defining soldiers diverge from those of civil society almost as soon as a recruit dons the uniform. Combat takes this divergence a step further by placing both individuals and groups under the terrific stress of constant life-or-death situations. Veterans who exit combat are changed people, living in the wake of old virtues temporarily abolished by the exigencies of war and, perhaps more important, by the persistence of these changes back into civilian life.

The nature of the warrior is thus transitional and subject to a host of important influences. The type of war he fights and the general social discourse surrounding it form the framework that determines issues of legitimacy and recognition. Beyond general context, a warrior's behavior also determines his legacy. Combat by its very definition demands the sacrifice of civilian virtues important to the majority of society. The extent to which a warrior pursues this path defines how far he must depart from social norms. In a similar sense, this journey also determines just how far a veteran must return to reenter the society that produced him.

These same considerations apply to the warrior and his image in

American history. In a country born of revolution and frontier conquest, the warrior has always figured prominently in the evolution of our country and its society. This was clearly the case after World War II. Veterans who exited the conflict received the imprimatur of a society celebrating victory in the "good war" against Japanese and German fascism. Public policy like the Serviceman's Readjustment Act of 1944 reflected public acclaim. In politics, military experience became a key litmus test for office. After World War II, Americans routinely chose veterans to be president. As Lifton notes, service, particularly in combat, was an extremely effective way to make a "claim on our emotions" to establish a commitment to public duty. Many political figures sought this path out of sincerity, understanding in part the risks it entailed. Senator John Sherman of Kentucky enlisted as an army private in 1942 at the age of 41 and went on to serve in Patton's Third Army. Representative Olin Teague of Texas ended the war with three Silver Stars and Three Purple Hearts after serving in the 79th Infantry Division.[11] Other modern leaders were more calculating. Service in war was an obvious path to political acclaim, something evident to those who were legitimate heroes (like John Kennedy) or men who decided to embellish their time in uniform (like Lyndon Johnson).[12]

The definition of a warrior proved to be transitional after World War II. Both Korea and Vietnam challenged conventional understandings of warfare even as the US military clung to doctrine familiar to veterans of World War II. The prospect of nuclear escalation overshadowed both conflicts, applying restrictions on commanders and their troops. In Vietnam, efforts to combat a guerrilla enemy resulted in a contest notable for both its intimacy and calculated, massive savagery. At home, the wars in Korea and Vietnam illustrated a growing gap between combatants and civilians. Neither war demanded or received full-scale mobilization as World War II had in 1941. Consequently, on the face of it, it seemed that the warriors produced by both wars "laid claim" on fewer and fewer emotions. Korea became a forgotten war even as it was fought. Vietnam invited controversy that would define two generations of Americans. The veterans who came home from these conflicts apparently differed in significant ways from the men and women of 1945.

Accordingly, this chapter first examines the factors that shaped American combat veterans in three separate wars from 1941 to 1973.

It focuses on the nature of conflict in the latter half of the twentieth century with careful attention to the "American way of war" after 1945. World War II, for example, reinforced a doctrinal penchant for employing massive firepower against an enemy, something improved technology embellished as the United States entered Korea and Vietnam. After 1945, the American way of war also included doctrinal reforms designed to enhance individual participation in combat. The warrior, by design, was intended to be a more lethal element in modern conflict.

A second focus is the individual combat veteran. Each generation that fought entered with preconceptions of war shaped by the legacy of previous conflicts. It is important to understand that these legacies—passed forward by fathers, families, and society—may have been as important as military doctrine in molding the warrior-to-be. In many instances, the separation between personal expectations and the realities of the battlefield determined the fundamental elements of personal stability once the combat veteran came home.

Finally, it is important to understand American society's role in defining the "collective glory" that awaited and eventually encompassed the combat veteran. The larger social discourse set the boundaries of what constituted a hero. World War II established a distinct model of such a person. How permeable was this definition of a hero in subsequent conflicts? Conversely, the American public also engaged in a distinctly different debate after 1945 regarding the potential threat posed by combat veterans. What forms did these perceived threats take? Were they valid and consistent?

The Warrior Image during and after World War II

War was a constant feature of American life in the forties. World War II drew millions into the military, and victory did little to alleviate the national focus on conflict. A combination of international events and official policy presaged a Cold War era of constant mobilization. Peacetime brought about a public debate over universal military training in 1945. Although universal military training failed to materialize, Cold War tensions grew and a peacetime draft became part of everyday life. A large standing military was deemed necessary to provide teeth for the Truman Doctrine, first applied to Greece and Turkey in 1947, as well as the subsequent creation of NATO two years later. The collapse of Nationalist China and the Soviet test of its first atomic bomb provided a dramatic backdrop for the Red Scare and partisanship that roiled the late forties. Global confrontation that might escalate to global annihilation defined the new American "normalcy," a time when moments of crisis regularly punctuated daily life.[13] Looking back, an almost constant stream of open clashes and barely missed disasters—the invasion of South Korea, Communist Chinese intervention in the war, Quemoy and Matsu, Lebanon, Berlin, Cuba, Laos, South Vietnam—established clear milestones marking a period of constant tension.

By the sixties, American leaders routinely sought out and embraced confrontation. David Halberstam captured the nature of foreign affairs in the Kennedy years in *The Best and the Brightest*: "Force was justified by what the Communists did; the times justified the kind of acts which decent men did not seek, but which historic responsibilities made necessary."[14] While they might not have celebrated it, crisis and conflict appeared to be a normalized part of American life.

The price of vigilance was constant, massive military readiness. While the American military never approached the colossal numbers generated during World War II, the reduced post-1945 peacetime forces were far larger than they were before Pearl Harbor. In 1936, the US Army numbered only 165,000 men. In 1947, the army alone retained more than one million individuals, joined by 558,000 in the navy and 108,000 marines.[15] To maintain these force levels, millions served by virtue of peacetime Selective Service. For most Americans, ongoing mobilization was a fairly mundane affair. However, periodic "hot" wars in Korea and Vietnam also punctuated military service. Overall, a total of 5.5 million eventually deployed to Korea. An additional 8.7 million Americans also served during the Vietnam era from 1964 to 1975.[16]

Amid the millions who wore the uniform, a handful of heroes stood out. Yet, even if their actions made them distinct, they maintained an important commonality with the country and an idealized version of American values. World War II established the basic model. Americans celebrated bravery under fire, quick thinking, and resourcefulness against the enemy. At the same time, they just as consistently emphasized the average nature, humility, and humble origins of American warriors.[17] In his autobiography, Audie Murphy, one of the best-known heroes of the war, made mention of his exposure to the war through his father, a farmer who quickly disabused his son of glorious notions. Asked to recount his time in World War I, he counseled his son, "If you want to fight, start fightin' these weeds." Speaking of his time in Sicily, Italy, and France, Murphy referred to his fellow infantrymen as "this unglamorous, greathearted fighting machine."[18]

War correspondents reinforced this vision of the humble hero. Bill Mauldin openly criticized the overglamorization of war by dispatch writers who indulged in phrases like "smashing armored columns" or "victorious, cheering armies."[19] *Time* and *Life* reporter Robert Sherrod deliberately avoided superlatives in his description of marines preparing to invade Tarawa in 1943: "They looked like any group of ordinary, healthy young Americans. The range of their backgrounds was as broad as America: farmers, truck drivers, college students, runaway kids, rich men's sons, orphans, lawyers, ex-soldiers."[20] Ernie Pyle, perhaps the most famous writer of the war, regularly applied the same standard to the men he wrote about in Sicily and Italy. His depictions of men in combat reflect an almost literal organic quality. When describing the 45th Infantry Division in Italy, he wrote: "The men of Oklahoma are drawling and soft-spoken. They are not smart alecks. Something of the purity of the soil seems to be in them. Even their cussing is simpler and more profound than the torrential obscenities of Eastern city men."[21] Pyle, like many war correspondents of his era, took great pains to illustrate the normality of his subject.

A similar standard applied to American leaders in World War II. In an October 1942 article in the *Saturday Evening Post*, an American colonel characterized Dwight Eisenhower in the following terms: "There's nothing romantic about him. He's never done anything spectacular. The public never heard of him until a few months ago, and most politicians have never laid eyes on him. But there is one thing about Ike Eisenhower—he is the Army's favorite general."[22] According to the piece, the Kansas prairie defined Eisenhower's character, guided by a mother who shaped his (and five brothers') work ethic on the family farm. She told the *Christian Science Monitor* in an interview that "there was always lots of work to do around the place."[23]

The values that Americans imparted to their heroes said a great deal about their approach to war before 1945. It would be easy to dismiss these characterizations as propaganda and self-aggrandizement. Writers employed by the Office of War Information were as interested in "selling" the war as Audie Murphy was in moving copies of his autobiography. However, it is possible that the common themes shared by these many other authors express a potentially deeper truth. Long before Studs Terkel defined World War II as the "good war," it was clear that Americans believed in their cause. Robert Sherrod argued that what made an American soldier distinct was his belief in the righteousness of the struggle to defeat fascism.[24] Matching personal and collective sacrifice against a fundamental evil embodied a consensus that World War II was a good war by any definition.

The means toward this end was also distinctly American. Sherrod, Pyle, Mauldin, and many authors consistently spoke of an egalitarian spirit that inhabited American soldiers. The war took their inherent sense of democratic participation in life and reinforced it. Conflict was the great leveler, where cooperation trumped personal ambition or individual quests for glory. These qualities applied as much to the marines invading Tarawa as they did for Eisenhower while he built an Allied army in Europe.

It is important to consider the fact that the values forming the core of an American warrior in World War II were those he brought from home. The generation of men and women who came of age during the Great Depression understood adversity and the virtue of sacrifice for the sake of cohesiveness. Exposure to the strain of combat augmented this understanding and served as the foundation that held units together through the worst days of the war. When the war ended in 1945, veterans quickly returned to these principles. The citizen-soldier who became the warrior understood that the value of peace would be determined by the virtues of home.

In the years following World War II, the conventional wisdom concerning what constituted a good war and a hero changed, largely not for the better. The postwar period is filled with popular literature written by veterans. Herman Wouk, James Jones, and Norman Mailer produced popular, classic treatments of World War II. However, in the pages of *The Naked and the Dead* (1948), *From Here to Eternity* (1951), and *The Caine Mutiny* (1951) there is not much that is ennobling about the military. The quality of life is often petty, cynical in garrison and terrifying in the field. In postwar films, directors like John Huston deliberately challenged the "warrior myth" in the portrayal of war in general. His *Battle of San Pietro* (1945) is notable for its lack of a grand vision of war, instead focusing on the common soldier and his individual struggles. Huston returned to the theme in *Red Badge of Courage* (based on Stephen Crane's 1951 novel), where he depicted battle as a precursor to confusion, personal crisis, and cowardice.[25] A number of postwar historians also chipped away at the gloss that surrounded depictions of World War II. John Toland's *Battle: The Story of the Bulge* (1959) built its narrative around a host of interviews with major commanders to common foot soldiers on both sides. Although Toland presented a familiar depiction of SS troops murdering American prisoners at Malmedy, he counterbalanced this story with an equally horrific depiction of 60 German POWs killed by soldiers of the 11th Armored Division in Chenogne on January 1, 1945.[26]

The Tainted Korea Warrior

These works, whether popular fiction or historical studies, revealed a changing perspective on World War II, one partly tempered by the passage of time and the opportunity to reflect but also the product of the evolving attitudes regarding American wars in general. Korea proved to be America's first direct military test during the Cold War, and, while Americans carried the optimism produced by World War II into Korea, it proved to be short-lived.[27] When Task Force Smith first met North Korean forces in June 1950, its soldiers were as confident as people at home that the United States would quickly prevail over the Communist threat. Military disaster followed and, with it, disillusionment and a chilling realization of the stakes involved in Korea. In August 1950, months before China entered the conflict, a Gallup Poll recorded that 57% of Americans believed that the United States was already engaged in World War III.[28] Rather than consider the Korean War a crusade to save civilization as World War II had been, many Americans contemplated the possibility that Korea might escalate to superpower confrontation and atomic Armageddon.

Because the Korean War lacked a nobility of purpose, much of the discussion surrounding it dwelled on its ugliness. John Osborne reported for *Life* magazine in August 1950:

Much of this war is alien to the American tradition and shocking to the American mind. For our men . . . are waging this war as they are forced to wage it and as they will be forced to wage any war against the Communists anywhere in Asia. . . . This means not the usual, inevitable savagery of combat in the field, but savagery in detail—the blotting out of villages where the enemy may be hiding; the shooting and shelling of refugees who may include [the enemy] or who may be screening an enemy advancing upon our positions.[29]

Osborne refused to separate North from South Korea. He saw both countries as equally culpable for the savagery of the war. Freda Kirchwey took this characterization a step further. Writing for the *Nation* in March 1951, she argued that recent history had changed Americans in a profound and negative way:

We were all hardened by the methods of mass slaughter practiced first by the Germans and Japanese and then, in self-defense, adopted and developed to the pitch of perfection illustrated at Hiroshima and Nagasaki by the Western allies, and, particularly, the Americans. We became accustomed to "area" bombing, "saturation" bombing, all the hideous forms of strategic air war aimed at wiping out not only military and industrial installations but whole populations.[30]

To Kirchwey, this callousness explained "the absence of protest against the orgy of agony and destruction now in progress in Korea." Few media sources questioned "the necessity for the vast slaughter of civilians, the burning of whole villages because a few Communist guerrillas were suspected to be hiding there, the systematic destruction of factories and water systems and transportation facilities—down, almost to the last ox-cart."[31]

In contrast to World War II, Korea was an ugly sideshow populated by a seemingly endless parade of human tragedy. The men who fought the war in Korea seemed to be engaged in an endurance contest rather than a great crusade against tyranny. What they endured—from bad weather, to difficult terrain, to a vicious enemy—inspired more public remorse than admiration. As one author recently put it:

If the notion that American troops faced hardships and death had circulated during World War II, the idea that they should be pitied for it, seemed new. Bill Mauldin's Willie and Joe and the GIs of Ernie Pyle's columns had invited sympathy and gratitude, but usually not pity. During the Korean War a grimmer form of stoicism—born out of the dire straits in which UN forces found themselves—would become as much a part of the GI's image in American culture as his fatigue and sorrow.[32]

Such stoicism was a common theme that often revealed a much darker side to sacrifice as the war dragged on. A 1951 *Time* article reflected on casualties suffered by West Point officers deployed to fight in Korea. By June of that year, 267 had been killed or wounded in combat, leading one officer to complain: "It is always the best men who get knocked off."[33]

Arguably, what ultimately tainted the Korean War was its inconclusiveness. Most Americans expected the conflict to be short. A July 1950 Gallup Poll noted that only 14% of the public believed that the war would last more than a year. When it expanded, alarmingly, with the addition of Communist China, public support for the war quickly evaporated. In January 1951, 66% of respondents said that the best way for the United States to resolve the war was to pull out. Only 25% believed the country should remain in South Korea.[34] While this diminishing support did not result in open protest, contemporary writers noted growing distance between the people and veterans. Indifferent, "even cold" public greetings awaited servicemen returning as early as 1951.[35]

The warrior who fought in Korea also suffered from the general backlash against a conflict that failed to produce decisive victory. In the public domain, a "police action" that resulted in an armistice was a poor substitute for the clarity punctuating the Allied triumph of 1945. For veterans of Korea, the absence of a final end point was perhaps a more bitter pill, something reflected in the memoirs of many Korea veterans. David Hackworth, a highly decorated infantryman who later served as an infantry officer in Vietnam, offered a blunt summary of Korea's legacy: "*What*, I asked myself, *is a war without a goal?* What was victory, if not something you could taste and breathe and feel. Instead, there'd just been three years of fighting—for nothing."[36]

More than 10 years later, the Vietnam War saw public acclaim for the military corrode into outright skepticism and open hostility. At its outset, the atmosphere surrounding American intervention had an almost surreal quality. Bound up as it was in the Kennedy mystique of Cold War confrontation, the warriors of the period were almost pop-culture heroes. This was especially true of special forces soldiers, who seemed to capture the spirit of the moment. A 1961 *Newsweek* story proclaimed:

> *From now on, President Kennedy told the Joint Chiefs of Staff, the Special Forces would no longer languish in the shade of the atomic missile, and they would, in fact, take on a series of new duties. The hard-muscled wielders of knife and garrote would teach their back-alley arts to fighters for freedom in the jungles of Southeast Asia, the savannas of Central Africa, wherever revolt and terror encroach.*[37]

The "hard-muscled wielders of knife and garrote" represented a caste of warriors who humanized the Cold War at a point when push-button nuclear escalation dominated the headlines. This was especially true during the respective crises in Berlin and Cuba. Special forces soldiers were real-life heroes in an era that celebrated spies and international intrigue. In early 1966, this romanticized Cold Warrior reached his apogee when the "Ballad of the Green Berets" went to number one on the Billboard chart and remained there for five weeks.

Much of this acclaim spoiled and fell away as the reality of the war in Vietnam reached American households. Television accounted for part of this erosion. Uncensored images of carnage on the ground no doubt shocked many into the true nature of war. The increasing cost of the war to taxpayers, hidden, but unavoidable after 1967, no doubt also played a role. The imposition of a 10% surcharge on corporate and individual income taxes and the subsequent conclusion in Gallup and Harris Polls that the war was a "mistake" was hardly a coincidence.[38] The most decisive factor, however, likely was the massive draft call-ups necessary to augment troop deployments to Southeast Asia.[39] It was one thing to vicariously celebrate the "hard-muscled wielders of knife and garrote" in song. It was another to be made to live his life.

What did the sacrifice of time, life, and limb earn in Vietnam? As in the Korean War, a massive influx of men and materiel as well as a sustained bombing campaign against North Vietnam failed to produce anything resembling a clear victory.[40] According to data made public in the *Pentagon Papers*, the Viet Cong (VC) and North Vietnamese Army (NVA) lost 344,000 combat troops between January 1965 and December 1967. Yet the overall strength of Communist forces in South Vietnam actually *increased* from 180,700 in December 1965 to 261,500 at the end of 1967.[41] Walter Cronkite's famous February 1968 declaration that the Vietnam War had reached a stalemate after the Tet Offensive was a reflection of the facts. In the wake of Tet, the conventional wisdom back home had simply caught up with the data.[42]

Stalemate in Korea earned its veterans the quiet derision of a nation. In Vietnam, the stalemate was underpinned by official deception, an approach that caused criticism to develop into overt contempt. Unlike contemporary conflicts in Iraq and Afghanistan, critics of Vietnam did not indulge in the "for the troops, but against the war" dichotomy. Fairly or not, Vietnam veterans wore the same stain created by their military and civilian leadership. Growing hostility to warriors returning home—apparent after World War II but particularly evident following Korea and Vietnam—would play an important part in veterans' eventual reassimilation.

The Nature of Combat in Three Wars

The general social context of wars is important in understanding their nature and those who fight. Equally important is the actual manner in which wars are fought. On this count, World War II, Korea, and Vietnam share many similar features. Overall, the weapons utilized in each were relatively similar. With the exception of jet aircraft, equipment in World War II and Korea was almost identical. In the sixties, variations in firing capacity, payload, or range reflected technological improvements. There are obvious exceptions. Helicopters used for medical evacuation and reconnaissance in Korea saw a much broader application during Vietnam. Laser-guided munitions appeared late in Vietnam and created their own revolution on bomb damage in the early seventies.

American forces involved in the three wars were remarkably similar. American units were overwhelmingly conventional in size and structure. Although Korea saw a brief reintroduction of rangers and Vietnam celebrated various types of special forces units, they were neither large in number nor decisive in their respective conflicts.

American doctrine, particularly its reliance on firepower, remained consistent between 1941 and 1973.[43] During the invasion of the Tarawa atoll in November 1943, the preparatory naval bombardment placed ten tons of shells per acre on Betio island.[44] After Tarawa, American commanders came to the conclusion that future casualties could be prevented by an even more deliberate use of naval and air bombardment. In Korea, firepower was a means to offset enemy numbers. During the defense of the Naktong River line in August 1950, American air units carpet-bombed North Korean forces with 900 tons of ordnance.[45] When Communist Chinese forces launched an offensive against the 2nd Infantry Division in May 1951, it had the entire X Corps artillery at its disposal. On May 16, US batteries fired 17,000 rounds at oncoming Chinese forces; the following day, American guns fired an additional 38,000 rounds, a practice one contemporary periodical called "meat-grinder tactics."[46] During Vietnam, the American military pushed the boundaries of firepower still further. Army search-and-destroy missions conducted during Operation Thayer I/Irving from September to October 1966 received support from offshore ship bombardments and 1,126 air force sorties that dropped 1.5 million pounds of explosives and 292,500 pounds of napalm on the enemy.[47]

World War II, Korea, and Vietnam all shared similarities regarding combat and the distinct culture it cultivated during wartime. Regardless of time, place, or branch of service, constant proximity to danger encouraged a common sense of a shared struggle. Sherrod, Pyle, and their generation of writers constantly referred to the camaraderie that existed amid combat units. More than 20 years later, Ronald Glasser wrote of medics in Vietnam: "suddenly tapped not for their selfishness and greed but for their grace and wisdom, not for their brutality but for their love and concern."[48] In the years following World War II, historians and social scientists such as S. L. A. Marshall, Edward Shils, and Morris Janowitz attempted to discern the factors that produced and preserved "primary groups" of soldiers engaged in war.[49] Understanding this particular component was critical to unraveling what made combat units effective at war. A 1951 Defense Department study put it in these terms:

> *The primary group is so important because it is the only face-to-face group to which the soldier can belong and he has an even stronger need to belong to such a group as a soldier than he did as a civilian. . . . Membership in a primary group helps the soldier by reducing his anxiety, by giving him a feeling that he counts as a person, and, in general, by enabling him to withstand the strains of army life which he might not otherwise be able to tolerate.*[50]

In the years following World War II, American military planners went to considerable lengths to reinforce the primary group to improve combat effectiveness.

In his classic 1959 work *The Warriors*, J. Glenn Gray considered the qualities that defined men at war without attempting to impose any systematic explanations to them. He explained the perverse attraction of the "atmosphere of violence," a quality that drew the casual observer motivated by simple curiosity but also, and more important, individuals who wanted to be direct participants in violence.[51] For Gray, combat could be a matter of choice and, over time, a status to be preserved and protected by its participants. The methods involved in this preservation were complex. Gray spends a great deal of time and effort articulating the relationships formed by men at war. He draws the contrast between comrades participating in a common effort and true friends interested in what he defined as "preservative love" or the direct concern for the well-being of another.[52] This latter type of relationship formed the cement that held individual units together over the course of World War II. According to Gray, "This love is, in men, evidently pervasive and immanent rather than ecstatic. It does not seize us from without, but arises out of our own nature. Hence it may be less periodic and more dependable than erotic love, though less able to dominate many men in moments of crisis."[53] An important point often missed is the broad application of this "preservative love." In combat, the quality of the relationship between warriors was the thing that held groups together in moments of enormous stress. However, what also gave this love perhaps greater value was its ability to preserve within the soldier a kernel of humanity amid the violence of combat. In other words, the preservative love provided an inkling of hope for the future veteran, both for himself and the society he was about to reenter.

As much as World War II, Korea, and Vietnam shared important similarities, the features separating them are also significant. During World War II, conflict was couched in the terms of "unconditional surrender" and the practice of total war. On the ground and through the air, the line that delineated combatant from noncombatant often simply ceased to exist. In 1950, individual civilians still enjoyed few protections from violence, but the Cold War required additional rules of engagement to prevent strategic escalation. In Korea, national borders served as the primary tripwires to avoid, particularly with respect to air combat.

Vietnam took these seemingly artificial and arbitrary limits and added still more. For much of the conflict, fears of escalation dominated civilian thinking. Consequently, as Harry G. Summers would point out in his critique of American military policy in Vietnam, *On Strategy* (1982), borders were again inviolate for most American forces, offering Communist forces ready sanctuaries.[54] American strategic bombing against North Vietnam reflected the same self-imposed limits, at least until 1972. For most of the ground war in South Vietnam, American commanders attempted to expand the rules of engagement to include tactical combat against Communist guerrillas and North Vietnamese regulars. While the goal was to protect civilians caught amid many combatants, contradictory objectives (e.g., creating a "body count," attrition against the VC and NVA) and practical circumstances made these standards difficult if not impossible to implement. Philip Caputo's 1965 memoir illustrated the larger dilemma:

> *The day before, a rifleman from B Company had shot a farmer, apparently mistaking him for a VC. To avoid similar incidents in the future, brigade again ordered that [rifle] chambers be kept clear except when contact was imminent, and in guerrilla-controlled areas, no fire be directed at unarmed Vietnamese*

unless they were running. A running Vietnamese was a fair target. This left us bewildered and uneasy. No one was eager to shoot civilians. Why should the act of running identify someone as a Communist? What if we shot a Vietnamese who turned out to have a legitimate reason for running? Would that be a justifiable act or grounds for a court martial?[55]

Responding to his men's questions, Caputo's company commander said: "Look, I don't know what this is supposed to mean, but I talked to battalion and they said as far as they are concerned, if he's dead and Vietnamese, he's VC."[56]

Combat in Vietnam subsequently contained the dominant features of both previous conflicts. While waging war in South Vietnam, American units enjoyed a massive advantage in firepower with the expressed intent of grinding down Communist forces. However, even as they relentlessly pursued the strategy of attrition, American combat forces in South Vietnam operated in what one author called "the absurd combination of certainty and uncertainty."[57] Improved weapons mattered little against an enemy that could not be found among the villages of the Mekong Delta or the Central Highlands. The VC and NVA controlled the operational tempo of the war on the ground. Communist forces consistently frustrated American efforts to find and fix them. According to a 1969 Central Intelligence Agency study of almost two million American, South Vietnamese, and allied small-unit operations, less than 1% resulted in contact with VC or NVA forces.[58] Self-imposed limits contributed to American frustrations. When US forces attempted to combine the "big war" of conventional maneuver units with the demands of counterinsurgency, the outcome was another "absurd combination" of winning "hearts and minds" while ramping up the enemy body count.

Military personnel policy during the Vietnam War also apparently separated it from the two previous conflicts. The most famous was the practice of rotating enlisted men out of Vietnam after completing a one-year tour of duty. During the war, sociologist Charles Moskos argued that the US rotation policy retarded the development of "primary groups" essential to the military, particularly smaller units at the squad and platoon levels.[59] When exposed to the stresses of combat, these groups provided what one historian described as "unities of time, place, or action."[60]

Rotation policy disrupted continuity and cohesiveness, according to Moskos. Instead of investing effort in their unit, soldiers became fixated on the "date eligible for return from overseas" (DEROS) date.[61] Many military analysts blamed the policy for the breakdown of the American military in Vietnam. One likened the army to "a recording tape that is erased every twelve months. It condemns us to learning the same lessons over and over again."[62]

Attempts to manage the combat tour of duty can be traced back to the Korean War and, to a limited extent, World War II. In Korea, the Pentagon introduced the rotation policy for individual soldiers as early as 1950. The reasoning behind the measure was fairly straightforward. Utilizing data from World War II, American planners understood that exposure to combat would create a "morale problem" if left unattended. Discarding unit rotation as impractical, the Defense Department focused instead on individual reassignment.[63] To return home, soldiers had to accumulate 36 points, with 4 points awarded per month to combat troops.[64] Unfortunately, the system proved poorly administered, confusing, and controversial from the start. In practice, Defense Department policy failed to differentiate between enlistees whose terms of service were extended for Korea, reservists involuntarily recalled to active duty, and actual combat soldiers.[65]

An American combatant could also be rotated or returned home during World War II. Selected air crews completing a prescribed number of missions earned a trip stateside. For the vast majority of US forces, however, this option was an extremely rare possibility. The army did not implement a formal rotation policy until 1944, allowing theater commanders the option of selecting "deserving" personnel, experienced individuals for use as training cadre, or soldiers "whose morale or health has been adversely affected by prolonged periods of duty under severe conditions."[66] By doctrine, the rotation quota was fixed at 1% of a unit's total strength each month. "Returnees" were another matter. Army personnel suffering from physical wounds or various forms of mental incapacity accumulated throughout the war at a fairly alarming rate. By V-E Day, more than 1.25 million had come back to the United States and approximately 500,000 were still there in uniform when the war ended in Europe.[67]

The returnee problem illustrates an important difficulty faced by some combat units in World War II, an extremely high casualty rate that was far more disruptive than the Vietnam-era rotation policy. In both Europe and the Pacific, a number of select elite units—the 1st Marine Division and the 82nd Airborne immediately come to mind—were constantly engaged in high-risk operations that produced an enormous attrition rate. During the 33 days following their jump into Normandy, the 82nd Airborne suffered 5,245 killed, wounded, and missing, almost half its assigned strength.[68] The evidence suggests that less elite units suffered similar losses. A War Department survey of four infantry divisions during the Normandy campaign revealed that after eight weeks in combat, 73.8% of officers and 59.6% of enlisted men assigned to rifle companies became casualties.[69]

Where does this put the primary groups cited by Moskos, Shils, and Janowitz? Combat units suffered high turnover rates in all three wars. Some were generated by deliberate policies that returned personnel for stateside duty, convalescence, or discharge. Combat units also saw their ranks fluctuate by virtue of significant casualty rates. Regardless of the reason, the prospect for men to build camaraderie within what J. Glenn Gray described as the "atmosphere of violence" seems murkier in retrospect. No doubt, some men forged strong ties that sustained them in times of dire need, but it is more difficult to project this cohesion to larger groups engaged in combat. In retrospect, it appears that World War II combat units may have experienced the same lack of cohesion as those in Vietnam and Korea.

Another factor that qualified primary groups of combatants in World War II, Korea, and Vietnam was their declining proportion within the military. War is a complex process. As they prepare for war, military institutions engage in the constant pursuit of self-improvement through modernization. New technology—applied to weapons systems, transportation, medicine, and a broad spectrum of functions—adds to this complexity. New capabilities demand additional logistical structures, a trend that influences the overall force structure. An infantry regiment in the American Civil War used almost its entire strength to fight. Personnel assigned to administrative and support duties were relatively small in number. By World War II, a growing army of clerks, mechanics, ammunition handlers, and medics followed the warrior into to combat. One study of the US Army that divided service according to combat, combat support, and combat service support assignments found that 60% of personnel were in the combat arms in 1944. During the next two wars, but particularly in Vietnam, the number of warriors diminished as the military institution became more complex and more dependent on logistics. By 1968, only 29% of personnel were assigned to the combat arms.[70]

These percentages do not provide a completely accurate picture. They fail to take into account the difference between combat assignments and actual combat *participation*. For example, many National Guard units mobilized for Korea actually deployed to Western Europe to free up regulars to fight in Asia.[71]

Similarly, in 1968, a soldier with the military occupational specialty (MOS) of infantry might have been assigned to duty in West Germany for his entire tour of duty without firing a single shot in anger. Taking these considerations into account, a 2007 study estimated that only 7.5% of the *total* army force structure actually fought in Korea. In Vietnam, the number was slightly lower at 7.2% of all army forces.[72] Consequently, while the total number of Vietnam-era veterans is a substantial 8,263,000 and those with service in the Vietnam theater amounts to 2,674,000, it is important to consider how few of these individuals were actually bona fide warriors.[73]

It is possible to refine this percentage even further. In 1947, S. L. A. Marshall published his famous study *Men against Fire: The Problem of Battle Command in Future War*. After conducting an extensive series of interviews with combat units in Europe and the Pacific, he suggested that only 25% of soldiers fired their primary weapons while engaged with the enemy.[74] In the many years since its publication, a host of scholars and military leaders have attacked Marshall's basic conclusion.[75] However, it is important to consider the historical context of his claims as well as their impact on the contemporary military institution. When Samuel A. Stouffer's far more rigorous study of the American military, *The American Soldier: Combat and Its Aftermath*, was published in 1949, one of its fundamental recommendations was for more realistic training, a conclusion derived from his own interviews with combat veterans.[76] Other official treatments of World War II and Korea cited the tendency to use unaimed artillery and small-arms fire to suppress enemy forces, a doctrine that came at the expense of marksmanship. Tactical countermeasures to increased firepower—dispersion, cover, and concealment—were also to blame. A 1955 army technical report pointed out that "the hastily trained replacement of World War II left much to be desired as a marksman, and frequently failed to fire at all."[77] The commander of the 2nd Infantry Division in Korea, Maj. Gen. James C. Fry, made the identical claim in his book *Assault Battle Drill*, published the same year.[78] Consequently, whether Marshall's research regarding the percentage of combatants firing their weapons was accurate or not, the military took him seriously when he characterized "the initiative to fire" as "the mainspring of successful minor tactics and hence of final victory in war."[79]

Throughout the fifties, in an effort to reinforce combat participation, military doctrine emphasized an "automatic habitual response to danger." There were recent, successful precedents to this approach. During World War II, army parachute training essentially took basic positive behavioral reinforcement techniques posited by psychologist B. F. Skinner and applied them to airborne candidates. At Fort Benning, instructors developed a process that progressively exposed airborne candidates to risk and overcame their not unreasonable fear of jumping out of an aircraft at altitude.[80]

During the Korean War, the Defense Department's Research and Development Board commissioned a series of papers that examined the broader application of fear to individuals and units in combat. In a 1951 report for the board, Yale psychologist Neal E. Miller framed the problem in terms of encouraging an "adaptive response" through training. Military doctrine needed to consider "not how afraid a man is, but what fear motivates him to do."[81] Like Stouffer, he recommended that training "should be made as realistic as possible" and should take into account "all factors including confusion and isolation." Miller believed trainees could overcome fear in moments of combat stress and function as a military unit through a gradual approach of exposure and proper reinforcement.[82]

Fry's *Assault Battle Drill* took many of Miller's behaviorist principles and applied them to post-Korea military doctrine. He argued that combat required actions that seemed, on their face to a civilian, counterintuitive at best or suicidal at worst. One example of this was in the concept that "Safety Lies Forward"; in other words, soldiers who closed with the enemy were more likely to survive combat.[83] Applied to the close proximity of ambushes or the movement of small units across open areas, survival was a matter of moving rapidly toward the enemy. For the remainder of *Assault Battle Drill*, Fry explains in great detail the construction and use of the "combat course" to encourage discipline and unit cohesion in time of real war.

The same conceptual model extended to individual training as well. After the Korean War, the army introduced the new "Trainfire" system to instruct new recruits in basic rifle marksmanship. The intent was to wean the institution away from outdated practices built around the pre-1939 bolt-action rifle. Trainfire included more time spent firing live ammunition instead of hours of "dry fire" exercises. More important, in response to problems identified in both World War II and Korea, army doctrine introduced a 16-hour module on "target detection" that included live soldiers in various forms of camouflage and cover on a simulated battlefield. Instructors provided guidance on how to find the enemy and "mark" a target for firing by relating its position to a fixed object on the battlefield. Finally, Trainfire also utilized automated pop-up human silhouette targets that appeared at random intervals, mimicking the lack of predictability on the battlefield.[84]

These measures were successful for the most part. During the Korean War, even before the army introduced many of its doctrinal reforms, S. L. A Marshall reported that 55% of combat infantry fired their weapons.[85] During Vietnam, after reforms were implemented, the percentage was significantly greater. David Grossman's 2009 *On Killing: The Psychological Cost of Learning to Kill in War and Society* claimed that fire rate in Vietnam was as high as 90%.[86] An earlier survey of 1st Cavalry troopers in Vietnam by Russell Glenn recorded a firing rate of 97%.[87]

While combat in World War II, Korea, and Vietnam shared important features, a number of distinct characteristics emerge in their comparison. The first one is the clearest: The US military rarely hesitated when the time came to apply massive firepower in almost any tactical situation. This characteristic carries through all three wars. The passage of time and improvements in weapons technology, from guidance systems to the actual size and composition of munitions, served to increase their lethality from World War II to Vietnam.

American doctrine after World War II was also clearly intent on building better warriors. The Defense Department took the recommendations made by Stouffer in *The American Soldier* seriously and attempted to address them at the end of the forties. While training focused on a number of qualities directly related to combat, from overcoming individual fear to improving unit cohesion, the goal was to train a warrior who was better prepared to fight.

Yet the overall number of warriors declined significantly in the years after World War II. The American military, particularly its nuclear-oriented incarnation in the fifties, embraced technology and all its logistical complexity. Support was the primary mission of a significant majority of soldiers, sailors, and airmen committed to war. Institutionally, the warrior became an increasingly rare factor, particularly those committed to actual combat.

If post-1945 warriors were better trained for combat, their battlefield became increasingly murky. Civilian casualties were a concrete part of the more conventional conflicts in World War II and Korea. Hundreds of thousands died as a result of aerial and artillery bombardments. Yet, because conventional forces dominated direct conflict between the United States and its enemies, the line between civilian and military at least existed and called for a degree of restraint, especially at the small-unit level. Marine and army units on Okinawa, for example, did not seek out civilians to kill and were horrified when American advances provoked mass suicides. In contrast, during the guerrilla insurgency that characterized much of the Vietnam War, the clear lines separating civilian from military and "the front" from the rear echelon did not exist.

The evolution of modern combat after 1945 left distinct marks on American veterans. The men and women shared a fairly consistent experience of just how much damage the "American way of war" could inflict on both enemies and innocents. In another important sense, however, direct involvement in combat became an increasingly concentrated and rarified experience by virtue of new doctrine and structural changes within the US military establishment. Combat veterans leaving Vietnam behind could relate to many of the same experiences of their fathers in World War II and Korea. What clearly differed in Vietnam was the complexity and ambiguity of a battlefield visited on an increasingly select few.

Combat, Veterans, and Society

In some respects, it is easy to measure the impact of combat on veterans. Three wars resulted in hundreds of thousands of wounded and injured service members all in need of treatment and some type of rehabilitation. After 1945, as medical technology improved alongside advances in weaponry, the likelihood of surviving wounds increased as well. During the two world wars, approximately two soldiers were wounded for every one who died. In Korea and Vietnam, the ratio was three to one.[88] The overall numbers are as impressive as they are daunting. By 1947, a total of 1.7 million World War II veterans received some form of disability payment. In 1955, the Veterans Administration provided the same assistance to 153,831 Korean War veterans. By 1977, an additional 496,815 Vietnam War veterans collected compensation for service-related disabilities.[89]

Military service also left a mark in less tangible but still important ways. Veterans expressed concerns regarding their suitability to return to civilian society. Stouffer's survey of soldiers at the end of World War II indicated that 48% of those interviewed worried that they would not be able to settle down and return to peacetime life.[90] Among combat veterans furloughed home in 1944 and 1945 because of wounds or exhaustion, hope was intermingled with disappointment and ambivalence. While overwhelmingly (88%) glad to be back in the states, a significant plurality (46%) claimed that it was "not as good as I expected it to be."[91] Some of these feelings persisted years later. A 1947 poll conducted by the National Opinion Research Center indicated that twice as many (48%) veterans believed that the war had made their lives worse as opposed to those who said it had made life better.[92]

During and after the Vietnam War, surveys were more sophisticated in dissecting distinctions regarding the impact of war on veterans. A 1981 study of Vietnam veterans, for example, recorded how much service personally affected them. White veterans were more likely than African American veterans to mention "maturation" as a benefit of service (29.2% versus 8.1%). In contrast, black Vietnam veterans considered service-related benefits (education, health care) more important (58.2% to 37.6%). The same percentages held when veterans of heavy combat responded to the same question. Regarding maturation, 36.1% of white combat veterans believed the military helped them, while only 7.4% of African American combat veterans agreed. Conversely, 63.6% of black veterans but only 31.0% of white veterans with heavy combat experience cited benefits as an advantage.[93]

Military experience and combat also had an impact on personal relationships, particularly between veterans and their families, although the results were not consistent for all three wars. In his 1951 examination of group dynamics in the military, anthropologist David G. Mandelbaum wrote that "the common experiences and the common stresses of military service are so pervasive in a life of a soldier and so unique to a soldier's life, that he finds little interest in civilian primary groups or little incentive to join them even if there is some opportunity to do so."[94] Just how far the military primary group displaced civilian families varied significantly between 1945 and 1973. According to a 2002 study by William Ruger, Sven E. Wilson, and Shawn L. Waddoups titled "Warfare and Welfare: Military Service, Combat, and Marital Dissolution," which incorporated data from National Survey of Families and Households, World War II veterans actually tended to have a lower divorce rate (8.7%) than nonveterans (11.6%). This was not the case for veterans who married after the Korean War between 1954 and 1957. In this cohort, 18.7% of veterans and 12.9% of nonveterans divorced. For most of the Vietnam War, between 1960 and 1973, veterans' marriages failed 21.4% of the time, about the same percentage as marriages among civilians (24.2%). However, veterans' rates spiked between 1974 and 1980 to 41.6%; the civilians' rate was 32.4%.[95]Among the three wars, the one great leveler with respect to divorce rates was combat experience. A veteran's exposure to combat increased the "hazard rate" for marriage by 62%.[96]

This research explained in clinical terms the significant strains that wartime experience created between veterans and their wives. Separation, infidelity, and the difficulties of raising young children while the father was deployed abroad all affected couples.[97] In many cases, an individual veteran's behavior, inexplicable to his spouse, made matters worse when he came home. James Jones reflected on this in his 1976 memoir of World War II:

> *Men still woke up in the middle of the night, thrashing around and trying to get their hands on their wives' throats. Men still rolled out from a dead sleep, and hit the dirt with a crash on*

the bedroom floor, huddling against the bed to evade the aerial bomb or the artillery shell they had dreamed they heard coming. While their wives sat straight up in bed in their new frilly nightgowns, horrified. An old buddy would have roared with laughter. There was no telling what the divorce rate was then, in the early year or two. Certainly a lot higher than was ever admitted.[98]

Contemporary clinical studies of World War II and Korea veterans found a correlation between exposure to combat and communication with spouses. Veterans with heaviest exposure were unwilling to talk about their experiences with their wives. Many were reluctant to expose loved ones to war's horror or their participation in it. Some men simply lacked the ability. Women, forced to cope with the symptoms of posttraumatic stress—such as nightmares and irritability—became less inclined to listen to their husbands over time.[99] This downward spiral destroyed many marriages.

The gradually increasing distance between husband and wife undercut what was the first line of support for returning veterans. During all three wars, families provided the foundation for efforts to mitigate the difficulties of veterans' reassimilation. Families helped reconstruct daily routines and provide a focus for veterans' energy when they returned home. More broadly, wives and family members were activists outside the home, forming the backbone of organizations from the Veterans Administration Volunteer Service and American Legion National Rehabilitation Program to the Navy Mutual Aid Association and Military Order of the Purple Heart.[100]

These networks of social support were a critical factor with respect to evaluating veterans and posttraumatic stress after World War II, Korea, and Vietnam. The initial points of contact between veterans and society were individual and personal. Spouses, families, and friends were the first to experience both the obvious physical handicaps created by war as well as far less visible degrees of mental disabilities. Most of these people were well-intentioned amateurs. Some groped their way toward fostering veterans' rehabilitation. Others found that the complexity of the problem overwhelmed the best intentions and faced impasses that stretched into years of silence. Official help eventually did arrive to deal with combat and mental trauma, but it would be the product of additional decades of debate within the professional community of doctors, clinicians, and therapists.

From Battle Fatigue to Posttraumatic Stress Disorder

The term "battle fatigue" was the label of choice for posttraumatic stress disorder (PTSD) during World War II. Contemporary medicine recognized mental disorders as a legitimate ailment and urged the Pentagon to improve screening practices for recruits. Unfortunately, they remained a significant problem throughout the war. Selective Service physicals conducted between 1940 and 1945 resulted in enormous numbers of American men being identified as psychologically unfit for military duty. Overall, 1,850,000 of 16 million men examined (12%) for service were rejected for this reason.[101]

Problems persisted among the millions who completed training and went overseas. In the army, battle fatigue accounted for one million hospital admissions and 300,000 medical discharges during the war. The navy and Marine Corps together generated 150,000 hospital admissions and 100,000 additional medical discharges by 1945.[102]

Historians have discovered some interesting trends within these statistics. Battle fatigue tended to be lower in elite units where high training standards and an increased sense of camaraderie shielded men from some of the effects of psychological trauma. The durability Stephen Ambrose observed in *Band of Brothers* among paratroopers in the 101st Airborne tended to be true for other similar formations during the war. Conversely, scholars also note a higher incidence of battle fatigue within segregated units that fought in World War II.[103] While these individuals enjoyed some of the structure created by their own primary groups, pervasive racial discrimination and official policy largely counteracted it.

As World War II progressed, military medicine adapted to the demands of battle fatigue. Clinical professionals became a regular part of medical staffs at the division level. Experience taught that it was better to treat mental trauma close to the front line and return soldiers to duty as quickly as possible. These methods were largely successful but limited in scope. While they improved the number of men eligible for combat duty, they did not address long-term psychological care.

Unfortunately, the American military had to relearn many of these limited lessons in Korea. At the start of the war, the initial psychiatric casualty rate for American military forces was 250 per thousand troops. In the early months of the conflict, there were no division-level psychiatric practitioners to treat such casualties. Evacuation to Japan and the United States was a common practice that resulted in fewer than half of battle fatigue casualties returning to duty.[104] By 1951, military medicine essentially reinvented the wheel. Psychiatrists again moved to forward units and began the same treatment regimen used during World War II. The military did make some adaptations to the circumstances of Korea. In the first full year of the war, doctors recorded an increase in combat exhaustion casualties with six months of service or more. The subsequent rotation policy implemented in 1951 was an effort to reduce the loss of combat veterans to what was euphemistically called "old sergeants syndrome." Between improved treatment and the rotation policy, return-to-duty rates rebounded to as high as 90% in the latter stages of the war.[105]

The overall initial incidence of combat-related psychological casualties in Vietnam was far lower than in the two previous wars. Where mental breakdowns had accounted for 100 casualties per thousand soldiers per year in World War II and 40 casualties per thousand troops per year in Korea, they amounted to only 12 per thousand per year in Vietnam. Losses varied from a low of 9.8 per thousand in 1967, when the ground war started to escalate, to 24.1 per thousand at the start of 1970, as American forces began their withdrawal. Contemporary medical professionals attributed success to more sophisticated treatment in closer proximity to combat forces as well as a rotation policy that was fully integrated into the military effort in Vietnam.[106]

For most of the 30-year period under consideration, veterans with mental disabilities constituted a significant portion of VA medical treatment. In 1958, patients categorized as "neuropsychiatric" composed the largest cohort—52,674 hospital admissions compared to 51,966 "general medical and surgical" patients—of individuals receiving VA medical care.[107] The proportion remained fairly consistent over time. By 1967, psychiatric patients made up approximately 46% of the total VA inpatient load.[108]

The sheer number of veterans experiencing persistent mental

trauma prompted the medical community to examine its causes and potential link with combat exposure. After the Korean War, clinicians developed an increasingly sophisticated understanding of linkage between combat and stress. One of these studies was the result of research by army major F. Gentry Harris and a team of doctors from the Walter Reed Army Hospital Department of Psychiatry. The team conducted extensive surveys of combat units serving in Korea during the last year of the war. The results, published in 1955, significantly refined the military's understanding of stress and the variety of mechanisms developed to cope with it. Harris argued, for example, that the "characteristics of the subculture of combat" varied significantly according to the type of fighting and an individual's proximity to violence. Moreover, exposure to combat involved more than a set period of days before an individual succumbed to stress. Harris's study concluded that a variety of factors mitigated the impact of combat on individuals and whole units. According to his research, racial integration appeared to have no effect. Consistent leadership was important, however. Units with stable squad, platoon, and company leadership tended to fare better in combat than units disrupted by internal transfers or men rotated back to the United States.[109]

During the sixties and early seventies, subsequent studies continued the process of differentiating between types of combat and their effects on wartime service.[110] As was the case in World War II and Korea, in Vietnam the short-term goal of military medicine was to preserve the fighting strength of units at war. However, the medical community also began to take a longer view on the effect combat had on individuals, particularly the correlation between combat exposure, individual stress, and subsequent "alienation" from civilian society.[111]

A number of factors extended the concept of traumatic stress from the battlefield to the home front. Diagnostic tools improved significantly in the latter stages of the Vietnam War. In his study of veterans' mental health treatment, Wilbur J. Scott reveals remarkable gaps in American medicine as late as 1968:

> *Mental health professionals across the country assessed disturbed Vietnam veterans using a diagnostic nomenclature that contained no specific entries for war-related trauma. The DSM-II nomenclature, used by hospitals, insurance companies, and the courts provided official diagnoses for sickness. VA*

physicians typically did not collect military histories as part of the diagnostic work up. Many thought that Vietnam veterans who were agitated by their war experiences, or who talked repeatedly about them, suffered from a neurosis or psychosis whose origin and dynamics lay outside the realm of combat.[112]

Perhaps a more powerful motive was the conflation of professional concerns with political opposition to the Vietnam War. Psychiatrists, like Yale University's Robert Lifton, argued that the tainted nature of the war was responsible for the psychological casualty rate among Vietnam veterans. Lifton first blamed modern military training for creating a "distorted, literalized, and manipulated version of the Hero as Warrior."[113] From his perspective, casting such individuals in the unconventional morass of Vietnam doomed them. "Sent as intruders in an Asian revolution, asked to fight a filthy and unfathomable war, they return as intruders in their own society, defiled by that war in the eyes of the very people who sent them as well as their own."[114] Unlike the veterans of World War II, a "more psychologically defensible" war in Lifton's eyes, the warrior who fought in Vietnam would be forever defined by his culpability and his guilt.[115] While Lifton did not speak for professional psychologists, the antiwar movement, or the country as a whole, he did articulate growing concerns regarding Vietnam veterans.

Ultimately, the combination of public controversy and considerable internal professional debate culminated in 1980 with the creation of the category of "post-traumatic stress disorder."[116] According to the *DSM-III: Diagnostic and Statistical Manual of Mental Disorders*, PTSD was the result of a "psychologically traumatic event that is generally outside the range of usual human experience."[117] The manual offered a laundry list of such "events," from "bereavement, chronic illness, business losses," to rape or assault, natural disasters, and military combat. More important than the causes of trauma were its long-term effects. According to the manual, individuals who experienced a "traumatic event" could suffer a number of chronic problems such as survivor's guilt, depression, or anxiety. More severe ailments could include "dissociativelike states" in which "components of the event are relived and the individual behaves as though experiencing the event at that moment." Such states could last minutes or days.[118]

Initially, the concept of PTSD was primarily applied to Vietnam veterans. One 1992 study speculated that as many as 470,000 Vietnam veterans (15% of those who served) suffered from some form of posttraumatic stress.[119] However, as additional research integrated data from veterans of World War II, Korea, and Vietnam, a number of similarities emerged. According to work done by Kathryn H. Andersen and Jean M. Mitchell, veterans of all three wars experienced the same rate (27%) of alcohol abuse. Korean War and Vietnam veterans reported depression at the same rate (4%), while World War II veterans' rates were somewhat lower (2%). The one factor that separated Vietnam from World War II and Korea veterans were instances of drug abuse. In the first two conflicts it was rare. Only 1% of veterans of Korea and World War II reported a problem, while 12% of Vietnam veterans acknowledged similar difficulties.[120]

Despite these similarities, there are plausible factors that might account for higher PTSD rates among Vietnam veterans. As noted earlier, individuals wounded in Vietnam had a substantially higher survival rate than their predecessors. The higher rate had a price. For many, surviving a wound was only the first step in a lengthy process of surgeries and rehabilitation. For many, recurring physical therapy was a lifetime necessity. Recent research has linked wound recovery—itself a "traumatic event"—as a trigger for the long-term onset of PTSD.[121]

The "life course" theory is a broader approach to separating the impact of Vietnam-era PTSD from experiences in previous wars. Generally, the theory asserts that social context is more important than individual trauma. That is, if the public accepts a war as honorable, its endorsement will mitigate the psychological damage caused to the warrior.[122] In essence, the life course theory offers the reverse of Lifton's approach. Defining a "just war" was not a function of its intrinsic characteristics. More important was what one author defined as the "post-military experience."[123] What defined a hero or a villain was basically the product of public perception.

Consequently, veterans of unpopular wars suffered as a matter of guilt by association rather than active participation.[124] This standard clearly applied to Vietnam veterans but also to those who served in Korea. In terms of the life course context, Korea occupies a middle ground somewhere between World War II and Vietnam. Edward W. McCranie and Leon A. Hyer note that Korea, as a "limited" conflict, lacked clear objectives and enjoyed far less public support than World War II. However, the lack of open, public controversy regarding Korea separates it from Vietnam. PTSD symptoms among Korean veterans reflect this middle status. According to a variety of measurements—PTSD symptom severity, general psychiatric disturbance, or poor "psychosocial functions" (i.e., alcohol abuse, unemployment, incarceration)—Korean War veterans consistently score higher than World War II veterans and either close to or lower than Vietnam veterans.[125] One important caveat with respect to Korean War veterans is the absence of systematic examinations of their immediate postwar adjustment in the fifties and early sixties. Existing studies have also tended to combine their data with that derived from World War II veterans.

World War II veterans have earned a few recent caveats. Members of the "greatest generation" were long held to be the most stable and well-adjusted group of the three because they enjoyed the most supportive context during and after their war. However, recent studies suggest that the life course theory takes on a new twist with advanced age and the onset of retirement. New evidence makes the point that PTSD rates among World War II veterans were lower because they were actively repressed by a lifetime of work and family obligations. In later life, without these external constraints and with more time to contemplate the past, these men appear far more willing to admit decades-old mental scars. Their trauma may be in actuality closer to the rates experienced in Korea and Vietnam.[126]

Female veterans deserve similar attention. Although proscribed from combat in all three wars, military policy did not successfully remove women from danger. In actual practice, it is clear that women's service likely increased their exposure to the consequences of combat without the option of responding in kind. This was no doubt true for nurses in World War II, Korea, and Vietnam, who treated traumatic injuries, disease, and mental trauma without relief during their overseas tours. Writing about medical personnel in Vietnam, Shelley Saywell noted: "What nurses saw in those operating rooms was an unrelenting procession of the bits and pieces of people arriving from the battlefields. What they felt, working twelve hour shifts in a kind of 'twilight zone' removed from the war yet dealing with its effects, was a sense of unreality, of helplessness, of anger."[127] Exposure to this "unrelenting procession" of trauma, compounded by isolation and recurrent sexual harassment, produced its own consequences for these women, although they were poorly understood at the time by veterans' institutions and the general public. Postwar examinations of army nurses in Vietnam indicated a high incidence of PTSD. One 1988 study indicated a PTSD rate as high as 20% among nurses exposed to "high war zone stress, e.g., exposure to enemy fire, death and dying, and environmental hazards."[128]

The historical record reveals a system poorly prepared to help women who experienced postwar trauma. In 1946, Omar Bradley quashed a pamphlet that addressed specific medical options for female veterans, arguing that the existing VA system was adequate for their needs.[129] The system, built for a male-dominated military, persisted into the Vietnam era. Clinicians regularly misdiagnosed PTSD symptoms in women. Administrative protocols proved confusing for female veterans who actively sought help. As late as 1982, a General Accountability Office (GAO) report indicated that VA hospitals failed to provide women with complete physical exams, domiciliary care, or psychiatric services.[130] Lacking both adequate institutional support and the peer groups available to men in need of assistance, women became a different form of "invisible veteran" after Vietnam.[131]

Veterans and the Criminal Element

While the discussion of posttraumatic stress highlighted individual suffering, the periods after World War II, Korea, and Vietnam each witnessed a debate about the threat posed by combat soldiers to American society. Pundits consistently argued over a 30-year span that military training, augmented by combat and the act of taking human life in war, would make the proper resocialization of veterans impossible. In his popular 1944 book, *When Johnny Comes Marching Home*, Dixon Wecter predicted that "a civilian can be licked into shape as a soldier by the manual of arms and a drillmaster, but no manual has ever been written for changing him back into a civilian."[132] More than a quarter century later, in an article titled "The New Public Enemy No. 1," *Time* magazine speculated that the country would face a crime wave as Vietnam demobilization sent thousands of maladjusted veterans back to the United States.[133]

Many writers assumed that military service and combat experience would foster a new criminal class in America. According to this school of thought, military service was a study in social regression. Entry into service required an individual to abandon civilized forms of behavior and interaction. Training, in its gradually more sophisticated incarnations over 30 years, rewarded not only antisocial but also violent behavior. Combat was the final stage in a deliberate process of deevolution. By encouraging what a 1946 publication described as "aggressive primitive urges expressed in hate, violence, destruction and the need to kill," combat made these newly constructed antisocial tendencies worse.[134]

According to this logic, three wars produced millions of veterans uncoupled from civilized standards of behavior toward life and property. War gave them a purpose, explicitly endorsing their violence for the sake of national survival. Absent a war, as one 1976 sociology study noted, the antisocial elements left over from the military experience persisted without any justification.[135] What was necessary for survival in war now threatened the public good. In *The Veteran Comes Back* (1947), Willard Waller believed that "sometimes the veteran has been so completely alienated from the attitudes and controls of civilian life that he becomes a criminal."[136]

Reality failed to match most of these dire predictions. A 1946 examination of prison inmates with prior military service found that the most important contributing factor to their imprisonment was not their veteran's status but a prior record of criminal acts. Further, researchers found no link between prior military service and violent crime. With one exception, combat veterans in the study committed robbery, larceny, or burglary.[137]

Research conducted on larger veteran populations came to similar conclusions. A 1948 study of crime in New York City incorporated a total of 907,638 veterans who returned to the metropolitan area after World War II. Taken as a whole, crime statistics actually show a significant increase in total offenses across the city. Most, however, were related to traffic accidents and illegal parking. The majority of serious crimes against people and property—robbery, larceny, and burglary—in the veterans' age cohort (21–30) actually decreased from prewar levels. An increasing incidence of offenses committed by individuals under the age of 20 indicated that New York's primary problem after 1945 was juvenile delinquency, not veterans.[138]

Similar patterns appeared across the country after World War II.

Nationally, violent crime decreased between 1945 and 1960.[139] According to statistics compiled by the Federal Bureau of Investigation (FBI) in its annual *Uniform Crime Reports*, instances of murder, manslaughter, and rape all diminished over the 15-year period.[140] From these data, it appeared that the approximately 20 million veterans discharged had little, if any, impact on crime in the United States.

This trend changed markedly in the sixties. The occurrence of aggravated assault and rape increased significantly between 1960 and 1970. Murder and "non-negligent manslaughter" rates doubled between 1963 and 1973.[141] On the face of it, popular predictions about the havoc returning home with Vietnam veterans might have been true.

The assumption is debatable at best. Veterans' social tendencies were the subject of numerous official research projects after Vietnam. An eight-year study published by the VA in 1981 found the record regarding criminality decidedly mixed. American men who joined the military were less prone to crime, according to the research. During the sixties and early seventies, the arrest rate for nonveterans under the age of 21 was more than twice as high (16%) as that for Vietnam-era veterans (6%) before they entered the military and higher than for veterans who had seen heavy combat (12%) prior to enlistment. Once they left the military, some clear distinctions did appear. For men between the ages of 21 and 25, the arrest rate for nonveterans was 14% but 17% for Vietnam-era veterans. Veterans with heavy combat experience had an arrest rate of 24%. However, the overwhelming majority of crimes committed by veterans in the survey (86.5%) were nonviolent.[142]

A more plausible source of crime in the sixties may be demographic in nature, specifically with respect to the age of perpetrators. According to *Uniform Crime Report* statistics, young offenders were the most important emerging problem of the postwar period. In the United States, juvenile arrests doubled nationally between 1948 and 1958.[143] As the baby boom came of age, this trend continued and worsened not just in America but also in other industrialized nations. West Germany, England, France, and Austria, countries whose respective baby booms lagged behind that of the United States by a few years, all experienced a surge in crime during the seventies.[144] None, perhaps with the minor exceptions of England and France, had any military commitments to Southeast Asia. Yet each struggled with increasing domestic instability. America and its Western allies share many plausible sources of internal unrest, from the "economic miracles" of the postwar period that triggered rising social expectations, to race and gender issues and contested Cold War foreign policies. Many factors contributed to what Herbert Marcuse would call, in 1964, the "Great Refusal."[145] However, it appears that veterans were unlikely to be the primary culprits.

War, Veterans, and Drug Abuse

Drug abuse is another aberrant behavior commonly linked to service in Vietnam. The conventional wisdom of the late sixties associated service in Southeast Asia with the greater availability of controlled substances—particularly marijuana and heroin—and a greater prevalence of use among its veterans. One correspondent wrote in 1971 that as many as 75% of soldiers in Vietnam regularly used drugs and that sanctioning marijuana would be like "trying to prohibit the inhalation of smog in Los Angeles."[146] Numerous commentators in the early seventies directly linked the national "heroin emergency" to troops returning home from Vietnam.[147] Senator Alan Cranston (Democrat, California), who chaired the Veterans Affairs Subcommittee on Health and Hospitals, estimated that 100,000 "addicted or drug abusing" veterans lived in the United States by June 1972.[148]

How close to the truth were public fears? Drugs were readily available in Southeast Asia at the time of the Vietnam War. As the military conflict wound down, US law enforcement, including the newly created Drug Enforcement Administration, rapidly escalated counter-narcotics efforts in South Vietnam, Laos, and Thailand with limited success.[149]

However, military drug use during and after Vietnam was not simply a function of increased availability. In fact, from World War II to Vietnam, drug use was the product of sanctioned, institutional research devoted to improve the modern warrior. During World War II, both Allied and Axis forces routinely issued stimulants to soldiers to enhance their fighting abilities.[150] Military medicine experimented with barbiturates, methamphetamines, amphetamines, and caffeine during the war to increase endurance, boost morale, and compensate for the new stresses imposed by modern war on the human body. Drug research in some cases focused on physical demands made by new technologies such as high-altitude manned flight. Throughout World War II, the US military conducted extensive tests to see if drugs could augment specific combat skills (e.g., marksmanship) and solve more prevalent problems like combat exhaustion. Although most of this research produced inconclusive results, it did not stop the US military from ordering as many as 250 million Benzedrine sulfate tablets by 1945. During World War II, an estimated 10% of all Americans serving may have used performance-enhancing drugs.[151]

On the home front, prescription drug use explosively increased in America after World War II. One historian estimated that civilians consumed as many as one million Benzedrine sulfate tablets each day at the end of the war.[152] Within a decade, domestic use reached staggering levels. In 1958, the total legal production of amphetamines alone was 75,000 pounds or 3.5 billion tablets.[153] By 1971, it had increased to 8 billion doses.[154]

Military use of amphetamines also continued and expanded after 1945. They were available to combat forces in Korea. During the Vietnam War, the military issued amphetamines to all branches of the military. Between 1966 and 1969, an estimated 225 million doses, primarily of Dexedrine, a more powerful form of amphetamine, were issued to personnel in Vietnam.[155]

In contrast to the massive expansion of drug use in the United States, the official number of addicts remained comparatively small. While statistics are limited, wartime military personnel screening does provide some insights. According to a 1958 federal report, the official rejection rate for military service because of narcotics addiction declined from 0.75 per thousand in World War I to 0.10 per thousand in World War II.[156] In 1964, the Department of Treasury's Bureau of Narcotics noted a total of 55,899 addicts across the nation, up from 44,146 cases between 1953 and 1957.[157] By 1967, the same agency identified a total of 62,045 "active narcotic addicts."[158] While the numbers are almost certainly low, if compared to national population statistics, it is clear that there was no drug "epidemic" on the scale popularized by pundits in the late sixties and early seventies.

Comparative studies of drug use among veterans of World War II, Korea, and Vietnam reveal some important trends within a muddled body of evidence. The 1992 study of personnel of all three wars by Andersen and Mitchell found drug abuse rates among Vietnam veterans (12%) was much higher than among World War II or Korea veterans (1% in both groups).[159] Twenty years earlier, the VA published similar findings from the Minneapolis VA Psychiatry Service. This study identified drug use as an "acting out" behavior, along with "alcohol problems," "suicidal or assaultive tendencies," and "civilian or military disciplinary problems." Veterans of World War II exhibited drug use 6.5% of the time, while 6.0% of Korean War veterans demonstrated the same behavior. The incidence of drug use among Vietnam-era veterans was more than twice as high at 16.5%.[160]

More-detailed studies of Vietnam-era veterans after the war revealed important distinctions regarding their drug use. According to a 1991 article published in the *Journal of Traumatic Studies*, Vietnam-era veterans had a lower incidence of use for marijuana, cocaine, amphetamines, barbiturates, and heroin than nonveterans. The study found, however, that postwar marijuana and cocaine use increased with combat exposure.[161]

The 1981 VA study mentioned earlier offers some interesting departures with respect to the available data. The authors offered the theory that drug and alcohol use more accurately reflected individual behavior before military service rather than resulted from it. By this metric, a very small percentage of Vietnam-era veterans attributed increasing drug (0.9%) and alcohol (3.6%) problems to their time in uniform. The effect of service in Vietnam was negligible. Veterans stationed in Vietnam reported a 1.1% increase in drug problems and a 0.4% increase in alcohol problems. Importantly, the impact of combat was nearly irrelevant, with no increase in drug use and only a 1% increase in alcohol abuse recorded in the survey.[162]

As was the case throughout the 1981 study, race had a distinct impact on both drug and alcohol use. For white veterans, service in Vietnam increased their likelihood of a drug problem by 1.3%. However, with respect to alcohol, time in country actually *reduced* alcohol abuse by 4.0%. African American veterans with service in Vietnam experienced a far greater increase in drug (9.4%) and alcohol (14.5%) problems. Interestingly, according to the study, combat exposure actually decreased substance abuse problems among African Americans and drug use among white servicemen in Vietnam.[163]

Finally, the evidence suggests that alcohol caused far more difficulties among all veterans than drugs. Andersen and Mitchell found identical rates (27%) of alcohol abuse for surveyed combat veterans in all three wars.[164] These findings correspond with a report to the Senate Armed Services Committee in 1973, which characterized 73% of junior enlisted men as "problem drinkers" or "heavy or binge drinkers."[165] The Minneapolis VA study cited previously noted disturbingly higher percentages of alcohol abuse as an "acting out" behavior for veterans of World War II (38.7%) and Vietnam (40.8%), with Korean veterans exhibiting the highest rate of difficulties at 48.0%.[166]

Drug use was indeed a distinct problem among Vietnam veterans, although the same is clearly true for the generation of Americans who grew up in the sixties. Contextually, it appears that the life course theory merits some consideration. Legal controlled substances permeated postwar American civilian and military life. The same was true of alcohol. This particular controlled substance was a far more predominant common feature of military culture than the amphetamines regularly issued to combat forces. The correlation between Vietnam service and increased drug use may be explained by the easier availability of drugs in Southeast Asia. However, as the 1981 VA study noted, individual tendencies regarding drug use may have had an equal if not more important influence on abuse. The same is true of alcohol use within the military, although some of the evidence indicates that combat exposure may have retarded rather than encouraged substance abuse among some types of combat veterans.

Conclusion

The warrior was a powerful figure in America after 1945. In the wake of World War II, the country celebrated his accomplishments. Dwight Eisenhower entered the White House in 1953 lacking a political record but enjoying the status as liberator of Europe. The veterans who voted for him basked in the reflected glow of their own contributions to the good war against fascism. When writers like Robert Sherrod and Ernie Pyle wrote about the nature of American warriors, they dwelled on the fact that conflict brought out greatness—duty, loyalty, and strength in the face of adversity—in the qualities of their countrymen. Military service in World War II represented the best of a nation and its individual citizen-soldiers.

This sense of accomplishment did not last. The greatness earned in Europe and the Pacific corroded in the hills of Korea. The inconclusiveness of the war, coupled with its brutality and potential for devastating escalation, confused and alienated the public as much as the men who fought it. Korea lacked the tangible, imminent threat of World War II. Although couched in Cold War rhetoric, it did not encompass America as a whole. Draftees filled out the ranks sent to fight along with reservists and the National Guard, but mobilization never fully reached the home front. At home, life moved ahead without rationing, or massive bond drives, or any of the facets that defined the previous war. In the end, the distance from Korea was as much a state of mind as it was a matter of geography.

The war in Vietnam witnessed this gap grow even larger. When combat units deployed to fight in 1965, the guard and reserves stayed home. Nor was the mission any clearer than in Korea. Stripped of rhetoric regarding "containment" and falling dominoes, the war in Vietnam cultivated little public confidence and growing restiveness once intervention developed into a stalemate by 1968. For veterans, Vietnam differed from Korea in that quiet doubts expressed in the fifties exploded into open controversy a decade later. By the time the conflict in Southeast Asia concluded, the image of the warrior, so easily burnished in 1945, invited almost reflexive controversy 30 years later.

As the status of the American warrior deteriorated, his prominence within the modern American military did as well, albeit for different reasons. Simply put, the number of men who did the actual fighting diminished with each passing year, displaced by new technologies and the necessity of maintaining them. This presented an interesting paradox by the sixties. As war became more and more lethal, it fell into the hands of fewer actual warriors in practice. For those who did remain to fight, new doctrine and improved training refined individual participation in the art of killing.

The circumstances surrounding the combat veteran of Vietnam were thus very distinct from those of his predecessors in Korea and World War II. His war was a combination of increased intensity, experienced by a minority of deployed forces, operating under very poorly defined conditions. Moreover, of the veterans of all three wars, he was the least likely to be publicly celebrated as one of the modest, "homely heroes," that seemed to populate World War II.[167] Korean War veterans existed somewhere between the two extremes, both with respect to public attitudes and operational conditions.

How did these circumstances affect the combat veteran's homecoming? Interestingly, despite the changing context, some consistent features are evident. Veterans, particularly those with combat experience, appeared to be easy scapegoats for what ailed civilian society after each war. Whether the discussion began in 1945 or 1970, veterans were fodder for public hysteria regarding crime, drug use, and other bad behaviors associated with exposure to war.

The facts do not appear to support these suspicions. Studies incorporating significant numbers of veterans fail to provide a causal link between military (or combat) service and crime. If viewed from a national perspective, it seems that veterans were a stabilizing force that gave way under the weight of the baby boom after 1945. Demographics are a more probable cause of increasing crime rates in the United States and many Western European countries during the modern era.

Individual suffering cannot be explained so easily. Terms like "shell shock," "combat fatigue," and "neuropsychosis" persisted over time because wartime trauma did generate significant short- and long-term problems for veterans. Understanding and comparing the impact of PTSD in veterans of World War II, Korea, and Vietnam with any accuracy is more difficult, however. Military and civilian medicine adapted well to treating wartime mental breakdowns for the purpose of returning combatants to duty. Developing long-term treatment regimes for veterans lagged behind these processes. The fact that PTSD did not enter into the mental health lexicon until 1980 speaks to the gap between mental health resources for veterans and their needs.

The life course theory applied to those with PTSD remains debatable. Public acceptance of military service may have influenced veterans' sense of legitimacy and subsequent feelings of guilt or justification. By this logic, World War II veterans should be the best adapted, with the fortunes of Korea and Vietnam veterans declining along with their social support. However, new evidence suggests that external social influences may have assisted World War II veterans in repressing or displacing their trauma rather than solving it. This is true for the majority of white, male veterans and possibly even more so for women and minorities who served alongside them.

Instances of veterans' substance abuse both challenges and supports the life course theory. Alcohol abuse among veterans, especially those with combat experience, is consistently high for all three wars. In Vietnam, it appeared that alcohol, rather than heroin or marijuana use, was the real crisis within the ranks, especially among African Americans. Lacking adequate treatment options in combat or afterward, many veterans likely reverted to the most available form of self-medication.

Tracking drug use among veterans, including those with combat exposure, presents a number of intriguing problems. Vietnam veterans clearly exhibited higher rates of drug use than World War II or Korea veterans did. However, that trend was true for American society as a whole. Applying this standard is more problematic with respect to combat veterans. According to the limited information available regarding World War II and Korea, it was a relatively minor problem. Information pertaining to Vietnam combat veterans is more extensive but seems to point to the absence of a link between drug abuse and exposure to wartime violence.

In the final analysis, the culture surrounding the veteran did change from World War II to Vietnam. Accolades awarded almost reflexively in 1945 changed into a broad spectrum of public responses to military service 30 years later. The treatment of combat veterans revealed more consistency, however. Much of the public discourse considered the warrior to be a threat even though the facts rarely justified this assumption. In reality, the combat veteran was more likely to be a threat to himself, his spouse, and people close by. With the exception of drug use, the personal responses to war among warriors were remarkably consistent over three decades. An important change and one reason for hope within this cohort were the advances in medical diagnosis and treatment that offered the possibility of long-term healing.

Soon after Japan's surrender, a steady stream of troopships made way for the United States. Here, veterans from the China-Burma-India theater mark their return home. Courtesy National Archives and Records Administration

The end of World War II saw millions of families reunited for the first time since Pearl Harbor. Courtesy National Archives and Records Administration

Victory parades awaited veterans returning from both Europe and the Pacific. Courtesy National Archives and Records Administration

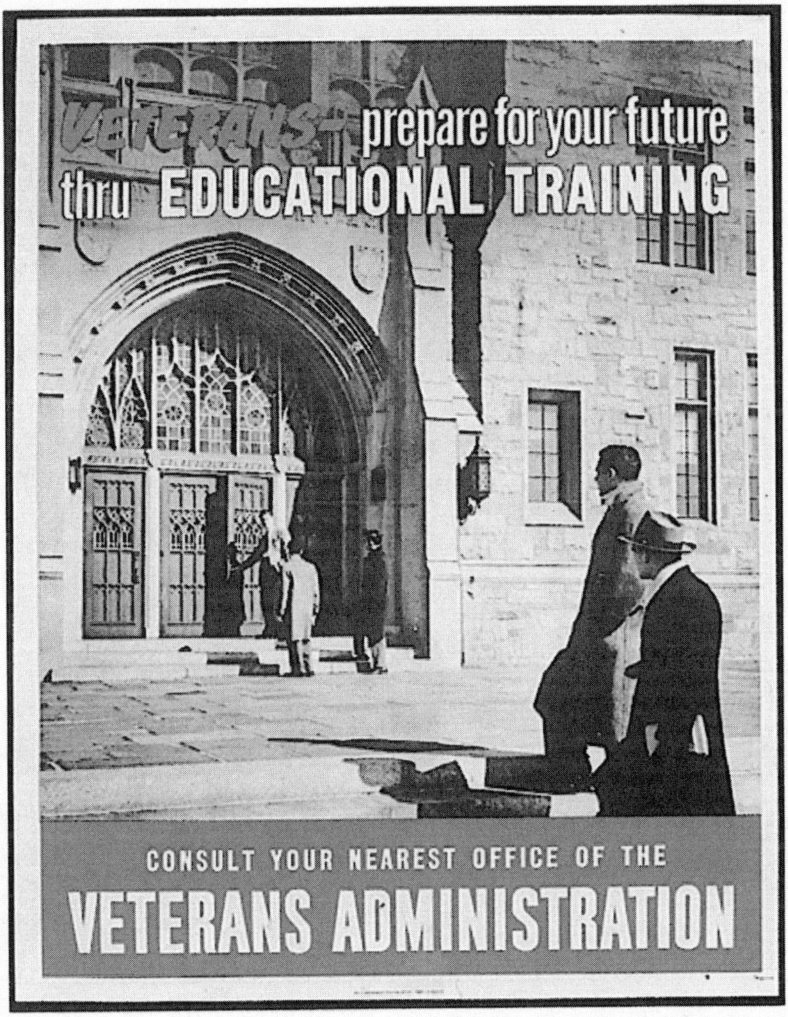

The 1944 Serviceman's Readjustment Act allowed a generation of Americans unprecedented access to higher education and technical training. Courtesy National Archives and Records Administration

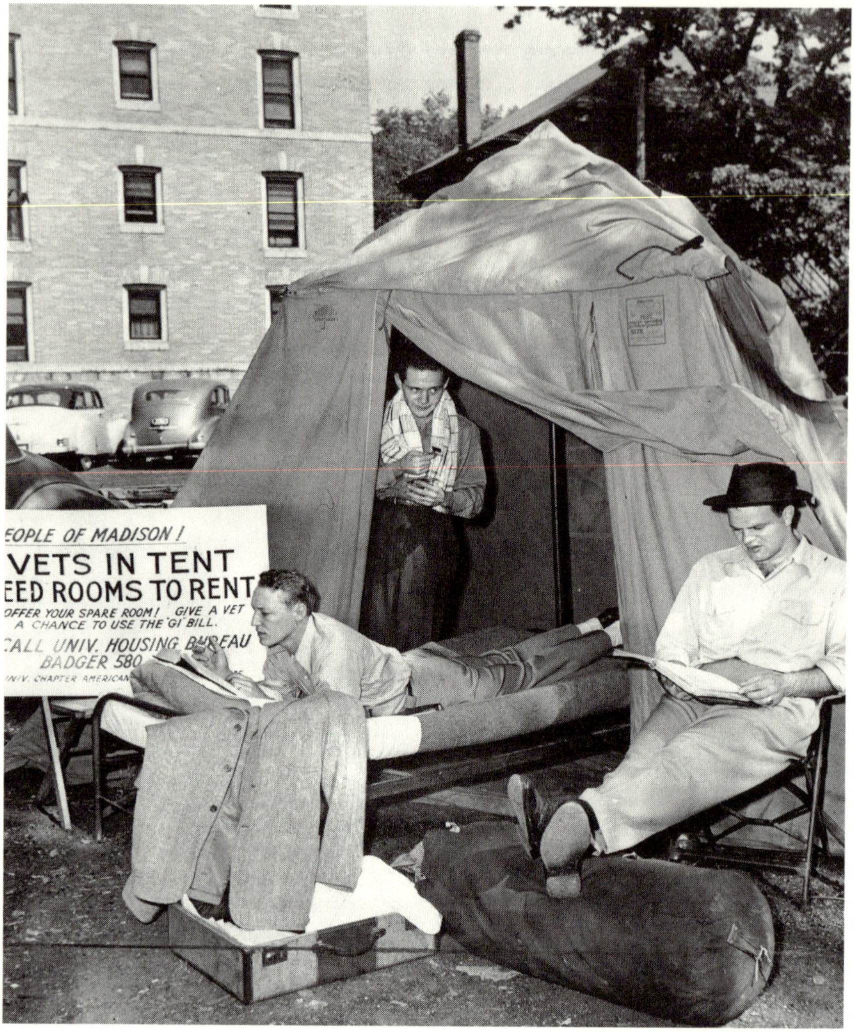

GIs bound for college quickly overwhelmed many colleges, such as the University of Wisconsin in 1947. Courtesy Wisconsin Historical Society-ID 3338

During the Vietnam War, many veterans joined active antiwar protests. Wounded combat veterans were prominently featured during Richard Nixon's 1973 inaugural. Courtesy Wisconsin Historical Society-ID 49679

The antiwar movement used a variety of approaches to illustrate their opposition, including artwork and full-page advertisements. (L.) Courtesy Library of Congress, Prints & Photographs Division, drawing by Edmund S. Valtman; (R.) Courtesy Daniel Cohen

After he returned from Vietnam, John Kerry joined the Vietnam Veterans against the War and became one of its prominent leaders. Courtesy Wisconsin Historical Society-ID 24631

'MY LAST EMPLOYMENT? — VIETNAM'

Vietnam veterans enjoyed a diminished version of the GI Bill with far fewer economic opportunities than returnees from World War II and Korea. Courtesy Library of Congress, Prints & Photographs Division, drawing by Edmund S. Valtman

CHAPTER 3
Veterans at Work

> *Here we have young, disciplined, competent men, a very salable commodity in any other time. Instead they have gone from untrained draft bait to unemployed infantrymen.*
>
> —*John Linton, Illinois Labor Department, 1971*[1]

Introduction

Work was a simple, yet critical method for veterans to reassimilate. It was a way to spend productive energy, to meet both personal ambitions and collective responsibilities. Work offered potential "normalcy" for many veterans. It allowed a distraction from the war experience. While some veterans sought out quiet and solitude, many more found comfort in deliberate effort and pursuing the economic opportunities that the country had to offer.

The exact nature of these opportunities was the problem. Hindsight allows the reader and the historian to see what waited for veterans when they came home. The post-1945 "boom" that defined much of the era is an accepted, if qualified fact today. However, no such surety existed in 1945 as the country faced reconverting to a peacetime economy that had not been prosperous since the Wall Street crash. In actuality, economic disruptions awaited veterans of all three wars. Although a second Great Depression never materialized, recessions were a constantly recurring feature of the postwar American economic landscape.

Veterans relied on a combination of their own talents and expanding state and federal support to navigate these circumstances. It was clear by the mid-twentieth century that modern militaries required an ever-increasing catalogue of technical aptitude. Even the combat arms relied on individuals who could adapt to complex weapons systems. In World War II and afterward, military training systems responded in kind, producing hundreds of technical and mechanical specialties. Many veterans subsequently left the military with new skill sets well suited for the civilian job market, itself increasingly influenced by the defense industry. For those who lacked adequate skills, help was available. The GI Bill was notable in that it moved far beyond traditional "old soldiers" pensions to an unprecedented series of readjustment programs dedicated to support the transition from military to civilian life.[2] GI Bill provisions for technical training and college education revolutionized learning in America.

As they made their way back into the economy, veterans also evoked major, largely unseen changes on the basic organization of the workplace. One of the most important legacies bequeathed by World War II was its constant, sometimes ruthless search for economic efficiency. Allied planners, full well understanding the essential value of industrial production to the war effort, relentlessly developed processes to enhance its efficiency from the factory floor to the battlefield. Victory proved the value of "operational research" to war planning. In the postwar era companies like RAND become pioneers who applied "operational analysis" to the challenges presented by the peacetime economy.[3]

Postwar Economies Awaiting Veterans

The economic disruptions that followed World War II were a case study of planning overcome by events. The wartime system of bureaus and committees painstakingly built to regulate labor, resources, finance, and investment, among a myriad of other details, came apart in the closing months of 1945. The unexpected abruptness of Japanese defeat held all the elements of a bureaucratic disaster as the Truman administration traversed the transition to peace. One author in 1944 accurately predicted that "the veteran of World War II will return to an industrial order in an unparalleled state of flux."[4]

Early indicators of the "state of flux" were truly alarming. America welcomed peace with massive layoffs. In the first 10 days following V-J Day, 1.8 million workers received their pink slips and 640,000 filed for unemployment compensation.[5] Secretary of Commerce Henry Wallace estimated that unemployment could rise to 7 or 8 million, returning the country to its prewar economic doldrums.[6] Although the jobless rate never reached predicted crisis proportions, it was significant. The economy shed 4 million manufacturing jobs by August 1946. These losses were cushioned by the fact that 3 million women and teenage temporary workers did not return to the workforce once the war ended.[7] Even with this shift, 1.2 million new people joined the ranks of the unemployed, increasing the rate to 4.9% by March 1946.[8]

Once wartime controls ceased, prices skyrocketed across the country. Between June and December 1946, food prices increased by 40%.[9] Wholesale prices for all commodities rose by 14.1% in 1946 and 22.7% in 1947.[10] Public discontent over market basket costs set the tone for the 1946 "Beefsteak Election" and returned Republicans to Congress in droves.

Labor strife also plagued the country after the war. Faced with the loss of earning power and declining short-term job prospects, unions flexed their postwar muscles. In the fall of 1945, auto, steel, and coal workers all joined picket lines, disrupting production and causing rolling power blackouts around the country. As the economy continued to stumble, labor stoppages grew. By 1946, 4.6 million workers went out on strike. Overall, the economy lost 116 million workdays to labor stoppages, three times that of the previous year.[11]

The economic problems emerging toward the end of the Vietnam War were similar in scale to the post-1945 era but more a product of planning that never kept pace with need. Outwardly, the American economy appeared strong in the late sixties, benefiting from both high productivity and employment.[12] Although defense spending increased significantly as the war in Vietnam escalated, a large defense establishment developed by the Cold War was present to manage it, something not present at the start of World War II.

Yet economic danger signals began surfacing with disturbing regularity throughout the sixties. As the decade moved forward, American global trade suffered, increasingly challenged by resurrected postwar European economies, particularly that of West Germany. In Asia, Japan led a regional economic resurgence and was joined by a number of lesser-developed nations.[13] By 1971, the United States had an unfavorable balance of trade, its first since 1893.[14]

The domestic economy also presented its own difficulties. As Doris Kearns Goodwin observed, while Lyndon Johnson was a genius at creating his version of the New Deal in the sixties, the Johnson administration did a terrible job of coordinating the Great Society with the Vietnam War.[15] The year 1965 was critical, when conventional ground forces began arriving in South Vietnam at the same time hundreds of new federal initiatives churned out of Congress. Combined, the two massive parallel efforts quickly overwhelmed policy makers responsible for them. The Pentagon struggled to divine the proper use of force against North Vietnam and Communist forces in the south.[16] Within the host of civilian agencies responsible for implementing the Great Society, officials confronted the problem of adequately understanding the linkages between deep-set socioeconomic problems and federally funded solutions.

In basic economic terms, the cost of these dual ambitions was enormous. The total amount spent on social welfare between 1965 and 1970 almost doubled, from $77.1 billion to $145.8 billion.[17] Just as the Great Society spending was beginning to hit its stride, Vietnam added tens of billions of additional unplanned dollars into the American economy. One author writing immediately after the war estimated that the direct cost of Vietnam was as high as $260 billion.[18]

Some important economic indicators improved, but progress was unsustainable. The poverty rate declined to 10% of the population by 1970. Disposal personal income per capita rose by 15% between 1965 and 1969.[19] However, one of the costs of progress was inflation. Prices that were relatively stable between 1961 and 1965 began to creep upward near the end of the sixties.[20] As the seventies began, inflation became a chronic, seemingly unbeatable problem.

National leadership proved unwilling or unable to prevent unfolding economic problems. Johnson delayed steps to slow down the overheating economy as defense orders matched military escalation in Vietnam. He waited until June 1968, three months after he withdrew his name from presidential contention, before finally signing an unpopular 10% surcharge on corporate and individual income.[21] Richard Nixon spent the early part of his first administration navigating difficult economic and political realities. Ongoing, popular domestic programs and a penchant in Congress for new tax cuts counterbalanced troop withdrawals from South Vietnam and defense reductions. White House staffer Daniel Patrick Moynihan quipped in 1969: "I'm afraid the peace dividend tends to become evanescent like the morning clouds around San Clemente."[22]

The systemic, poorly coordinated decisions of the sixties bequeathed what pundits in the seventies would label "stagflation," a time of simultaneously increasing inflation and unemployment. Billions spent for Vietnam and the Great Society flowed into the economy, trickling down through vast civilian and military bureaucracies that took years to disburse funds for thousands of expensive and complex projects. At the same time, private-sector retrenchment and peace in Vietnam translated into a surge in unemployment. Between 1969 and 1970, 1.2 million people lost their jobs, increasing the national unemployment rate from 3.5% to 4.9%.[23] For most people, very little about the future seemed promising. In 1970, there were 7.9 million students enrolled in American colleges and universities, a massive group eventually bound for the troubled job market.[24] Added to these were millions of newly demobilized veterans, some gravitating to higher education but most entering an economy that proved far less welcoming to them than it had for their fathers.

The economy that greeted Korean War veterans stood somewhere between the two extremes presented by World War II and Vietnam. When North Korean forces advanced across the 38th parallel in June 1950, the act surprised more than the American foreign policy community. Massive wartime mobilization triggered a concurrent surge in federal spending. Between 1950 and 1953, the US defense budget grew from $39.5 billion to $74.1 billion. As early as 1951, "national security expenditures" were more than all private-sector investments combined.[25]

Cash poured into a home front lacking the economic controls mandated during the previous war. Opportunities abounded as manufacturers expanded to keep pace with war orders. Jobs linked to defense industries increased accordingly. However, as occurred during the Vietnam War, economic danger signals also appeared, albeit much more quickly. Between June and September, public grumbling rose along with a 2.6% increase in the consumer price index.[26] In contrast, when peace returned, it introduced a familiar wave of defense cuts. As military spending dwindled toward peacetime norms, a brief recession followed the Korean armistice. A combination of returning veterans and defense industry layoffs caused unemployment to spike from 2.9% in 1953 to 5.5% a year later. After meeting his promise to conclude the war, Dwight Eisenhower made repairing the economy his next priority.[27]

Preparing Veterans for the Post–World War II Economy

Veterans preparing to return home have traditionally presented an economic dilemma for their countrymen. In past ages, limits placed on local militia service mitigated the disruptions concurrent with their return. Peasant levies returned to their fields after relatively short campaign seasons, as did freeholders in the American colonies. Small professional armies generally retained the men who served in them under long contracts. Overall, the impact of military demobilization on the civilian economy was fairly small.[28]

This pattern changed with the mass mobilizations of the Napoleonic Age. European systems of national conscription included millions of citizens. With the arrival of peace, these same millions enjoyed limited and inconsistent veterans' benefits, a problem many countries continued to struggle with after World War I.[29] Although the United States generally avoided the economic problems associated with mass demobilization, even after the American Civil War, the twentieth century eventually presented its own challenges, a point reinforced by the onset of the Great Depression in 1929.[30]

Fears of a second Great Depression greeted American veterans returning from World War II. An army survey addressing the postwar situation in 1945 indicated that half of respondents worried about "the problem of earning a living."[31] Most men who responded did not set the bar very high. Soldiers seemed less interested in embarking on new careers than the need to meet basic responsibilities for themselves and their families.

Civilians at home seemed even less sanguine about the future state of the American economy. In his dystopian 1944 *The Veteran Comes Back*, Willard Waller argued that economic problems would be only a starting point for the veteran. Waller flatly declared that "military skills are useless for peacetime living" and that the American "class economy" would consign veterans to menial jobs. He believed that with little prospect for promotion, and subject to civilian work rules, veterans would create cleavages that would destabilize society in the late forties in much the same way returning German soldiers had ruined Weimar Germany in the twenties.[32]

Other less dire but still important concerns percolated through the postwar discourse. One particular target was the Veterans Administration's "52/20" program that provided an unemployment benefit of $20 per week for up to a year. Critics derided what they considered federally subsidized laziness. One author writing in a September 1946 article titled "Are We Making a Bum out of G.I. Joe?" for the *Ladies' Home Journal* noted: "Work is a habit, and these payments get the veteran out of the habit of working."[33]

Obviously, not all the commentary was negative. Many writers were optimistic about the positive impact the war might have on peacetime, particularly with respect to the veteran's part in it. In GI Bill provisions for small-business and farm loans, they saw hundreds of thousands of veterans as future entrepreneurs prepared to husband the economy back to a prosperous normalcy.[34] Other commentators believed that leftover military discipline and professionalism might impart a better quality of work in America, where home-front standards had begun to noticeably slip.[35]

In a sense, both sides were correct concerning their predictions about veterans. Without question, mobilization for World War II profoundly altered the nature of work in America, in terms of both its type and the processes guiding it. Yet the optimists were right in the sense that veterans returning home from war in Europe and the Pacific did prove to be a critical, dynamic element in the postwar economic boom that traveled through America for almost 30 years.

Massive industrial and manufacturing growth was key to defeating the Axis during World War II. While the United States was already a formidable industrial power before the war, military production brought new plants and manufacturing complexes to nearly every corner of the country. Rural states like Mississippi and Alabama, for example, saw their manufacturing workforce nearly double during the war.[36] Industrial centers in Michigan, Ohio, and Pennsylvania grew in concert with new opportunities that appeared throughout the Sunbelt states. A 1947 study by the VA estimated that the postwar California labor force would remain more than 30% higher than its 1939 levels (4.2 million versus 3.0 million). The new economy promised opportunities aplenty on the Pacific coast.[37]

The war also altered the systems that governed American work. "Simplification" and "efficiency," not new concepts to industry, became the watchwords of World War II. Early in the war, American manufacturers adopted the British concept of "operations research" to improve output.[38] It involved more than a modern gloss on standardized parts and Ford's prewar assembly-line process. Operations research and concepts like it encouraged planners to think beyond specific products and more about strategically managing both resources and talent. As the war progressed, the idea expanded beyond individual industries to a dedicated attempt to coordinate the national economy.[39]

Training new entrants to the industrial workforce was instrumental to this goal. During World War II, the Department of Labor promoted the Training within Industry Program, which offered "job instruction training" to millions of people entering manufacturing and industry for the first time. For the sake of portability and efficiency, new doctrine reduced the work process to "utter simplicity" so that an individual completely untutored in industrial work could quickly understand the cadences of the factory floor. Between January 1942 and October 1945, 9.8 million workers received this training, among them millions of women who were joining industry.[40]

The program meshed well with concurrent military instruction conducted for millions of service members during the war. Over the course of a remarkably short five-year period, the War Department proved adept at screening, selecting, and training an enormous cohort of specialists. Between 1940 and 1945, the army and navy produced 1.3 million men with expertise in technical and scientific fields as well as 324,510 mechanics and craftsmen.[41] The accomplishment was important in two respects. In one sense, the military was providing a substantial bloc of trained workers with the technical skills that a modern postwar economy would likely demand. Perhaps more important, civilian and military training systems increasingly shared a pedagogy that reflected modular, simplified instruction.

In the postwar period, the GI Bill picked up the threads of this integrated relationship. When the VA surveyed veterans' college and university enrollment in 1946, it found an increase in accepted applications from 26,333 to 162,485.[42] By the time the 1947 school year began, 1.1 million veterans were college students.[43] Subsidized by federal tuition payments, these graduates provided an immense reservoir of talent for the postwar economy. Many became professors themselves to pursue private and public research. More than a few sought out careers focused on teaching. Taken as a whole, these men made up a core group in academe awaiting the baby boom when it went to school in the sixties.[44] Many of the remainder pursued technical expertise that shaped and guided nearly every sector of the American economy. Between 1945 and 1950, the number of engineers in the country almost doubled from 297,000 to 543,000; the number of draftsmen increased from 82,000 to 127,000.[45]

The largest group of veterans, approximately 3.5 million, never attended college, instead taking training courses and certification programs through the GI Bill. With these new and refined skills they became the plumbers, carpenters, electricians, and bricklayers who built the new suburban developments and retail shopping centers. They entered the growing ranks of organized labor in the northeastern auto industry. When Adm. Ben Moreell, who served as chief of the Navy Bureau of Yards and Docks, became president of the Jones & Laughlin Steel Corporation in 1947, he oversaw a company that contributed 12,689 of its employees to the armed forces during World War II, many of whom returned to work in Pittsburgh under the provisions of the GI Bill.[46] New industries offered additional opportunities for veterans. Expanding domestic aircraft production opened employment in a host of technical specialties. After World War II, the number of aircraft mechanics nearly tripled from 28,000 to 75,000.[47]

Although training and education were important contributors to veterans' employment prospects, they were not the only means toward that end. At the state level, "local veterans' employment representatives" provided counseling and placement for individuals returning to the job market.[48] The federal Veterans Employment Service largely mirrored these efforts through a small cohort of field representatives available in each state.[49] Between 1945 and 1955, state and federal veterans' employment agencies received 23.6 million job applications and managed to place 15.3 million veterans in jobs.[50]

Progress on this scale would have been impossible without private-sector cooperation. In the years following World War II, corporations across the spectrum rallied to the idea of supporting returning veterans. The Jones & Laughlin Steel Corporation approved promotions for veterans who had lost seniority due to their military service.[51] Other companies, like Ford, Bulova, International Harvester, and Westinghouse, with prompting from Omar Bradley as VA administrator, readily joined federal initiatives to train and employ disabled veterans.[52] In the postwar period, 1.2 million disabled veterans entered job-training programs at a higher rate (57%) than veterans without disabilities.[53]

Patriotism no doubt motivated corporate leaders, but their decisions also reflected a series of shrewd economic calculations. When private industry contemplated postwar expansion to meet rapidly increasing consumer demand, it needed to tap into the reservoir of talent, then being subsidized by the GI Bill. More broadly, entrepreneurs also understood the makeup of the new peacetime marketplace. In a tract published immediately after the war, Shell Oil cultivated solidarity with the public by claiming that it "merely acted in the line of duty in doing better than its best to speed the war's end."[54] By appealing to a sense of mutual wartime service, companies like Shell very carefully positioned themselves in a postwar boom dominated by millions of veterans.

The sum of these efforts proved to be remarkably successful for the American economy, the business sector, and individual veterans. Fears of a second depression proved to be unfounded. Although subject to considerable stresses, the postwar economy recovered and grew in a remarkably short time. Some 10 million veterans rejoined the economy in the year following the Japanese surrender. Their "absorption into civilian jobs proceeded smoothly," according to a later Labor Department study, facilitated by the withdrawal of millions of women from the labor force and the departure of millions more veterans to school.[55] Pent-up consumer demand, measured by the $140 billion sitting in individual savings accounts, found ready outlets after the war.[56] Triggered by the rapid expansion of suburban development, employment in trades and services, light manufacturing, and building materials boomed. Construction employment more than doubled by 1946 as contractors attempted to keep pace with new subdivisions.[57]

Job security also improved in general and for veterans in particular. Increasing union membership, with its attendant contractual salary structure and benefits, introduced many Americans to the middle class for the first time. Veterans, by virtue of the GI Bill, also gained greater control over their employment. The right to return to jobs left behind before the war was an important provision to the Serviceman's Readjustment Act. For men interested in moving beyond their old jobs, the GI Bill created a way station in college or technical school, which allowed veterans to pursue their ambitions. For minority and women veterans, simply having these options was a major departure from the norm. For them, the GI Bill became a means to break into previously restricted vocations and establish a permanent place in the American workforce.[58]

Most Americans had real reasons to be optimistic after 1945. Upward mobility, facilitated by billions in federal benefits, became a basic reality for the majority of people. For a growing plurality, the GI Bill offered training and education that translated into new skills and better incomes. A 1956 examination of veterans' programs found that former service members between 25 and 44 years old consistently earned better annual salaries than comparable civilians.[59]

Veterans' expectations rose along with those of the rest of the country. Hope was perhaps more pronounced for minority veterans. The GI Bill was blind with respect to race and access to education, for example. The prospect of educational achievement was a boon to African American veterans, who generally entered the military with less education than their white counterparts.[60] However, hope for the future competed with long-standing racist practices. As much as it was groundbreaking legislation, the GI Bill did not prevent school segregation at any level. Consequently, large numbers of minority veterans found themselves channeled into a far smaller array of poorly funded colleges and technical schools than were white veterans.[61] Even so, the number of African Americans attending college tripled between 1940 and 1950.[62] Similar obstacles prevented equal access to work once they graduated. Labor unions around the country proved reluctant to admit minorities. A 1946 study by the National Urban League of African American veterans' readjustment in 50 cities reported that training and apprenticeship were rarely made available. Job placement through the US Employment Service tended to focus on menial, "traditional Negro jobs."[63] Regardless, only 15% of African American veterans returned to their prewar jobs in the first two years of peace, according to one 1947 study.[64] Ten years later, a report by the American Veterans Committee noted persistent resistance by labor and management to minority hires in skilled or technical work in Alabama and Mississippi. This same resistance also prevented on-the-job training allowed by the GI Bill.[65] When individual state employment offices failed to act on behalf of minorities, the undermanned federal Veterans Employment Service offered a poor alternative.

Women veterans of World War II negotiated a similar path. In the aftermath of the war, the general expectation was that women would return to traditional roles as mothers and homemakers to reconstruct the social foundations of the country. A spike in the national divorce rate, rising juvenile delinquency, and the prospect of caring for more than 600,000 wounded veterans as well as unknown numbers of men affected by "battle fatigue" all attracted national attention.[66] Many women in fact did depart the job market for the sake of their families and children. However, although the overall number of women at work shrank significantly in the immediate aftermath of World War II, 18 million remained employed outside the home by 1947 (28% of the total workforce), and their numbers increased with each successive year.[67]

Female veterans pursued two divergent courses in the postwar American economy. Family and childbearing were two of the most often-cited reasons for women to leave the military, a trend that continued for the next 30 years.[68] Conversely, many women actively pursued careers after 1945. Some remained in the military, where they lobbied for greater opportunities but largely failed in that effort. Others attempted to parlay skills gained in the military into civilian careers. In this instance, they had greater success. Corporate America welcomed women who were responsible for the "billions of facts, recorded individually," according to historian Doris Weatherford, that were integral to the management of military operations during World War II.[69] This was particularly the case with entrepreneurs who were veterans, men who could readily identify military skills with business applications. As one 1946 publication claimed, "GI Jane's stoutest advocate in civilian life is her ex-commanding officer."[70] Sharing as they did a common experience with male veterans, in many cases in the same campaigns in Europe and the Pacific, women enjoyed a degree of credibility that their peers lacked. Given these opportunities, many undertook professional careers and never looked back.[71]

Unfortunately, ambition, training, and a degree of acceptance did not automatically translate into a broad range of professional careers for women veterans. According to the 1950 census, most fields, from dentists to engineers to pharmacists, included practically no women, veterans or otherwise. In that year, two job categories encompassed almost two-thirds of employed women: teacher and nurse.[72]

In sum, veterans of World War II benefited from a rare combination of economic opportunity and cooperation between the public and private sectors. Opportunities proliferated as the postwar boom took hold and expanded in the years and decades following the end of the war. Employers readily welcomed a well-trained workforce created by virtue of the US military and the GI Bill. Both potential and realized earning power drove the optimism and higher expectations of the era.

However, the abundant economic potential of the postwar period was also a source of frustration and ongoing discontent. For hundreds of thousands of minority and women veterans, equal opportunity under the law was lost in translation when they entered segregated classrooms and an unequal marketplace. These veterans made some progress, but the grudging advancement that resulted in higher college graduation rates for African Americans or new white-collar opportunities for women only highlighted entrenched inequities. The abundance achieved by millions of veterans remained tantalizingly out of reach for many if not most of these isolated groups, a reality that would fester throughout the fifties and sixties.

Veterans' Economic Fortunes after Korea

The economic context surrounding the Korean War was markedly different from that of either World War II or Vietnam. Its most notable feature was the general absence of contemporary concerns about prosperity. The war began in a decade defined by growth, when America's real gross national product increased by 51% between 1949 and 1960.[73] By 1950, the economic teething problems experienced in the year following V-J Day were largely solved. The conflict in Korea impacted the economy but on nowhere near the same scale as World War II. Even as it conducted a pell-mell mobilization for Korea, the Truman administration deliberately avoided rationing, wage-price controls, and most of the measures that governed the home front after Pearl Harbor. The 1951 troop rotation policy, initially adopted to ease the burden on reservists and World War II "retreads," also had the additional impact of returning veterans to the economy gradually over the course of the Korean War. Fears of massive unemployment after the war never materialized

The Korean War separated civilians and veterans into two distinct economic spheres. As the fighting raged on, people at home took advantage of the many opportunities presented by American business, particularly in sectors enjoying the surge in defense spending, such as steel, electronics, and aviation. For Americans in the military, it was a different story. Professional career soldiers were already separated from the civilian world, living in military housing and shopping in military commissaries. Young draftees lived much the same way, but temporarily and generally before they embarked on postsecondary education and civilian careers. Those most affected by the Korean War were the reservists and National Guard. These "retreads" from World War II had, for the most part, finished their schooling and moved on to careers and families. Their world before June 1950 was filled with mortgage payments, education funds, and competition for promotion. Mobilization ended that pursuit. For more than a million men, pay cuts were the order of the day. A new private (E-1) earned $75 a month in 1949. A lieutenant entering the army for the first time made $213.75.[74] Military compensation was a far cry from comparable civilian wages. More important, these veterans lost seniority, opportunities for training in civilian fields, and the ability to network in the booming American economy. For them, Korea was a time of lost years.

Disparities in pay tainted postwar prospects for military recruiters and retention in general. When asked about joining the air force, one young man responded, "But I don't want security, I want to make a living."[75] Keeping highly trained technicians was another problem. One air force sergeant groused to Bill Mauldin in 1955 that the service was "training the whole damn' television industry."[76]

The economic separation of Korean veterans from civilians took many forms after the war, some more obvious than others. An August 1953 *New York Times* article written by George Barrett described the typical soldier returning from the war in terms that combined military service with many contemporary features of the modern workplace:

> *Raised as sixth-graders to family tales of the mechanized fighting of World War II, mechanically conditioned then and later to the push-button concept of living and the cosmic-ray concept of fighting, sent very young with other very young soldiers to a country they had never heard about to fight a war they did not understand, the new veterans are disquieting, machine-like products of their special time, and products particularly of the impersonalized low-pressure but deadly war that they have been waging.*[77]

He further characterized the Korea veteran as having "an amazing amalgam of first-class fighting competence and an almost eerie disinterest in a job or surroundings or relationships."[78] Barrett makes an interesting cultural statement, one that took the features of economic progress, celebrated during World War II, and turned them on their head. Korea veterans, produced by the best-crafted systems of training and fighting, emerged from the war seemingly as cold fish, almost a different species.

Barrett obviously exaggerated his point for effect. More than a few veterans were extremely bitter about their lost years. Writing for the *American Legion Magazine* in 1952, Gene Gilmore put a common complaint in the following terms: "You find your job has shrunken in your absence, become a vestigial organ. Your take-home pay is considerably less than it was two years ago, and what is left doesn't go very far. The law that guarantees a veteran his old job and his old salary doesn't work out as intended. You are financially penalized, and not only for your time in the Army."[79]

The economic forces separating veterans from civilians also appeared in very tangible ways after Korea. The economy was fundamentally more stable in 1953 than it was in 1945. There was no waiting deluge of new veterans to overwhelm the job market. Consequently, the early fifties lacked the sense of urgency regarding national demobilization in general and veterans in particular. "Belt tightening" was the catchphrase of the 1952 election that propelled Dwight Eisenhower into the presidency. While the new president wanted to make sure Americans understood he was not a "mindless slasher," to use James T. Patterson's phrase, no program was off the table.[80]

The 1952 Korean Veterans' Assistance Act (PL 550) reflected this thinking. The "Korea GI Bill" was perhaps best characterized by an ongoing commitment to reward military service that was increasingly subject to budgetary limits. It provided slightly more money ($26 per week instead of $20) for unemployment insurance but cut its availability from one year to six months.[81] Another sign of retrenchment was what the American Legion called a "drastic curtailment" of funds for the Veterans Employment Service, whose overall number of field offices declined throughout the fifties.[82]

The most important sign of encroaching restrictions concerned veterans' educational benefits. The 1944 GI Bill had paid up to $500 annually for tuition directly to the school in addition to a $75 monthly allowance to single veterans without dependents. Instead of paying tuition directly to schools and a stipend to the veteran, the Korea GI Bill allowed the VA to provide veterans with a lump sum for all expenses: $110 per month for individuals, $135 for veterans with one dependent, and $160 for veterans with two or more dependents.[83] For individuals without dependents, this was a significant cut even before accounting for inflation between 1944 and 1952. William P. Tolley, chancellor of Syracuse University, described the benefits plan as a "shabby deal." The Association of American Colleges voted unanimously, and unsuccessfully, in January 1954 to increase the subsistence allowance for veterans.[84]

The sheer number of veterans in the United States, 22 million by 1955, was a significant problem for the Eisenhower administration as it explored measures to reduce the federal budget. Midway into his first term, the president appointed Omar Bradley to lead a commission that would examine the long-range budget impact of accumulating veterans' health, education, and disability benefits. Eisenhower also wanted to parry lobbying for new spending that would provide full old-age pensions for all veterans.

The Bradley Commission's final 1956 report was an attempt to dampen expectations regarding benefits. One of its main findings concluded that "the ordinary losses of time and opportunity while in military service must be regarded as part of the responsibilities of a citizen and only extreme or extraordinary handicaps should be regarded as creating an obligation on the Government."[85] In practice, the commission reaffirmed the country's commitment to individuals disabled by military service but drew a clear line against extending a pension or new benefits to the remainder. The American Legion and Veterans of Foreign Wars challenged even these conclusions and managed, with a host of other veterans groups and their allies in Congress, to forestall major cuts in the VA budget.

Regardless, retrenchment proceeded in quieter ways for the remainder of the fifties. Lawmakers made no effort to upgrade funding for education through the existing GI Bill. The Eisenhower administration also oversaw the closing and consolidation of VA facilities around the country. By 1957, nearly 5,000 beds had been withdrawn from the VA hospital system.[86] In some cases, a rather bizarre (at least in retrospect) Cold War logic sufficed to justify the cuts. The VA, for example, proposed closing a hospital in Cleveland,

Ohio, because it cost too much to renovate it to withstand a nuclear blast.[87]

The economic prospect for veterans in the years between the Korean and Vietnam Wars was notable for its regress and progress. The time immediately after the Korean armistice was particularly troubling. In October 1954, of three million discharged veterans, 835,000 had applied for educational benefits and only 200,000 were attending college full-time. Korea veterans who actually attended classes had higher dropout rates than civilians, particularly among married veterans. National economic trends appeared equally problematic. Two additional recessions, in 1957–58 and 1960–61, bracketed the ongoing cuts in veterans' benefits.[88] A marked decline in auto production and housing starts characterized the first. In August 1958, unemployment rose to a disturbing 7.6%.[89]

Fortunately, veterans proved adaptable to their circumstances. Lacking the generous 1944 educational payments, Korean War veterans enrolled in cheaper public colleges and universities, a trend that continued into the sixties. Over time, gradually accumulating numbers made the move to school. By April 1955, a total of 587,000 veterans were receiving training, the largest component in college (325,000) followed by technical training (178,000).[90] Three years later, 600,000 were enrolled in some type of educational program, with 400,000 in college.[91]

The number of Korean War veterans in school never equaled the tidal wave of GIs who engulfed colleges after 1945. In part, this situation was a simple function of the total number of personnel mobilized, but it was also affected by the fact that a third of veterans discharged after 1953 were veterans of World War II who had already used their benefits. Changes in the Selective Service law also allowed more student deferments and permitted college students to complete their education during the war.

Despite suffering three recessions in the fifties, the underlying strength of the US economy also proved to be a decisive factor in veterans' favor. Although growth began to noticeably slow in the last half of the decade, the labor market was able to absorb both skilled and unskilled workers.[92] Moreover, when confronted with potential economic calamity, Eisenhower proved to be a pragmatist and a closet Keynesian, willing to jump-start growth with increased federal spending for highways, education, and defense.[93]

The decade ended on a positive note for most veterans. The hard data indicate that Korea veterans achieved economic success after their war in the same manner as the earlier World War II cohort. In 1954, the median income for veterans who were 25 years old and over was $4,039, and for civilians, $3,087.[94] Despite curtailed funding, continuing training and education benefits in the 1952 version of the GI Bill helped pave their way into the booming middle class.

Not all the economic news was good, however. When it expired in 1955, the Korea GI Bill left unaddressed veterans' peacetime benefits over the long term. As the Eisenhower administration intended, a robust private sector was responsible for veterans' economic integration. As the fifties moved into the sixties, it proved adequate to the task of reassimilating the shrinking number of men and women departing military service. Although few realized it at the time, industrial obsolescence, declining productivity, prohibitive labor costs, and trade imbalances produced by encroaching foreign competition would soon take away this cushion for veterans and the general public alike.

Vietnam Veterans and American Economic Decline

Veterans of the Vietnam War suffered from a combination of poor economic circumstances made worse by poorly crafted and executed federal policy. Although the American economy of the late sixties and early seventies remained sound in many ways and continued to lead much of the world, signs that it had begun to unravel appeared by the time the war in Vietnam was over. The times presented veterans with a frustrating dilemma. Generally better educated but younger than the individuals who served in World War II or Korea, Vietnam-era veterans found a systemically weaker economy that was not prepared for them and, in some cases, treated military service as a liability. Missing from the early seventies was the as-yet-untapped potential for economic growth of 1945 or the depth apparent in manufacturing, industry, and service work that awaited Korean War veterans. For Vietnam veterans, a time of increasing need and declining prospects was their basic reality.

National economic policy often compounded these difficulties. In many respects, the Johnson and Nixon administrations as well as the Defense Department repeated many of the same fundamental mistakes committed in 1945 and 1950. Although Vietnam draft calls benefited the job market by removing excess labor, it was a poorly managed process, one that became increasingly apparent after Richard Nixon reversed course on the war in 1969. Officials did little to coordinate the rapidly increasing number of discharges—from 496,000 in 1965 to over one million by 1970—with private-sector demand.[95] Moreover, as the draft wound down, inducting 152,000 men in 1972 and only 25,000 a year later, Nixon and his primary advisers tended to see the issue of manpower in political terms, linking the measure to his 1972 reelection prospects rather than considering the economic impact on veterans as a group.[96]

Veterans' programs operated in fits and starts during the Vietnam era. When Lyndon Johnson escalated troop deployments in the mid-sixties, his administration was taking a budget axe to veterans' programs. When the 1st Cavalry Division received its mobilization orders, a backlog of 17,000 disabled veterans waited for access to VA hospitals. Due to budget cuts, VA contact offices responsible for facilitating job placement and benefits were reduced from 215 in 1960 to only 10 by 1965.[97]

Vietnam-era military policies also complicated veterans' employment prospects. First among these was the Pentagon's response to the concurrent challenges of declining discipline and a significant uptick in military drug use. At first, commanders attempted to draw a hard line against both, sanctioning behavior in the hope of deterring bad acts. As the *Nader Report on Vietnam Veterans* explained it, "Drug use in the military has always been a crime, but until recently it was nothing else. All programs, all directives, all actions taken by military authorities were predicated on that fact. Having defined the drug user as a criminal, the military traditionally felt no responsibility toward him." A sergeant major in the 173rd Airborne Brigade put the matter another way in 1971: "The thing we really need . . . is a way to get rid of these people as soon as we discover them. Be able to eliminate them."[98]

The effort largely failed and was, at least with respect to military drug use, replaced with internal treatment programs under the Nixon administration. In the meantime, sanctions produced a noticeable increase in administrative discharges. Between June 1970 and June 1971, for example, almost one in five sailors left the navy under terms that were "general," "undesirable," "bad conduct," or "dishonorable."[99] These types of discharges followed veterans immediately into civilian life. A dishonorable discharge automatically forfeited readjustment benefits under the Veterans Readjustment Benefits Act of 1966 (PL 89–358), known as the "Cold War GI Bill."[100] Military careers shortened by other types of discharges automatically impacted the total number of months veterans could receive educational support. Veterans discharged for drug use could also lose medical benefits at the discretion of the VA.[101] Other sanctions, for drug use or bad conduct, persisted on a veteran's record and tainted future job prospects.

As the military crackdown on drug use proceeded, civilian policy makers added to the portfolio of veterans' assistance programs. In 1967, the VA began Operation Outreach, an aggressive attempt to provide transition counseling for military personnel about to leave the service. VA representatives traveled directly to South Vietnam to meet with service members preparing to return home. Over the course of three years, they eventually met with 1.1 million personnel. Approximately one-third of disabled veterans received counseling while still hospitalized for their injuries. Once they left the military, contact continued through direct mail and phone calls.[102] By 1970, VA staff were available seven days per week at 311 separation points around the country. Veterans who could not travel could also take advantage of free phone service to regional VA offices.[103]

Civilian policy makers in the Pentagon also attempted to ease the path to civilian life for veterans. Project Transition was a Defense Department initiative first begun to assist enlistees and draftees with low aptitude scores find work after they had left the military. It eventually expanded to offer counseling and job training on half the military bases in the United States and overseas. By 1969, Department of Defense officials claimed that 250,000 personnel received job training and an additional 1.5 million personnel had undergone counseling.[104] To further facilitate job placement, the Pentagon also sponsored direct connections with businesses that were defense contractors, such as IBM, to employ discharged veterans.[105] In June 1971, the Nixon administration took this idea a step further by encouraging the National Alliance of Businessmen, which represented almost 30,000 companies, to provide 100,000 jobs for Vietnam veterans.[106]

Both the VA and the Defense Department cooperated with numerous Great Society projects intended to ease veterans' transition from the military to civilian life. Programs for employment placement in police and fire departments, Volunteers in Service to America (VISTA), and Job Corps were all folded into "veterans in public service careers" (VIPS) initiatives. During the Nixon years, the Defense Department funneled veterans into Department of Labor vocational training as well as the US Office of Education's Career Opportunities Program.[107] The VA encouraged veterans to serve as teachers in the "deprived areas" of rural America as well as the inner city;[108] Project Remed and Operation MEDIHC (Medical Experience Directed into Health Careers) attempted to recruit military medical specialists in the civilian medical professions.[109]

By all official accounts, the overlapping layers of federal programs touched millions of Vietnam-era veterans. Just how deep an impact they had was the subject of both controversy and no small amount of resentment among their target group. For all its grand claims, for example, Nixon's effort with the National Association of Businesses was purely voluntary and netted only 20,000 new jobs for veterans in 1971. The *Nader Report* found veterans' programs under Nixon to be poorly funded, sometimes with money taken from other job programs.[110] Government-sponsored job fairs commonly attracted far more veterans than available positions. In May 1972, veterans destroyed kiosks in what one witness described simply as a "riot."[111] Word of mouth, family, friends, and personal initiative accounted for the vast majority of employment, according to one Harris Poll.[112]

Veterans' unemployment emerged as a major issue at the end of the Vietnam War. Although it stood at only 4% in late 1969, two years later, with the national economy in the teeth of another recession, the rate for younger veterans aged 20–24 was 12.4%. For all veterans, it was more than double the national figure.[113] Joblessness was far greater for minority veterans. Ironically, the vocations that offered higher rates of promotion in the military—the combat arms—translated as "low-skill occupational specialties" in the civilian sector. This, combined with higher rates of less-than-honorable discharges among African American veterans, made employment far more difficult.[114] According to testimony by the National Urban League before the Senate Committee on Veterans Affairs, black veterans' unemployment was 22.4% in the first quarter of 1972.[115]

Employers, buffeted by encroaching hard times and dubious about the prospects for the newest crop of returning soldiers, proved reluc-

Table 3.1. Post-1945 comparison of unemployment rates

	Veteran (%)	*Nonveteran (%)*
August 1946	8.0	3.6
November 1954	7.9	5.3
January 1969	3.7	3.4
February 1971	11.0	5.9

Source: Paul Starr, *The Discarded Army: Veterans after Vietnam: The Nader Report on Vietnam Veterans and the Veterans Administration* (New York: Charterhouse, 1973), 203–4; *Monthly Labor Review* 63 (November 1946): 673–74; Bureau of Labor Statistics, https://www.bls.gov/data/.

tant to assist veterans. When the 1970 "Jobs for Veterans" initiative sent out a mass mail appeal to 900,000 businesses to encourage hiring, it received a 2% response rate. Undersecretary of Commerce Rocco Siciliano put the matter bluntly in June 1970: "It is hard to imbue businessmen with a social conscience when business is bad."[116] Unions proved equally reluctant to allow returning rank-and-file members with little seniority to jump the line ahead of hundreds of already laid-off men.[117]

Youth was a serious handicap regarding employment of Vietnam veterans. Men under the age of 24 had less education and experience than their World War II or Korea counterparts. After discharge they were poorly positioned to enter an economy that demanded better technical skills and training.[118] Alternatives in relatively unskilled work, such as the building trades in the forties or manufacturing in the fifties, were lacking after Vietnam as industry retrenched and the Rust Belt grew in scope and scale. Military skills garnered by young veterans, particularly draftees channeled into the combat arms, also proved poorly suited for the civilian job market. A 1969 University of Maryland survey reported that only 16% of army veterans and 28% of navy veterans used their military training in the civilian sector.[119] The result was a persistently higher unemployment rate for the age 20–24 veterans' demographic. In March 1971, it stood at 14.6% for veterans and 10.8% for nonveterans and remained above 10% even after the economy staged a recovery later that year.[120]

As was the case in World War II and Korea, Vietnam veterans

had a chance to explore higher education before work, albeit with substantially reduced opportunities. The Cold War GI Bill reversed earlier Bradley Commission recommendations by making veterans' benefits retroactive to 1955. It kept veterans' preference for federal employment as well as established home and farm loans. The 1966 version of the GI Bill similarly rejected an important Bradley Commission conclusion when it expanded hospitalization to include non-service-related disabilities.[121]

However, in regard to education, the Cold War GI Bill was frozen in time. It kept the key provision committing the federal government to pay for 36 months of school, but it allotted only $100 a month for tuition, fees, and "subsistence" for a full-time student with no dependents. Veterans who attended classes and had two or more dependents received a monthly stipend of $150.[122] Even though they had effectively cut benefits from 1952 levels even before inflation, lawmakers assumed that Vietnam-era veterans would use education, particularly college, in greater numbers than the previous generation. At the time Lyndon Johnson signed the Cold War GI Bill, approximately 3.8 million men and women qualified for educational support.[123]

American legislators proved to be half right about their assumptions. Vietnam veterans were better educated and better prepared for higher learning than those coming home from the two previous wars. According to a 1977 VA study, 59.1% of Vietnam veterans, 26.3% of World War II veterans, and 43.5% of individuals who served in Korea had at least four years of high school. The same was true with respect to college. Where fewer than 1 in 10 (9.6%) World War II veterans attended classes in colleges and universities, 13.0% of Vietnam-era veterans could say the same. Korean War servicemen and servicewomen were again in the middle at 11.1%.[124]

Unfortunately, even with Vietnam veterans' stronger credentials, the Cold War GI Bill did not result in a surge in school attendance. As the Vietnam War proceeded, college participation remained low. The most straightforward cause was the disparity between VA funding for school and its actual cost. Officials in Washington cited other reasons. The Nixon administration placed part of the blame firmly on veterans. In 1970, the President's Committee on Vietnam reported that 22% of veterans had no high school diploma and 30% of those who did scored worse on AFQT tests than those without diplomas. The VA attributed low attendance rates to the relative youth of Vietnam veterans and the fact that they tended to be discharged as individuals rather than groups in a mass demobilization. Years after cutting back more than 95% of its local contact offices, the VA complained without any sense of irony that authorities lacked access to veterans as they processed out of the military.[125]

American campuses offered fewer solutions to veterans seeking an education. Private and public colleges in the early seventies presented a drastically different environment for veterans than that of the earlier postwar periods. The deferment provisions built into the Selective Service System in the fifties and sixties allowed most university-bound baby boomers to pursue higher education without the burden of military service. Consequently, although the Vietnam-era military contained the highest proportion of college-educated recruits in its history, higher education was dominated by a generation of students without direct military experience.

Veterans became a distinct minority in this environment. A 1969 study by the University of Wisconsin, Madison defined them as "another sub-group in the population," a term that offers a number of insights on the status of contemporary veterans.[126] The report noted that 1,000 veterans obtained benefits to attend college during the fall 1968 semester, only a fraction of those eligible, and a tiny part of 34,670 students enrolled at that time.[127] The study attempted to explain the root causes of this phenomenon. Again, economic circumstances were the most obvious factor. Most veterans simply could not afford to attend an elite school like the University of Wisconsin. Personal finances were inadequate to close the tuition gap left open by the 1966 GI Bill. The study also considered cultural and educational factors affecting veterans. Many individuals returning from Vietnam and other active duty elsewhere were unwilling to consider college because of family obligations or a lack of preparation in college-track courses while in high school. The university administration identified them as "veterans whose motivation has changed as a result of service experience and maturity."[128]

Collectively, the University of Wisconsin categorized Vietnam-era veterans as "disadvantaged students," comparable to individuals eligible for Upward Bound. The label is meaningful for a number of important reasons. In contrast to the attitude of higher education after World War II and Korea, which openly cultivated veterans' admissions en masse, by the late sixties, their service was being treated more as a disadvantage than an asset. To address this need, university officials in Madison recommended outreach centers similar to those created for minorities and economically underprivileged students. In this manner, veterans could be recruited and mentored with attention to gaining college credit for past work experience and obtaining occupational experience while attending classes and meaningful employment while enrolled. These steps were no doubt sincere, but they also illustrate a final point. The situation at the University of Wisconsin was mirrored in most other colleges and universities across the country. Where veterans occupied a prominent place on campuses in the forties, by the early seventies, they were but one among an increasingly diverse array of competing constituencies.

Despite this new reality, the educational narrative began to improve. Congress finally addressed the tuition gap in a 1970 amendment to the GI Bill. That year, single veterans in school received $135 a month, while veterans with two or more dependents saw their monthly stipend improve to $210.[129] Increasing numbers of veterans took advantage of training and education under the GI Bill as the seventies proceeded. By 1970, 736,000 applied for school support, up from 542,000 in 1968.[130] By June 1973, roughly half of Vietnam-era veterans took advantage of GI Bill education and training. Overall, 51.2% of post-Korea and Vietnam-era veterans attended college, higher than after Korea (50.7%) and World War II (28.6%).[131]

Federal funding for veterans' education continued to lag behind need for most of the seventies. Even after Congress increased benefits for tuition and living expenses again in 1974, they were still grossly inadequate. That year, a single veteran received $1,980 for all college expenses even though tuition alone cost about $890 for state colleges and as high as $5,000 for private universities.[132] Renewed economic troubles following in the wake of the energy crisis and a concurrent spike in inflation soured the Ford administration on what it saw as an unnecessary burden. Only a few months into his term, the new president vetoed a new GI Bill that attempted to close the benefits gap. Although massive majorities in the House and Senate overrode Ford, he successfully obstructed additional spending increases for the remainder of his time in office.[133]

In the end, Vietnam veterans suffered from a stigma that clung to them when they returned to work and school, one that took many years to overcome. Employers thought twice about hiring a generation of soldiers stereotyped in the media for their bad behavior. Stories of rampant drug addiction and disgruntled troops "fragging" their leaders took hold of the public imagination and impeded progress by cultivating fear and distrust. Public leaders who might have checked the spread of these stereotypes sometimes reinforced them. Senator Alan Cranston's claim that 100,000 to 150,000 servicemen returned home as heroin users became an accepted part of the conventional wisdom. In a declining economy, few businesses wanted to accept such a risk regardless of individual merit. Richard Dix, who returned from Vietnam in June 1970, captured the frustration of many veterans in an interview with *Business Week*: "Employers tell me it's not their problem that my military service cut me out of the job market. They say I've got no work experience. It's the old tired circle of no experience, no job, no job, no experience. People don't care. They just don't care."[134] Despite these obstacles, Vietnam veterans endured and, in many cases, defied the odds. Existing data indicate a mixed record with respect to their postwar economic fortunes. One 1981 study recorded Vietnam veterans' unemployment rate in 1977 at 8%, more than that of Vietnam-era veterans (5%) but almost equal to that of surveyed nonveterans (9%). Race continued to be an important determinant of employment. Joblessness for African American veterans of Vietnam was more than five times that of white veterans.[135] Underemployment also remained a chronic problem unseen in the statistics. Combat veterans were already well versed with the problem of translating military skills to civilian work after discharge, but this dilemma also affected individuals with technical skills, particularly women. Although trained in literally hundreds of military occupations, female veterans discovered their most likely employment reduced to "clerical and kindred work."[136] Twenty years later, military nurses who rejoined hospital staffs found the transition from valued colleague to "handmaiden" a difficult process, as one historian has observed.[137]

Studies of Vietnam veterans' earning power illustrate some departures and dispel a few myths. Obstacles specific to Vietnam-era veterans, from parsimonious readjustment benefits to the troublesome core of poorly educated men within the most advanced military in the world, created significant economic difficulties. In some respects, veterans experienced the same problems as their boomer generation; their incomes suffered from a glut of young applicants entering a soft economy in the seventies.[138] Unlike the much stronger periods of growth following World War II and Korea, it took time for veterans to recover. Yet, through a combination of improving economic times and individual initiative, they did regain lost ground. One comparison of Korea and Vietnam veterans indicates that while the former group earned slightly more than comparable civilians, Vietnam veterans had not fallen behind their nonveteran peers at the end of the seventies.[139] One more recent (2003) evaluation of approximately 30,000 veterans noted distinctions between Vietnam-era draftees and volunteers according to their race. Overall, men in the sample saw a 1.5% reduction in wages compared to those of their civilian peers. White draftees suffered the largest losses (-5.0%), while African American draftees (+3.0%) and volunteers (+7.5%) recorded the largest increases over comparable nonveterans.[140]

Military Influences on the Postwar Workplace

When Robert S. McNamara made the transition from the Ford Motor Company to the Department of Defense in 1961, contemporary media reports generated a great deal of commentary about just how much corporate influence, more specifically "systems management," became an integral part of the military's institutional culture. A January 1961 profile of the incoming Kennedy administration by the *New York Times* noted that McNamara's task was "to bring efficiency to a $40 billion enterprise beset by jealousies and political pressures while maintaining American military superiority."[141] In reality, the exact opposite was true. When McNamara arrived at the Pentagon, he was returning home to the place where he originally found his managerial spark two decades earlier when the country struggled to find a way to win another war.

American mobilization during World War II required a consistent form of what could be best described as ruthless efficiency. In order to prevail over the Axis powers, the United States had to develop both the mass production of war materiel while simultaneously promoting qualitative improvements in military technology. An obvious means toward this end was to apply science to the "instrumentalities of war."[142]

One of the individuals responsible for this approach was Vannevar Bush, director of the Office of Scientific Research and Development (OSRD). Bush oversaw research divisions devoted to chemistry, physics, and metallurgy as well as applied psychology studies responsible for the selection, classification, and training of American military personnel. The OSRD did so, recognizing that "tests devised to eliminate the emotionally unfit from induction prevented the wrecking of many lives and the fruitless expenditure of much time, effort, and money."[143]

One of OSRD's most important objectives was to foster what it called the "man-machine system." During the course of World War II, it became abundantly clear that machines designed to move (on the ground and in the air) and kill had largely outpaced the ability of their users to control them. Consequently, researchers on both sides expended considerable resources to meld human effort with existing technology. Researchers focused in particular on "stimulus and response" thresholds, the ability to differentiate between types of information under conditions of extreme mental and physical pressure.[144]

In practice, this meant reducing physical actions to quantifiable standards that could be predicted and integrated with mechanical systems, a contemporary update of ergonomics. Throughout the war, OSRD research applied to a broad spectrum of man-machine interfaces, from procedures to match hand-eye coordination with gunsights, to aircraft gauges and control levers that were readable under high g-forces, to the development of a spoken lexicon that facilitated group communication within the confines of a heavy bomber in combat.[145]

Taken individually, these systems were important solutions to the dilemma that "the least efficient element of a machine is often the man who operates it."[146] A 1946 report from the National Defense Research Committee (NDRC) on antiaircraft weapons spoke to the problem of the human element: "First, antiaircraft action is so rapid, the problem is so complicated, and the results are required to be so accurate that simple human skill is utterly useless."[147] Research sought out a process to perfect the combination of man and machine, or, in the 1946 parlance, "the essential dynamical unity of a *complete* fire-control system."[148]

Looking back, American and Allied researchers produced remarkable results with the comparatively primitive analog technology of the day. More important was the emerging faith in the ability to creatively and positively wield modern science and technology to solve *any* problem. Few saw an upward limit to what successes the future might hold.[149]

Allied victory was a final and critical stamp of approval to this concept. During the war, American corporations went to great lengths to advertise their contributions to mobilization and conspicuously link their success with future civilian consumption. A Shell Oil publication in 1945 noted "winning the war is a full-time job" and that "regardless of all other considerations, the Company would devote all its energies and all its resources toward helping with the war." This patriotic fervor had derivative benefits for the postwar economy. "There will be brand new products too, rising from the increased knowledge of Shell's research scientists."[150] Plastics, and other petroleum-based compounds created to beat the Axis, were the wave of the future. Similarly, postwar advertisements were careful to highlight the fact that their products were "battle tested," making the case for durability clear for a consumer who had fought the war.[151]

The endorsement went far beyond advertising copy. In the post-1945 period, the systems that won the war traveled directly into the American corporate sector. In part, billions of dollars in government Cold War defense contracts reinforced this process. Former military men who moved into corporate leadership also promoted the transfer of ideas. Postwar corporate rosters read like a virtual who's who of American wartime leadership. Omar Bradley chaired the board of Bulova Research Laboratories. Douglas MacArthur held the same position for Remington Rand. Eisenhower's former chief of staff Walter Bedell Smith served as vice chairman of the American Machine and Foundry Company board of directors.[152]

The sheer number of veterans among the company rank and file allowed military standards to proliferate throughout the corporate structure. During World War II, the Grumman Aircraft Company worked especially closely with the US Navy, a relationship wherein military personnel, company management, and workers integrated their skills to produce fighters for the military. Once the war was over, Grumman welcomed navy veterans back into its ranks for their technical expertise and ready understanding of government contract processes.[153]

Tested by war and endorsed by victory, military practices became corporate practices. Companies quickly adopted standardized employee screening along the lines created for military personnel during the war. The National Association of Manufacturers adopted rating systems that gauged objective factors such as attendance and quantity of work along with more subjective matters like "gets along with others," "work habits," and "judgment."[154] Employee training followed a similar logic. The Pittsburgh advertising firm Ketchum, MacLeod & Grove argued that military training could be easily adapted to civilian circumstances in that it was "selling" an idea en masse. They also believed that army's use of visual material to convey an idea was perfect for postwar mass marketing.[155]

More broadly, postwar corporate America embraced the wartime concept of continuous innovation applied to technology and organizational structure. "Systems management," derived from World War II innovations sponsored by the OSRD, became the catchphrase for success in the late forties and fifties. When Robert McNamara arrived at Ford in 1946 accompanied by a cohort of officers from the Army Air Corps Statistical Control Office, he revolutionized the company's cost structure and organization.[156]

He was not alone in this endeavor. In 1950, Remington Rand promised that its new UNIVAC combined "both management and science" and could facilitate "analysis of computed results in accordance with management-established rules."[157] In essence, Remington Rand proposed not only to further the rational systems constructed during the war but to continue melding man and machine. Over the next 10 years, it examined management systems that applied to human behavior. In 1961, this rationality applied to what Sperry Rand described as "life science systems." Its research facilities studied "perception and control; adaptation; behavior under stress; communications; reliability; vulnerability."[158]

The American media popularized many of these methodologies during the selection and training of the Mercury astronauts in the late fifties.[159] However, practical application extended to a far larger array of purposes after 1945. "Engineering psychology" was a booming field in postwar America. It envisaged the rational use of space, an idea engineers applied to the aircraft industry, but also to subjects as diverse as the national highway system, city planning, and the organization of office space.[160] In some respects, the workplace became akin to a

Skinner Box. Industrial planners considered lighting, temperature, ventilation, and a host of inputs that affected worker productivity.[161]

The ruthless efficiency demanded by systems management and engineering psychology left a significant and largely negative impact on corporate culture. Systematic approaches to managing costs and the workplace eventually began to affect the structure of authority and relations between managers and employees. One 1955 publication recommended that budding executives apply "content analysis" to organize the way they communicated in the office.[162] Such a structure, cleanly delineated by facts, offered the promise of predictability and efficiency, both of which led the way toward better profits and promotions.

Yet there were unseen costs to this approach. When Robert McNamara rebuilt the Ford Motor Company, he constructed clearly delineated, centralized lines of authority that improved decision making as it created better short-term revenues. In the process, he eliminated input from plant managers, foremen, and line workers. Although the old method of doing business was often sloppy and sometimes adversarial, it was able to spot design flaws during the assembly process and offer innovations for future Ford models.[163] Ironically, systems management undercut morale at Ford, while over the long run it began to significantly undermine its competitiveness.

It is also arguable that American companies lost a good part of their souls during this period. The link forged between efficiency and profitability came at the cost of creativity in many workplaces. The constant drive for predictable, uniform standards of behavior resulted in a demand for conformity that conflated workplace culture with personal behavior. The intrusiveness of this process eventually reached absurd levels. The type of suit a man wore, his voting preferences, leisure activities, or the exclusiveness of his suburban development all became intrinsic components supporting advancement up the corporate ladder.[164] In 1963, Betty Friedan famously described women shackled to their "comfortable concentration camps" in the suburbs.[165] Men, chafing under corporate workplace rules, risked their employment and economic viability if they demanded too much autonomy at home or on the job. A man seeking greater control over his terms of work also risked his social role as a provider, something that could (and did) create considerable friction within marriages.[166]

Corporate America only belatedly recognized the scope of this discontent. By the sixties, "operational design" was the new management theory in vogue. It offered advice on how best to develop "a true unfolding of human potentialities."[167] This revamped approach was a clear movement away from the "science" of the workplace. Instead of narrowly applying systems management for the sake of resulting profit margins, operational design argued that a worker craved "a sense of dignity, self-worth, self actualization, and participation in shaping his own future."[168]

For many members of corporate America, this change was largely too late. As early as 1951, C. Wright Mills criticized the "minutely subdivided organizations" that had "replaced the bustling interest of work in well-known groups."[169] In *The Lonely Crowd* (1950), David Riesman talked about the growing penchant toward deliberate self-manipulation to achieve success within corporate culture. Riesman argued that in the new service economy, tangible skills mattered less than the ability to sell yourself and be a "good teamworker." Success essentially meant abandoning a known craft for the uncertainty of bending personal relationships to your economic ambitions.[170]

Navigating his way through this rising tide of discontent was Sloan Wilson's "man in the gray flannel suit." Although veterans did not represent a uniform constituency, they did retain some consistent characteristics. Few, for example, questioned the epistemology of the organizational systems that had won World War II and propelled America into its postwar economic boom. Even when this boom slowed in the sixties, they assumed that their systems required adjustment, not wholesale abandonment. Veteran corporate executives such as Ben Moreell, who led companies like Jones & Laughlin Steel, did so at a time when American companies were beginning to lose traction in an increasingly more competitive global economy.[171] Many of these leaders clung to the efficiencies promised by systems management and other theories for the sake of recapturing competitiveness.

Veterans who made up the rank and file were a different constituency, but one that reflected a similar focus. Vested in the value of picking up the lost threads of normalcy, millions of veterans embraced the two entwined pillars of life: work and family.[172] With respect to the former, most veterans invested their jobs with a combination of accepted cultural norms prevalent in the forties as well as the structure and discipline retained from their time in uniform. Overall, they were pragmatists, willing to accept the strictures of corporate life in exchange for job security and the prospect of advancement. Consequently, qualities defined with "consistency," "uniformity," and "conformity" became embedded in the American workplace, where they continued to define this generation decades later.[173]

Veterans' dedication to work produced additional, unintended legacies over the long term. The degree of conformity most veterans were willing to tolerate established the basic parameters of generational conflict that dominated much of the sixties. When the *Port Huron Statement* was first published in 1962, it excoriated American society for its "superfluous abundance" and complacency.[174] Whether the accusation was fair or not was beside the point. The Students for a Democratic Society and those who followed it placed the blame for this system on the keepers of the postwar status quo, a constituency dominated by working veterans of World War II.

Recent medical studies have focused on a more personal legacy. PTSD is a relatively recent categorization, normally applied to veterans of Vietnam and subsequent conflicts.[175] However, in the past decade, clinicians have addressed the impact of posttraumatic stress on World War II combat veterans. According to their findings, veterans like James Bradley were typical of many of this generation. When they engaged in the responsibilities of work and family, these men effectively repressed, or "disassociated," their PTSD symptoms. However, once World War II veterans began retiring in the nineties, these problems resurfaced. In the present day, these men have joined their younger compatriots from Iraq and Afghanistan in addressing the latent problems created by war.[176]

Conclusion

Peace presented its own unique set of economic challenges for veterans exiting World War II, Korea, and Vietnam. The problems that followed victory in 1945 centered around the transitions necessary to convert a massive industrial base from war production, while simultaneously reincorporating millions of discharged military personnel. Absent national mobilization for war eight years later, Korea veterans wrestled less with broadly felt economic cleavages than the prospect of losing a step in the booming Cold War economy of America in the fifties. Vietnam veterans returned home to a country increasingly defined by the end of the postwar boom; encroaching economic stagnation dictated their opportunities. The one common thread that does hold the three periods together, however, is the ongoing state of economic flux that veterans confronted after their return home.

Helping veterans along the way was a lineage of federal readjustment programs. The 1944 version of the GI Bill set a precedent for expansive, inclusive benefits that used training and education as bridges to employment security and upward mobility. The generosity of these benefits, combined with the broad array of opportunities generated by the sustained post-1945 economic recovery, revolutionized the American standard of living for the World War II generation.

However, as the 1944 GI Bill progressed and succeeded, it encouraged increasingly higher expectations. By the fifties, in the wake of the Korean War, the public discussion moved from readjustment benefits for wartime veterans to a full-scale lifetime pension plan for all former service members. The Eisenhower administration balked at the potential cost of such a plan and appointed Omar Bradley's commission in 1955 as a brake on these expectations. It proved to be an imperfect solution for all sides. As the *Nader Report* noted 20 years later, successful lobbying from veterans' groups preserved benefits for those who served in World War II and Korea, but subsequent generations of veterans faced fiscal retrenchment and resistance to parity with the old GI Bill. In terms of federal help, a generation gap appeared well before the height of the Vietnam War. By the early seventies, veterans could rely on fewer resources and less private-sector cooperation amid an increasingly crowded landscape of special interests and government beneficiaries.

Even while recognizing the ebb and flow of national economic trends and the evolution of federal assistance policy, it is also important to recognize the specific importance of the individual veteran. Looking back, we often take for granted how these men and women successfully negotiated significant transitions in life and work. If there is a common thread among veterans of these three wars, it was their ability to adapt to the new burdens imposed by new opportunities. Some elements of the individual experience were unique, however. Many of the economic opportunities presented to veterans broke with old, established social precedents that could be all at once uplifting, dangerous, and frustrating. Right-to-work provisions in federal law established the potential for employment stability for minority veterans. Race- and gender-blind education and training programs granted the ultimate prospect of upward mobility. But what the law could create, it could not implement. The economic opportunities established by the 1944 GI Bill remained subject to prejudices of state officials, unions, and employers, obstacles that took additional years of struggle to address and incompletely overcome.

One final economic impediment was a veteran's age when departing military service. By definition, age dictated experience as well as capability in the workplace. While the law protected employment, it could not impart additional value to an entry-level job. Nor could policy create the maturity necessary to succeed in training, education, or the market. Scholars and official reports have chronicled the declining average age of veterans from World War II to Vietnam. The quality was clearly important to combat exposure and the incidence of PTSD, but it is equally relevant to postwar economic opportunities. Vietnam veterans, already handicapped by declining American economic fortunes, also faced a crowded job market that placed a premium on skills that many youth could not provide. Consequently, individual economic recovery was not just a function of economic circumstances but also of the passage of time.

Finally, it is interesting to note just how much the military systems permeating corporate culture after World War II promoted success and frustration among veterans. The penchant for "systems management" that took hold during World War II benefited from both its practical efficiency and the gloss lent by victory over the Axis in 1945.[177] The millions of veterans returning home rediscovered the military in the offices and factory floors of the peacetime American workplace. Ironically, the various incarnations of the "man-machine system" proved vulnerable to the very success it fostered. Increasingly affluent veterans, illustrated by Sloan Wilson's "man in the gray flannel suit," bridled at the prospect of conformity for the sake of efficiency. Years before baby boomers would reach this same conclusion, veterans were already realizing one social fissure that would contribute to the emerging generation gap. Despite the difficulties presented by the postwar economic transitions, inconsistent readjustment policies, persistent social prejudice, and individual limitations, on balance, veterans generally enjoyed economic success during the period under consideration.

CHAPTER 4

The Veteran as an Activist

Our travels have taught us much. . . . People, action, thoughts, scenery, idealism, and conflict have created a ponderous juggernaut which strangely has not destroyed us. Rather, it has reformed, reshaped, in substance as well as spirit, our peculiar scholastic idealism. It made us realistic idealists.

—Army veteran, 1946[1]

He is a man accustomed to discharging duty and exercising responsibility. He is used to commanding the respect he has justly earned. And these are the spoils of battle he will bring with him when he returns to America. This time the Negro veteran will return to his native land shorn of his old sense of stunted purpose. This fact poses some deep questions.

—Whitney M. Young, National Urban League, 1967[2]

A Daughter of the American Revolution approached one of the VVAWers [Vietnam Veterans against the War] and said, "Son, I don't think what you are doing is good for the troops." Replied the VVAWer, "Lady, we are the troops."

—An exchange during the 1971 Dewey Canyon III protest[3]

Introduction

A strong thread of volunteerism runs through American history, comprising a combination of political, religious, and civic involvement that touches nearly every corner of life. The often-quoted passage from Alexis de Tocqueville that in America "there are not only commercial and industrial associations in which all take part, but others of a thousand different types—religious, moral, serious, futile, very general and very limited, immensely large and very minute" was timely in the nineteenth century and equally relevant more than 100 years later.[4]

The period after World War II saw a distinct surge in volunteer activism that extended well beyond the forties. In part, this growth may be attributed to the circumstances of the times. Membership in the Parent Teacher Association grew (and dissipated) in concert with the maturation of the baby boom through the public school system. Generally, however, more Americans made a deliberate decision to invest increasing amounts of time and resources in civic participation after 1945. When Robert D. Putnam examined American volunteerism in *Bowling Alone*, he constructed a representative sample of membership in an array of 32 national chapter-based organizations from the Elks to B'nai B'rith, the Red Cross, and the Girl Scouts. As a group, all saw their numbers grow in the postwar period and peak at the start of the sixties.[5]

Veterans clearly were part of the growth in postwar volunteerism. Putnam includes the American Legion and the Veterans of Foreign Wars (VFW) in his survey of dynamic organizations, although membership in both peaked much earlier in 1945. When they did, the Legion and the VFW together encompassed one-third of the total veteran population in the United States.[6] As discussed later, the two organizations made up a powerful, well-funded lobby that successfully promoted veterans' issues in public policy for years. Their influence on the various evolving incarnations of the GI Bill is a testament to that effectiveness.

How far did veterans' activism extend? Was it narrowly defined within the confines of deliberate self-interest? Or, as Whitney M. Young offered, was military service a transformational event that left veterans individually or collectively prepared to challenge the social status quo after returning to civilian life?

Negative stereotypes pervade both models. Throughout the post-1945 period, a series of articles and books addressed how the military experience might shape and taint activism in the civilian world. Speculation extended to both the means employed by veterans and their ultimate ends. In his 1944 work, *When Johnny Comes Marching Home*, Dixon Wecter speculated that returning veterans would essentially import militarized cultural standards into the public domain and become the catalyst for fascism in the United States. More than 30 years later, another author cited almost identical concerns. He agreed that veterans likely would be more "authoritarian" in their approach to social causes and prone to accept violence as a method to achieve that end.[7]

This chapter tests characterizations regarding goals, methods, structure, and generational approaches to veterans' activism to see how far they stretch before breaking apart. A substantial proportion of veterans' advocacy may have been captured and directed by American Legion and VFW lobbying efforts, but it is important to understand how much veterans' activism extended beyond traditional institutional boundaries. How far did veterans venture forth to engage in causes that did not represent their direct self-interests? The methods employed by veterans also deserve similar scrutiny. As discussed in the previous chapter, veterans' organizations transferred many facets of military culture into the civilian sphere. In many basic ways, the local VFW, the American Legion, and other organizations reflected military lines of hierarchy and authority. Post "commanders" led by following a structured process of establishing concrete objectives, setting benchmarks and deadlines, and allocating resources. The more effective leaders learned to consult with the rank and file and delegate responsibilities. However, overall, the system employed a process that was conservative by its nature to the point of being almost pedantic. Did this conservative element permeate veterans' organizations as a rule, or were there significant departures from the norm?

Finally, one part of the stereotypical model of veterans' activism tends to be monolithic, politically conservative, and socially constructive, particularly in the VFW and American Legion during the forties and fifties. On the opposite end of the scale are Vietnam veterans, a group largely defined by images of public protest and a lingering conglomeration of bitterness, cynicism, and alienation.[8] Were these stereotypes based on fact? Or are there significant departures from this story line based on changing times and veterans' actions that remain to be understood?

Traditional Veterans' Activism

The historical purpose of American veterans' groups since the founding of the country was to win recognition for their wartime sacrifices. In one respect, organizations like the Grand Army of the Republic or the American Legion dedicated their energies to public celebrations and the commemoration of service. In a more tangible sense, these groups pursued compensation from state legislatures and the federal government, a combination of medical care, pensions, survivor benefits, and domiciliary care.[9] Their goal, as expressed by an official American Legion statement on the 1944 Serviceman's Readjustment Act, was to compensate for war when it "disrupted the everyday living of all of the citizens, and especially those who were called to arms."[10]

The GI Bill, as it quickly came to be known, was a triumph of traditional veterans' activism. Representatives from the Military Order of the Purple Heart, Disabled American Veterans (DAV), the VFW, and the American Legion all worked closely with the House and Senate as the legislation evolved into the final law signed by Franklin Roosevelt on 22 June 1944. As the two largest organizations, the VFW and the American Legion assumed the most important positions at the table, crafting language for the bill in concert with lawmakers while deflecting concerns emanating from the smaller veterans' organizations. In 1944, the Legion and VFW agreed to include a specific figure for Veterans Administration hospital expansion of $500 million over the objections of the DAV, which was lobbying for a higher figure. The Legion was also able to reconcile divergent plans regarding veterans' unemployment compensation and educational benefits.[11]

Their combined efforts proved wildly successful. Money poured into "readjustment benefits," with an increase from $295 million in 1945 to $2.1 billion in 1947.[12] Readjustment became one of the central pillars of the GI Bill. Funding went to education, business and home loans, and unemployment compensation, all with the intended purpose to ease veterans back into a stable, productive civilian life. The growth of American colleges and trade schools and the subsequent infusion of intellectual capital into the post-1945 economic boom is a well-known story. The second pillar attended to the immediate costs of hundreds of thousands of men wounded and disabled during World War II. Again, the massive expansion of budgets for "hospital and domiciliary facilities" tells a similar story, increasing from $17.9 million in 1945 to a staggering $242.8 million just two years later.[13] In the years following World War II, the VA hospital system developed some of the best programs in the world for wound treatment, physical rehabilitation, and mental health.[14]

Once the GI Bill became law, both the American Legion and the VFW became its guardians. They defended it against fiscal retrenchment in the years before the Korean War with mixed results. After the United States went to war in Korea, veterans' organizations led the call for a new GI Bill for the conflict. The subsequent 1952 Korean Veterans' Assistance Act (PL 550) covered service between 1950 and 1955. It essentially replicated the same financial and program commitments made by the earlier version of the bill, but with a few cuts to employment assistance and educational benefits.[15]

This form of traditional activism proved highly popular. According to an October 1954 Roper survey of veterans, a strong majority favored not only the existing array of programs but also special additional consideration from lawmakers. The poll recorded the highest support for expanding payments for service-connected disabilities, the right for veterans to return to their former jobs after their Korea deployment, veterans' preference in federal civil service applications, and improved VA payments for school and training. Overall, 68% of the Roper sample agreed that veterans' groups were doing a "fine job in keeping the country well prepared" by encouraging a strong benefits program for military service.[16]

The Korean GI Bill also signaled a looming clash between veterans' expectations and the government's willingness to expand veterans' programs, particularly on the issue of lifetime pensions. In 1955, Dwight Eisenhower appointed Omar Bradley to chair a commission tasked with studying veterans' benefits. It was the second time in Bradley's career that he was tapped by the White House to address the pressing problems of American veterans. Ten years earlier, Harry Truman recalled Bradley from command in Europe to rebuild the VA for the purpose of serving the needs of millions of soon-to-be discharged service members. The rapid expansion of VA capabilities and the many reforms implemented during Bradley's tenure were a testament to his success.

However, the Bradley Commission's mission in 1955 was distinctly different. As was the case with most federal programs during the Eisenhower years, the main concern was cost, both the escalating expenses of two GI Bills that now covered approximately 22 million individuals and the expectation, fostered by the likes of the American Legion and VFW, that additional benefits were on the way. In particular, the White House balked at the idea of a full retirement pension for all veterans regardless of service in peace or war. Administration budget analysts estimated the new costs for this program alone would be $762 billion.[17] Eisenhower's 1956 budget message pointedly identified veterans' benefits as an ongoing and increasing expense that needed "constructive reconsideration."[18]

Bradley's task in 1955, therefore, was reform through retrenchment. Rather than lend his significant public prestige to expanding veteran readjustment and medical programs, Bradley became a counterbalance to the power of veterans' groups that traditionally rejected any attempts to disrupt the benefits status quo. As mentioned previously, the Bradley Commission did not recommend the same draconian cuts under way in the US military at the time. Instead, it advocated prioritization, drawing a distinction between "programs which take care of the needs arising directly out of military service" and other normal problems of aging and infirmity.[19] While the VA could take care of the former responsibility, the commission argued that the existing social welfare system should take charge of the latter. Duplication was inefficient and also extremely costly. The Bradley Commission noted that commitments to pensions, compensation, and benefits totaled $140 billion in 1956.[20]

Regardless of the commission's limited goals, criticism began as soon as the commission released its findings and recommendations. Individuals lambasted the report as well as the process. George J. Pickett, administrator of Albany County, New York, veterans' service center, stated that veterans were "tired of being used as petty pawns to be moulded [*sic*] and shaped by the slimy and filthy hands of the money-changers; the worshipers of the almighty dollar, and the so-called economizers and penny-pinching crackpots at their every whim and fancy."[21] The strongest negative response came from the

American Legion, which attacked the commission's report as "filled with cliches, self-contradictions, inaccuracies, looseness of expression, non-sequitors [*sic*], statistical monstrosities."[22] The VFW characterized commission recommendations as "impractical, contrary to national tradition and replete with distortions and exaggerations" and an "attempt to reverse the traditional national policy of the United States with respect to those who have served in the Armed Forces."[23] Smaller veterans' organizations also contributed to the dialogue, although not all sided with the Legion or VFW. The DAV was critical of the commission before it issued the report and cautioned Bradley against "a disgraceful campaign for economy in government, mostly at the expense of all our war-disabled."[24] However, the American Veterans Committee offered a more positive assessment. Writing to Bradley in July 1955, the AVC hewed to the idea that the commission's conclusions should represent the "best interest of the country as a whole."[25]

Collectively, the individuals and veterans' groups who expressed their dissent managed a stalemate with the Eisenhower administration that was eventually reversed in their favor. As the fifties proceeded, the VA witnessed small cuts, to educational funding and VA bed space, but overall the 1957–64 period saw consistent spending increases, from $4.8 billion in 1957 to $5.3 billion in 1960 and $6.0 billion in 1964.[26]

The accomplishments of traditional activism had two important future consequences. In some respects the Legion and the VFW were victims of their own success. By the mid-fifties, both versions of the GI Bill touched veterans and their families, a total of 81 million people, or nearly half of the country.[27] What had started as a campaign for appropriate compensation and recognition in 1943 had developed into an important component of post–World War II American normalcy. Despite the Bradley Commission's pointed recommendation that federal policy makers divine a way to prioritize funding and limit programs to individuals directly affected by military service, the actual constituency was far broader. Almost 10 years before the Great Society expanded social welfare in the country, the continually expanding GI Bill was already solidifying the expectation that federally funded benefits were the rule rather than an exception to national policy.

Timing is important in another sense. In the 10 years preceding Vietnam, this large cohort of Americans, protected by the constellation of organizations led by the American Legion and VFW, became a vested interest intent on protecting their benefits, a position that eventually placed them at odds with the next generation of American veterans. When it examined the core problems impacting veterans, the 1973 *Nader Report* constantly identified the generation gap between World War II and Korean War veterans and younger men and women exiting the Vietnam conflict. The report noted in particular that "the larger part of the benefits go to veterans who never saw combat, at ages when their readjustment needs have passed, and for problems unrelated to military service."[28] When the Bradley Commission failed to refocus programs and funding solely on service-related needs, it deferred a serious opportunity cost to the future whose outcome was predictable and tragic. The gigantic constituency ostensibly led by the American Legion and VFW was organized, well funded, and entrenched in policy circles. It defended the enormous costs of unrestricted veterans' programs at the expense of those who came next. Traditional activism, guided by generational self-interest, failed Vietnam veterans at a time when need reached its greatest point in postwar America.

Table 4.1. Veterans Administration expenditures, 1956–64 (thousands of dollars)

Year	*Amount*	*Percent change*
1956	4,801,885	—
1957	4,884,506	+1.6
1958	5,205,941	+6.5
1959	5,343,711	+2.6
1960	5,389,378	+0.8
1961	5,567,531	+3.3
1962	5,636,630	+1.2
1963	5,866,233	+4.0
1964	6,008,129	+2.4

Source: US Bureau of the Census, *The Statistical History of the United States: From Colonial Times to the Present* (New York: Basic Books, 1976), 1146.

Traditional veterans' activism extended far beyond promoting specific self-interests. Veterans' organizations were constant actors involved in community outreach projects at the local, national, and international levels. They were an integral part of American philanthropy, continuing the established tradition of promoting social welfare through private charity. Community outreach also served as part of a savvy public relations stratagem for veterans' groups, providing periodic reminders of their positive contributions to the greater good.

Veterans were first responders when disaster struck parts of the country. Volunteers from American Legion Post 1 in Portland, Oregon, rendered aid after a local dam burst in 1948. In 1947, Maine Legion posts provided firefighters and auxiliary police for forest fires. When floods struck Fort Worth, Texas, and tornadoes ravaged parts of Arkansas, the Legion responded by dispatching volunteers and raising money for local residents in need.[29]

A number of projects attempted to foster long-term permanent reform at home. In 1949, the American Legion began the Community Development Program, which stressed sustainable employment and affordable housing.[30] In Baton Rouge and New Orleans, American Legion posts formed corporations to develop hundreds of housing units in suburban subdivisions. The Legion also purchased and rehabilitated community hospitals in Louisiana.[31]

Charity work periodically extended overseas. The Legion launched its Tide of Toys program in 1950 to provide three million gifts to children in Europe.[32] The VFW launched its People-to-People program in 1955 and 1956 to distribute books in Latin America and Europe.[33]

Veterans' organizations dedicated considerable effort to American children. Both the VFW and American Legion sponsored local chapters of the Boy Scouts, Boys Clubs, 4-H Club, and Girl Scouts.[34] In 1954, the Legion created the Child Welfare Foundation, a project dedicated to medical and educational research that would "collectively fight the many ills confronting our nation's young people."[35]

The health and well-being of baby boomers was a particular preoccupation of veterans' organizations after World War II. Part of what motivated them was likely the lingering problems of the Great Depression. During both the Korean War and World War II, the millions of men rejected by Selective Service for physical ailments resulting from poor nutrition were a constant reminder that the next generation deserved healthier lives. But veterans were also concerned about some of the social and political "ills" that followed in the wake of World War II: teenage delinquency, the breakdown of the family, sexual promiscuity, and political subversion that seeped from the Cold War abroad into America at home.[36]

An ongoing emphasis on strengthening American citizenship became the preferred antidote to some of these problems. It is not hard to see why in retrospect. Sex education traversed too many contemporary social taboos. By approaching citizenship from the high social vantage point of former military service, veterans' groups hoped to influence political and social cohesion from a position of authority. Toward this end, the American Legion sponsored state and national chapters of Boys State, which provided instruction in citizenship, governance, and trips to Washington, D.C. In 1960, 18,000 boys visited the nation's capital under Legion auspices.[37]

Another popular venue for citizenship was baseball. For most people alive at the time, baseball was synonymous with the American way of life.[38] It represented all the best virtues of individual merit and collective effort. In many respects, it was for these reasons and others that baseball exercised such an important grip on the US military during World War II.

For a largely draftee military, baseball maintained an important link with civilian life. The sport preserved the idea that men were fighting for "America's pastime" and all the benefits associated with the game and the country.[39] Perhaps more fundamentally, the prospect of playing a game without life or death constantly at stake allowed soldiers and sailors a welcome respite from the hard realities of war.

The American military institution saw its own benefits in baseball. The sport promoted "health and efficiency" through physical training. The fundamentals of baseball also reinforced basic military skills such as running and throwing. By participating, recruits could understand and aggressively push their physical limits.[40] Moreover, during the frequent lulls stateside and overseas, baseball was a means to maintain morale. A number of major league stars like Joe DiMaggio and Phil Rizzuto spent their time in the military playing exhibition games for the troops on bases scattered around the world. Overall, the American pastime translated well in the environment of

World War II. According to a War Department survey, 75% of service members played or watched the game during the war.[41]

Baseball remained incredibly popular in the postwar period. Returning veterans like DiMaggio, Ted Williams, and many others rebuilt the major league for a peacetime audience ready to celebrate the sport. In the meantime, amateur leagues surged throughout the country, augmented by thousands of veterans who wanted to play themselves or, increasingly, volunteer to teach and coach the leading edge of the baby boom. By 1947 alone, approximately five million boys played through the auspices of the American Legion.[42] In local leagues and national organizations men who wanted to coach saw an opportunity to mentor boys through a passage of life. Baseball became a vehicle to inculcate adolescents with the virtues of masculinity.[43] On the practice field and at game time, teams focused on aggressive competition within the bounds of good sportsmanship, leadership based on merit, and disciplined physical prowess.

Veterans' organizations added one additional virtue to the game. When it began in 1926, American Legion youth baseball was intended as a civilizing experience for both veterans and their young charges. Veterans, whose military experience embodied what one historian called the "essence of good citizenship," had the opportunity to pass these values on to the next generation.[44] American Legion baseball endorsed the idea that good character could be taught. Its sponsorship of the sport combined two articles of faith common to the time. The first reflected the old progressive ideal that an individual could learn something by doing it. Second, Legion leaders believed that well-disciplined training, incorporating the simplicity and practicality that defined their own military experience, could lead to a defined outcome.[45] In essence, by joining a Legion team, a young boy could improve both his athleticism and social virtues.

After World War II, the Legion counseled its coaches that teamwork and the "spirit of competition" were more essential than winning on the field, adding, "When an attempt is made by some leader to take all the stars from a group of teams and with them form a team solely for the purpose of winning championship honors, it destroys the very foundation upon which the program is built."[46] To these ideals, the Legion added what it considered even more important features. Its national leadership saw baseball as a critical contributor to citizenship: "The good sportsman has learned teamwork. The good citizen has also learned teamwork, which is merely another name for co-operation. A nation of individualists would pass swiftly into anarchy."[47]

On its face, American Legion baseball was an ambitious program. It appeared intent on producing both well-balanced individuals and contributors to a stable society. It was a good case study of the inherent confidence that historians have identified as the foundation of the American postwar consensus. Moreover, like the conventional wisdom that informed the possibility of building a better "human fighting machine" during World War II, Legion baseball is also an excellent example of the contemporary faith in the malleability of humanity through social engineering.[48]

This multifaceted investment begs the question, "How well did it work?" It is clear that the Legion devoted serious attention to the ideal of good social and political behavior. However, in actual practice it was also equally clear that competition outweighed principle. Instead of focusing on character building, Legion teams focus on winning. Throughout the forties and fifties, the organization constantly celebrated its outstanding athletes.[49] The American media did much the same. Legion baseball box scores were regular features in national publications like the *New York Times*.[50]

More interesting and perhaps more troubling were the lengths to which Legion teams would go to win. Recent scholarship has catalogued the recurrent and widespread problem of cheating in Legion leagues throughout the country. Legion posts regularly accused each other of cheating. It was fairly common for players to use fake birth certificates to avoid the standard maximum age requirement of 17. Coaches also routinely poached talented players to bolster their prospects in Legion tournaments.[51]

In regard to activism, most veterans leading American Legion baseball were more vested in mainstream standards of winning and losing than any effort to remake society from the grass roots. While coaches certainly imparted a degree of military culture in team training regimens, it is likely that this was intended to enhance physical endurance and group cohesion. It is equally likely that a significant number of Legion veterans adopted the basics of sportsmanship on the field. However, when the time came to articulate the particularities of good citizenship, it is clear that victory on the field won out as the most important end of all.

In the final analysis, the strengths and weaknesses of American Legion baseball are analogous to veterans' philanthropy in general. Most efforts originated with publicly expressed high-minded principles: better employment opportunities, good housing, strong communities, the health and welfare of children, the passage of virtue from one generation to another. As is the case for most reform movements, translating intention into practicality was often difficult. An extensive array of state and federal programs offered more consistency and better funding to the social welfare safety net than start-up efforts sponsored by the American Legion and VFW. Cultural standards proved resilient to change. Baseball remained the national pastime but proved a poor vehicle for making better citizens. However, even when success proved elusive, veterans continued their pursuit of positive reform. Lacking good results from traditional means, many began to consider more unorthodox approaches.

Challenging the Status Quo

It is common to assume that military culture lends itself to conservatism or, at the very least, moderation before entering into public debate. Part of this tendency may be based on historical tradition. Open disdain for standing armies was a strong colonial precedent that carried forward well into the modern era. Americans and their armies put a great deal of effort into making sure that the latter maintained an outwardly apolitical stance in regard to free discourse between citizens.[52]

A second component might be derived from the internal culture of the military. Recruits learn from the very moment they enter basic training that the military is not a democracy. Sacrificing individual preference for the sake of collective discipline forms the backbone of military doctrine. Perhaps more important, militaries are intolerant organizations by definition. The primary mission of the military is the destruction of lives and property. Some branches, like the army and Marine Corps, engage in this task personally, in direct proximity to combatants and noncombatants alike.[53] These factors add up to the mistaken assumption that military service leaves a fundamentally conservative stamp on individuals who become veterans. In reality, military experience did not restrain men and women interested in challenging the post-1945 American status quo.

Military dissent over basic American policy decisions frequently spilled over into the public domain after World War II. Senior navy officers prompted the so-called revolt of the admirals in 1949 when they broke with the Defense Department over budget cuts that led to canceling the new carrier *United States*. Subsequent congressional hearings revealed much of the internal squabbling that dominated postwar military policy making.[54] In the fifties, it was the army's turn. Matthew Ridgeway and Maxwell Taylor, bona fide heroes of World War II, become vocal critics of the nuclear-dependent New Look, its reliance on the air force, and the Eisenhower administration for allowing cuts to American ground forces. Shortly after his retirement, Taylor used his memoir to denounce airpower "dogma" given the polish of "Madison Avenue trappings."[55] During the Vietnam War, the penchant for senior officers to publicly criticize official policy continued unabated. When Gen. David M. Shoup finished his career as commandant of the Marine Corps, he regularly spoke and wrote in opposition to American involvement in the conflict.[56]

Most senior officers were motivated by a desire to promote institutional reform. Taylor, for example, believed that a nuclear-reliant military possessed far too few capabilities for the increasingly unconventional demands being imposed by the Cold War. To his mind, embracing nuclear deterrence at the expense of other more flexible options actually increased the likelihood of thermonuclear war with the Soviet Union. Shoup questioned the effectiveness of counterinsurgency applied to the Third World as a waste of finite resources. He openly challenged the domino theory, itself a Cold War dogma at the time. In official testimony before the Senate Foreign Relations Committee in March 1968, he said, "It is ludicrous to think that just because we lose Vietnam, the Communists will soon be knocking at the doors of Pearl Harbor."[57]

Shoup and other generals maintained their faith in traditional solutions even when they broke faith with the establishment. James Gavin entered politics after his retirement but quit the Advisory Council of the Massachusetts Democratic State Committee over the Vietnam War in 1967. In his 1968 book, *Crisis Now*, Gavin criticized the destructive tactics used in the war and the fact that "so much of our physical wealth and human energy should be diverted from our urgent domestic problems."[58] Yet, rather than lend his name to the emerging antiwar movement, Gavin briefly considered a run for president as a Republican.[59] Rear Adm. Arnold E. True publicly opposed US policy in Vietnam but also avoided siding with protesters. Rather than join what many considered the fringe, he conducted his own speaking tour against the war in 1967.[60] Such faith had limits, however. As the war ground on and public frustration rose, a number of retired senior officers were more than willing to endorse the protest movement. Shoup did just that in support of a five-day "encampment" in Washington against the war in 1971.[61]

The rank and file within the American military was much less reserved in saying what it thought about the status quo. For all of its emphasis on discipline, the American militaries of World War II, Korea, and Vietnam, whether draftee or volunteer, were citizen armies largely defined by the understanding that service was something to be tolerated rather than embraced. As a result, an egalitarian, antiestablishment undercurrent runs through all three wars. It was captured in the candor of Ernie Pyle regarding the sacrifices of common soldiers evident throughout World War II. It was present when Bill Mauldin wrote about the rough, honest style of newspapers published by infantry divisions on the front line.[62] Writers like Mauldin himself embodied the irreverent spirit of the troops when poking fun at authority. In his wildly popular book *Up Front*, he congratulated reporter Ken Dixon, who "roasted the pants off the general who commanded Naples, charging unfairness to combat troops."[63] As the war ended in Europe, so did a great deal of journalistic self-restraint. When Andy Rooney wrote his last column for *Stars and Stripes*, it ran under the headline "Good! When Do We Leave This Hole and Go Home?"[64]

The younger veterans who left World War II behind kept this sense of restlessness when they approached activism in the forties. Men and women interested in joining established veterans' organizations like the American Legion or the VFW were welcome to do so, but with an important caveat: a wide generation gap between the rank and file and their leadership. One article published in July 1945 put the problem this way:

> *A former doughboy can pat a war-aged man of 25 on the back just so many times and buy him just so many drinks, but he'll*

tell him about hardtack and the Argonne and the legendary Mademoiselle just once too often. The confused—and no doubt bored—GI is going to turn his back and go out and hunt up someone of his own time who's tasted saki, or who could tell the difference between the sound of a B-25 and a B-29 motor, or who's also wondering if he'll ever have enough money to get married.[65]

Bill Mauldin looked beyond divergent wartime experiences to point out the root problems of "old" organizations like the American Legion, their fundamental conservatism and undemocratic methods. Mauldin characterized speeches made by Legion leaders as "a mixture of National Association of Manufacturing advertising and a Hearst editorial page."[66] Newly arrived veterans of World War II had little voice. A few took charge of local chapter commands, but national leadership remained closed to them. A senior delegate to the American Legion 1946 national convention in San Francisco put it in these terms: "This is a billion-dollar corporation. You don't turn something like that over to a bunch of inexperienced kids."[67]

Hundreds of thousands joined the American Legion and the VFW regardless, ready to accept the prospect of local camaraderie above meaningful participation in leadership of the whole. Those who did not gravitated toward dozens of new organizations that began to appear almost immediately after the war. The late forties saw the Nationalist Veterans of World War II, the United Nations League, the American Order of Patriots, and St. Sebastian's Brigade, among many others, join a crowded landscape of veterans' groups.[68]

One of the strongest and longest lived of these new organizations was the American Veterans Committee (AVC). When it was formally founded by a group of World War II veterans in 1944, the AVC was intended to be the antithesis of the American Legion. Its charter, headlined by the motto "Citizens First, Veterans Second," focused primarily on serving the greater good for American society rather than the vested interests of veterans.[69]

The AVC adopted a progressive stance on social issues and activism from the outset. It built working relationships with a spectrum of organizations, such as the AFL-CIO, the National Conference of Christians and Jews, and the B'nai B'rith.[70] In practice, the AVC did not shy away from controversial or difficult issues. As early as December

1945, the committee's legal staff assisted city colleges in New York that were protesting tuition and fees charged to veteran students in violation of state law.[71] Less than a year later, the Hollywood chapter of the AVC joined in an AFL strike against seven movie studios that devolved into a full-scale riot involving hundreds of police.[72] A Minnesota AVC chapter picketed the Minneapolis Real Estate Board when it banned a Nisei veteran from purchasing a home. In 1947, the AVC unsuccessfully attempted to add race to a Minnesota law that banned restrictive covenants on property purchases and rentals.[73]

One of the AVC's strongest alliances was with the NAACP. From the time of its founding, the AVC served as an advocate for minority veterans and their surviving family members denied disability benefits by the VA and state governments. The American Veterans Committee Legal Aid Project provided black veterans with help to file and receive claims. AVC lawyers frequently assisted the NAACP by filing amicus curiae briefs in federal court.[74] This legal relationship continued for years. At the conclusion of the sixties, the AVC claimed a place at "the forefront of the fight for school desegregation, civil rights legislation, the war against poverty, and efforts to improve the social welfare programs for our old people, and those unable to work."[75]

While this work targeted segregation and discrimination in public and private institutions, it also inevitably led the AVC to expose racism within national veterans' organizations. Overt segregation was a common practice among local chapters of the American Legion and VFW in the postwar era. This was particularly the case as the NAACP and other civil rights groups began to gain legal traction after the *Brown v. Board* decision. A 1954 resolution by the VFW Clark-Lyon Post 4731 of Indianola, Mississippi, for example, promised "to aid all Races but not at each others [*sic*] expense. To provide equal but separate schooling for the Black and White Races. To prevent mongrelization of our nation by avoiding conditions that foster and promote intermarriage of races. To uphold Segregation in the states that desire it and whose social structure requires it."[76] Practices like this drew a constant and public stream of criticism from the AVC national office and additional amicus briefs, a strategy that further solidified its alliance with the NAACP. Nor did the American Legion escape scrutiny. In 1955, the AVC attacked its "false patriotism" for tolerating segregation through its affiliate organization, the Forty & Eight.[77]

The AVC's willingness to challenge the status quo made it a ready target for reactionaries in the federal government and veterans' organizations. During the late forties, as the Red Scare grew in momentum, the AVC seemed ripe for investigation. Communists were part of the original post–World War II membership, although the national leadership moved in 1948 to ban these individuals from its ranks. Nevertheless, the FBI conducted an in-depth investigation of the organization between 1947 and 1950 and reported that the AVC had been "subjected to Communist infiltration in local chapters."[78]

Despite these official suspicions, the AVC mounted an aggressive counteroffensive against its critics in the federal government. The AVC was a rare voice among American progressives willing to challenge Senator Joseph McCarthy. In June 1950, the AVC National Planning Committee demanded McCarthy's impeachment "for high crimes and misdemeanors" committed during his anticommunist investigations. Over the next four years, the AVC cited McCarthy's damage to free speech, civil liberties, and overall American resilience in the Cold War.[79] Once the Eisenhower administration took charge of the White House and began a new series of background checks on federal employees, the AVC publicly counseled the president to make a distinction between "undesirables" who threatened national security and the need to protect the enthusiasm of loyal civil servants.[80] The AVC applied similar scrutiny to other veterans' groups, particularly the American Legion. When he became national chairman of the AVC, Bill Mauldin called out the "antics of certain self-styled 'veterans leaders' who were sounding off in all directions," acting like "Junior FBI, amateur GPU, or hooded Dick Tracys."[81] In 1954, the AVC proposed a jointly drafted code of conduct to mitigate the ongoing animosity between itself and other veterans' groups. However, neither the American Legion nor the VFW accepted the idea, leading Mauldin to comment that the latter organization "appears committed to continuing this 'now you see it, now you don't' spook hunt as an out-and-out publicity gimmick to gain new members."[82]

There were limits to just how far veterans could challenge the status quo. Former generals and admirals, once retired and on the outside of the military establishment, soon discovered how little relevance and influence they retained as civilians. As Maxwell

Taylor, James Gavin, and many other officers discovered, military tradition, obedience to civilian leadership, and simple inertia proved to be powerful obstacles to change despite the prestige and storied careers of would-be reformers.

Organizations composed of veterans from the rank and file experienced their own trials as they contested America's status quo after 1945. The men and women who joined the AVC were not unlike their peers in the forties. They left the military after the war, retaining a respect for authority tempered by ingrained skepticism and a sense of impatient hope that the country could be made better in the immediate future. Some of the problems they saw were long-standing and familiar to the World War II generation. The AVC's campaigns for fair housing, labor rights, and education benefits echoed the type of American liberalism embodied by the New Deal and the GI Bill. In an important sense, the AVC was less concerned with breaking new ground than advancing reforms already won.

Advocacy for civil rights was a different matter. The problems of discrimination, segregation, and outright racism were embedded in American history and culture. In the years surrounding World War II, the issue of race was a bright line that many contemporary liberals avoided, a tendency reflected in the New Deal as a whole and in specific programs like the GI Bill. When the AVC pursued the interests of Asian Americans and African Americans, it crossed that bright line, inviting controversy and resistance.

The status quo defined and, at the same time, marginalized much of what the AVC tried to accomplish in the postwar period. When the AVC sought out better-defined and protected veterans benefits from the GI Bill of Rights, it joined a large chorus of groups like the American Legion and the VFW already making the same demands, albeit with far more resources at hand. The vast majority of veterans sided with the two larger organizations, something reflected in the AVC's membership, which rose to 100,000 by 1947 and plummeted to approximately 35,000 only three years later.[83]

The AVC's willingness to directly confront the status quo is another clear reason for its gradual marginalization. The 1950 campaign against Joseph McCarthy reflected a defense of the best American principles. To a political pragmatist, however, it also risked political suicide at a moment when the senator from Wisconsin was nearing the peak of his influence. At the very least, the prospect of attacking

McCarthy with impeachment gave many veterans, and people in general, more than a moment's pause when contemplating membership in the AVC. The same collision of principle and practice was at work with respect to AVC support of civil rights. It joined in with the NAACP to preserve a set of fundamental freedoms enshrined by the good war, but in doing so provoked deeply set social prejudices.

Veterans and the Civil Rights Movement

When they challenged the status quo and were repeatedly rebuffed or marginalized, many veterans underwent a transition familiar to any activist movement; they became radicalized. Sometimes this transition was the product of historical circumstances and the contemporary conventions under attack. At other times, radicalism was a deliberate choice by veterans.

The historical post–World War II evolution of African American civil rights movements offers a window to both. Clearly, the context of the immediate postwar period was framed by the high expectations stemming from official statements like the Four Freedoms, which connected the country to the principle of universal rights.[84] Moreover, throughout the war, public officials used the changing status of African Americans to rhetorically connect a previously disenfranchised minority to the great accomplishments being produced by the crusade against fascism. A statement by an aide to Secretary of War Frank Knox in May 1945 spoke to the fact that "Negroes are, first, Americans. Our futures are inescapably bound up with the progress of the United States. Our soldiers overseas have been indelibly impressed with this. They are a part of a great team."[85]

Once African American veterans returned home, they tested the limits of this rhetoric and very quickly rediscovered the entrenched realities of racism. The immediate history of postwar America is peppered with tragic stories of African American veterans returning home to violence at the hands of local authorities and society. Perhaps the most famous is the story of Isaac Woodard, an army veteran blinded by police in South Carolina after his arrest for alleged disorderly conduct.[86] Sadly, Hayes's story was not unique. In February 1946, rioting broke out in Columbia, Tennessee, after a black navy veteran, James Stephenson, attempted to intervene against a white resident, who attacked his mother when she complained about his repair of her radio. Both the state highway patrol and the National Guard were eventually called in to cope with escalating violence that followed their arrest.[87] Later that summer, African American veteran Maceo Snipes was murdered in Taylor County, Georgia, after voting in the July 1946 primary.[88]

On the face of it, none of these actions on the part of African American veterans should have provoked violence. In every case, returning soldiers, sailors, and marines simply were exercising what should have been the mainstream social, economic, and political rights celebrated and embellished during World War II. Black veterans coming home and in need of transportation challenged local practices governing public transport. Wounded and disabled veterans demanded equal access to the VA hospital system. In Mississippi, which waived the poll tax for veterans without considering their race, hundreds of African American veterans besieged local authorities when they attempted to register to vote.[89] Still others, with GI benefits in hand, sought out the same educational and housing opportunities awaiting millions of white veterans.

Yet when they pursued what should have been sanctioned components of postwar American normalcy, African American veterans and other minorities who had served were breaking with long-standing economic, social, and political practices. In this context, self-improvement was a radical alternative to the status quo. African Americans' ambitions to make better lives for themselves and their families ran against a combination of generational prejudice and institutional inertia. The clash between the two provoked a national crisis that stretched far beyond the Old South and eventually reached into nearly every neighborhood, classroom, and business in America.

Little help from Washington was forthcoming. Federal officials adopted the early refrain that they had little interest in interfering with state and local prerogatives. Veterans Administration head Frank Hines buried this sentiment in a dense paragraph when he wrote to the NAACP in April 1945 regarding ongoing segregation and property rights:

> *I assume you are aware of the fact that in some States statutory restrictions are prescribed as to ownership of real estate by members of certain races (other than Negro or Caucasian); and also that in many deeds covenants may provide for reversion if*

sale be to persons other than of prescribed race, or for use of the property for certain purposes. It would be no favor to a veteran to promulgate regulations so loose as to induce him to become a burden with an illegal contract or deed, with resultant loss and disappointment.[90]

Omar Bradley followed a similar line of reasoning in a December 1945 speech, albeit in simpler language regarding the limits of federal power: "Washington alone can no more reestablish the veteran than Washington alone could win the war. While we can assist with benefits and offer guidance, it is the community that must do the grass roots work."[91] This stance was a simple recipe for continued inertia. VA policy remained largely unchanged. The National Urban League noted in March 1946 that African American veterans lacked confidence in the US Employment Service to place them into anything but old, traditional, menial employment.[92]

A decade later, the same attitudes persisted with the same results. The AVC reported in 1956 obvious disparities in VA programs defined by race. That year, for example, the VA insured home loans for 14.3% of white veterans, compared to only 4.2% of black veterans. In the Deep South, particularly Mississippi and Alabama, this disparity was even greater.[93] Education programs reflected equally troubling trends. Efforts to get on-the-job training to obtain higher skills and pay were thwarted in Georgia, Alabama, and Mississippi by a combination of managers who refused to hire African Americans and labor unions that refused them membership.[94] In Montgomery, Alabama, the VA maintained traditional policy and employed no African American as "clerks, counsellors [*sic*], or in any other technical positions," instead keeping the old practice of offering jobs only as custodians.[95]

Activism in the form of self-help continued because there were few if any alternatives. African American veterans joined the NAACP in droves, rapidly expanding its membership to more than 450,000 in 14,000 chapters by 1946. Amzie Moore, Aaron Henry, and Medgar Evers all left the military to add their leadership.[96] These individuals fought for voter registration as early as 1946 and launched political reform campaigns against white southern Democratic machines in Georgia, Tennessee, Louisiana, and Arkansas.[97] Through the NAACP and with the active support of other progressive groups like the AVC, they challenged labor rules and educational policies in court throughout the fifties.

The sixties obviously were a different decade in terms of the status quo, minority rights, and the changing definition of radicalism. Great Society programs openly tested an array of American conventions through federal programs and law. However, as many scholars have since noted, transferring the spirit of the law from its letter took time and additional struggle.[98] Objective rights like the vote proved more easily established than social equality or equal economic opportunity. Minority veterans saw these gaps between promise and practice no less than minorities in general.

As the Vietnam War wound down, veterans' employment illustrated the distance between proposed change and actual reality. The 1966 version of the GI Bill kept the provision for veterans' preference in federal hiring. As mentioned previously, new training and job placement programs available through the Departments of Defense and Labor supplemented older employment benefits.[99] Regardless, many African American veterans were openly concerned about their job prospects in what they considered a hostile market. According to a Harris Poll taken in 1971, 66% of white veterans but only 50% of nonwhite veterans believed employers would be "very interested" in offering them jobs.[100] Significant numbers were pessimistic about their economic futures. A far larger percentage of African Americans (26%) than whites (9%) believed that veterans status was a stigma for prospective employers.[101]

The facts seemed to bear out these suspicions. In 1972, Lewis C. Olive, director of the National Urban League's Military and Veterans Affairs Division, noted that unemployment rates for African American veterans was nearly double that of white veterans. According to Olive, it was a problem "equal to if not greater than any similar period during the Great Depression of the 1930 s."[102] During the first quarter of 1972, the unemployment rate for African American veterans aged 20–24 was 22.4%.[103]

Once again, African American veterans turned to private efforts for help. The National Urban League was a relative newcomer to this audience, having established a Military and Veterans Affairs Program only in 1967.[104] Nevertheless, it had created a broad collection of initiatives in the final years of the Vietnam War. The Military and Veterans Affairs Division lobbied the VA in Washington and the Federal Aviation Administration in Atlanta for federal assistance and job placement for African American veterans.[105] National Urban League chapter offices also reached out to the corporate sector, promoting hiring veterans by major companies such as United Airlines, Xerox, Westinghouse, and Mobil.[106] By 1974, the national headquarters claimed to have assisted 78,000 African American veterans.[107]

It was a depressingly small number given the hundreds of thousands who served during the Vietnam era. It was also a number that illustrated marginal economic progress despite the best intentions of African American veterans and activists. Part of the problem was rooted in the structural changes under way in the American economy, which was moving into a postindustrial phase that placed a premium on education and skilled labor. Federal programs could counterbalance hard economic times and this transition to a point, but their influence was limited. In part, this was also the fault of programs like Project 100,000 and general military recruitment policies, which opened service to minorities without adequately addressing their educational needs or future job prospects. Major sectors of the American economy, representing the business community and labor, were literally fighting for their lives after the Vietnam War. Contemporary hard times, in addition to latent prejudice, were formidable additional obstacles to economic progress.

"A Proud Restless Group"

There were times when armed self-defense defined veterans' activism. Documented instances of this choice are rare but present in the post–World War II period. During the bloody 1946 election year, as white extremists wreaked havoc in African American communities, some World War II veterans refused to passively accept aggression. When the Klan began a campaign of open harassment in Bennettsville, Georgia, African American veterans responded with armed patrols of their part of the town. The *Atlanta Daily World* described them as "a proud restless group" that was "tired of being booted about."[108]

As the dynamic of violence against the civil rights movement continued and worsened, particularly in the early sixties, a similar response appeared in the form of the Deacons for Defense and Justice. Initially formed to counter officially sanctioned violence against civil rights workers and the local population of Jonesboro, Louisiana, the

Deacons counted on African American veterans for the bulk of its initial membership. Their shared military background lent a basic coherence to the organization. White supremacists were easily identifiable as the "enemy." The Klan's ready use of violence translated the nature of the threat into a form easily understood by servicemen and combat veterans. Subsequent planning focused on the armed defense of individual civil rights workers, their residences, and movement. Discussion centered on practical concerns such as acquiring weapons and ammunition, assigning shifts to ensure round-the-clock security, and the like. Historian Lance Hill notes that, as an organization, the Deacons for Defense was almost entirely utilitarian and tactical in nature. It addressed immediate needs rather than long-term strategy, a feature that defined the group for most of its existence.[109]

The Deacons presented civil rights leaders with an interesting dilemma. One marcher commented years later that he felt "rather reassured" by an armed presence.[110] This was no small comfort. Armed veterans accompanied marchers and organizers who faced the constant, imminent threat of death and injury throughout the sixties. The Deacons were providing bodyguards for Sammy Young, a navy veteran, when he was killed attempting to register voters in Macon County, Alabama, in 1964.[111] Thus, years later, another civil rights activist could speak to an important aspect of the Deacons' value: "The Deacons took the fear out of it, because they taught them [civil rights workers] that the same bullet that will kill you is the same bullet that will kill somebody else. There's no difference. There's no difference. But it also shows that you don't look for trouble, all you do is protect yourself."[112] However, the idea of "protected nonviolence" deeply disturbed members of the civil rights movement, who based their advocacy on nonviolence as an unbreakable principle.[113] The Deacons' militancy and the prospect of armed self-defense openly alienated many members of the Congress of Racial Equality (CORE) active in the South at the time. Martin Luther King was reported to have been "deeply upset and concerned" about Deacon activity. In contrast, Jackie Robinson, writing for the *Chicago* Defender, was "1,000 percent" in favor of the Deacons.[114]

The debate within the civil rights community was underpinned by a greater fear of what might happen if veterans escaped the boundaries of "protected nonviolence" into more dangerous behavior. Media in the sixties consistently invoked the potential threat posed by African American veterans returning from Vietnam. Many journalists reflected on the impact of racial strife in the United States on troops fighting the war. A May 1968 *New York Times* article written by Thomas A. Johnson reported on the likelihood that the discharged African American veteran would "be approached by black ultra-militants eager to capitalize on his battle skills and on his resentment."[115] Other authors attempted to strike a balance. While recognizing racial strife at home and abroad, a *Chicago Daily Defender* article written that June noted that common sense and cool heads would prevail, quoting one Vietnam veteran as saying, "Rioting has done more harm than good. You don't prove anything with rioting."[116]

Despite the search for balance, public concerns increased, particularly in the escalating violence of 1968. An army unit deployed from Fort Hood, Texas, to provide security for the Democratic National Convention ran into trouble when it arrived in Chicago. Some 43 African American soldiers (including 26 Vietnam veterans) refused to comply with an order to deploy for riot duty. After the division commander personally failed to break the impasse, they were placed under arrest.[117] A *Time* magazine article noted that "generals are troubled by the possibility that black soldiers will find that they owe a higher fealty to the black community than to the US Army."[118]

Public fears were drawn to incidents like this not so much for the actual danger they posed but because of their potential for it. Race sharpened existing anxiety about the Vietnam veteran. If the perceptions that combat and widespread drug use had already warped veterans were true, how much more dangerous could racial hatred make them?

Fear of the African American veteran subsequently became both a cautionary tale and a threat. It was not uncommon for social activists to use them to illustrate the consequences of failing to meet the needs of all African Americans. National Urban League director Whitney M. Young made this point plain in a 1968 interview: "It would then be realistic to expect such experts of mines and booby traps and all other forms of destruction to find good reason why they should use these skills and risk their lives against the enemy of personal injustice as they did against the enemy of communist aggression."[119] Young did more than intimate the potential cost of unmet expectations; he speculated that if African American soldiers "return to find the conditions they left unchanged, these Negro veterans might become an interested audience for the preachers of violence—and one capable of being organized into a major national threat."[120]

Groups like the Black Panther Party were willing to take this threat a step further. The Black Panthers did not envision African American veterans as a potentially dangerous consequence of poverty, social prejudice, or government inaction. They saw their military skills, personal discipline, and, most important, combat experience as a means to add what one author called the "the element of calculated action" to their movement.[121] In other words, the threat of the veteran was something that could be proactive and not just reactive. Military training and experience were thus the means toward the end of reinforcing the Black Panthers' militant credibility when confronting the American establishment.

Wielding the image of the threatening African American was not just a vicarious fear produced by a public engrossed in the mythology of the Vietnam veteran; it was a deliberate product created by groups perfectly willing to use fear as a weapon. Charles E. Cobb observes that the Deacons for Defense and Justice were most effective as a political organization.[122] By illustrating the need for armed self-defense, they focused media attention on the necessity to counterbalance white terrorism against the civil rights movement.[123] Their struggle also lent the Deacons an air of brief nobility. One journalist writing in June 1965 described them as an "armed, tough-minded league of Negroes."[124]

The image of armed activism could also be used for simple intimidation. If the Deacons could "take the fear out of it" for marchers, they could put the fear of God into white supremacists. They used a number of methods. The Deacons regularly inflated membership numbers to exaggerate their reach across the South.[125] When rumors spread that a Louisiana chapter of the Deacons had come into possession of explosives and was seeking automatic weapons, leaders did nothing to allay them. When rumor was not enough, the Deacons did not shrink from openly threatening retaliation against Klan violence in public meetings.[126] As time passed and the political atmosphere deteriorated, such rhetoric became increasingly common. Speaking of African American veterans in March 1968, Carlos Russell, leader of the black caucus of the Chicago New Politics Convention, said: "White America will do everything to make them turn their backs on their black brothers, but it won't work. They have been trained to kill; if rebellions break out and they see their black brothers and sisters slaughtered by racist cops they will come to the defense of their own."[127] Not surprisingly, manipulating belligerence rather quickly produced a backlash, as fear outpaced efforts to control it. The constant drumbeat that African American veterans might use their skills to promote violence began to resonate with journalists, the public, and law enforcement in largely negative ways. As the civil rights movement began to fragment by the mid-sixties, it became increasingly easy to attribute its problems to the groups that promoted violence. By 1966, when the Deacons for Defense and Justice arrived in Chicago to form a new chapter, the *New York Times* referred to them as a "vigilante group."[128] As the decade proceeded, writers were increasingly prone to speculate that black veterans might use military skills to promote violence. Sol Stern, writing in March 1968, noted:

> *If they are inclined to take part in ghetto uprisings, using the skills they were taught by Uncle Sam, it is not the kind of thing they are likely to talk to an interviewer about. If there is one thing they have learned in the service it is how to play it cool. More likely than not, however, they don't yet know themselves how they will react if violence breaks out in their ghetto this summer.*[129]

Journalists drawn to high-profile sensationalism began cherry-picking instances of African American veterans involved in violence, much in the same way that media outlets reported on veterans committing crimes after World War II. One popular story involved Fred Ahmed Evans, a former Korean War combat veteran, arrested in Cleveland and accused of leading an armed group that killed three Cleveland police in July 1968.[130] It was not uncommon to see analogies drawn between violence in the streets and open warfare. One author writing for the *Saturday Evening Post* said that clashes between police and militants in Cleveland "could be best described as an engagement between infantry patrols."[131] Television reporting on tanks patrolling the streets of Detroit in the aftermath of rioting conjured up similar imagery.[132]

The combination of real and imagined threats predicated a reaction from law enforcement at nearly every level across the country.

Responding to rumors of impending riots and armed confrontations, police departments in Los Angeles, Tampa, and Chicago began stockpiling weapons, armored vehicles, and equipment as early as March 1968.[133] Once riots broke out in Cleveland, the police were convinced that "black nationalists" possessed a "tripod mounted, belt-fed machine gun" that would be used against them.[134]

As local and state police agencies mobilized, the FBI began its own well-documented campaign against "black nationalist, hate-type organizations." Federal authorities used a broad brush when applying that particular definition. In 1967, a COINTELPRO (Counterintelligence Program) report included the Deacons for Defense and Justice in the same category as other groups considered radical and dangerous; a year later the FBI revised its assessment, listing them as "extremely militant."[135] In one fell swoop, the FBI lumped the Deacons into the same category as the Black Panther Party, the Black Legion of the Republic of New Africa in Detroit, and the Black Liberators in St. Louis.[136] Subsequent federal investigations (some conducted extralegally) and prosecutions also made no attempt at drawing distinctions between self-defense and armed belligerence.

Attempts to use veterans as a device to either deter violence or threaten it for the sake of political leverage proved dangerous and ultimately self-defeating. The ongoing debate between pragmatic self-defense and principled nonviolence badly split the civil rights movement. The loss of key leaders like Martin Luther King, coupled with an ongoing procession of "long, hot summers" where violence engulfed cities around the country, made the prospect of healing the rift almost impossible. Nationally, Americans seemed paralyzed by fear at the prospect of former African American soldiers joining in, or leading, a violent rebellion against the status quo. If anything, this fear added the additional element of race to the already accumulating negative stereotype surrounding the troubled Vietnam veteran.

Veterans and Antiwar Movements

Veterans have been an integral part of American antiwar movements in the twentieth century. As noted previously, after 1918, military service contributed to public skepticism regarding intervention at the start of World War II.[137] Veterans' organizations clearly impacted public reluctance to enter World War II. In September 1939, the American Legion renewed its call for armed neutrality at its national convention in Chicago. As late as December 1940, James E. Van Zandt, a former commander of the VFW (1934–36), was making speeches at public rallies in favor of peace.[138]

Both the American Legion and VFW retreated from the approach to neutrality as public opinion shifted in favor of the war. At the Legion's 1940 convention, bitter floor debates broke out between traditional advocates of neutrality and delegates who wanted condemnation of "aggressor nations." Alfred Kelly, department commander of Oregon, condemned the old policy using pointed terminology that would become familiar in the Cold War: "The people of America want courage from the American Legion, not appeasement. Strength, courage and idealism will keep us at peace; weakness, compromise and appeasement will lead us to war." In the end, the convention "roared down" a resolution calling for neutrality and endorsed a substitute offering "the fullest cooperation" to nations threatened by aggression.[139]

The lasting impression left by Pearl Harbor, the accepted sanctity of the good war after 1945, and the onset of tensions with the Soviet Union made antiwar organization difficult in the late forties. Despite these obstacles, small numbers of veterans remained willing to challenge the conventional wisdom on overseas conflict and American intervention. During the early years of the Cold War, the minuscule veterans' antiwar movement clung to the same principles as isolationists before World War II. Veterans Against the War, which was formed once fighting erupted in Korea, characterized itself as "a group of pacifist veterans who seek to crystallize revulsion against war into positive peace action."[140] The organization adopted the past as a touchstone, claiming kinship with World War I veterans disillusioned with war in the thirties.

Veterans Against the War kept its activism on a relatively low boil. It advised members to individually interview returning veterans and encourage them to join the peace movement. It kept in touch with veterans and men of draft age, attempting to dissuade the latter from joining the military. The group avoided mobilizing large, public protests against the Korean War. The only evidence of a public campaign was letter writing to local newspapers.[141] This strategy reflected a great deal of common sense. During the heyday of McCarthyism, even small-scale, low-profile activism carried tremendous risks.

The aversion to risk ended with the Vietnam War. As was the case during Korea, the antiwar movement comprising veterans was small and took time to accumulate support. In its earliest stages, many of the veterans who turned against Vietnam did so motivated by the same reasons as former Marine Corps commandant David M. Shoup. They reiterated his concerns that US counterinsurgency doctrine was ineffective to the degree that popular support from the Vietnamese people would never be forthcoming.[142]

Retired special forces sergeant Donald Duncan followed this particular line of thought. Duncan created a sensation in 1966 when he publicly revealed US involvement in torture and efforts to send forces to infiltrate Laos and North Vietnam. In a widely cited article that appeared in *Ramparts*, Duncan argued that anticommunism was dominating every other American priority in Southeast Asia. He asked the basic question about "whether communism is spreading in spite of our involvement or because of it."[143] What lent his commentary perhaps even more credibility than Shoup's was his firsthand experience in Vietnam. This feature of his service, in addition to Duncan's acknowledged expertise as a special forces soldier, likely also provided him with greater leeway when directly criticizing the American war effort.

This same combination of credibility and discretion is what inspired early organizers of the Vietnam antiwar movement to consider including veterans in their marches. A December 1965 letter from the Ad Hoc Committee of Veterans for Peace in Vietnam makes the point: "No doubt you will agree with us that such veterans components would serve, over and above their obvious positive impact, to inhibit some of the obscenities ('coward,' 'traitor') recently hurled at us peace demonstrators. To this end, we urge you to contact us to organize veteran participation in any significant peace activities your organization undertakes."[144] Small groups of Vietnam veterans joined older men who served in the world wars and Korea as recurring participants in antiwar demonstrations as early as 1965. In addition to lending gravity to the event, they also shielded the marchers from hecklers.[145]

One of the groups that eventually joined in these marches was the Vietnam Veterans against the War (VVAW). The VVAW started as a very small group that joined larger antiwar protests in 1967. In its earliest incarnation, the group maintained a relatively conservative approach to activism; they kept their hair short and wore suits when they met and spoke in public. The tone of their statements was respectful in much the same way as that of earlier veterans groups contesting US conflicts overseas. As a rule, the VVAW attempted to advance its agenda through accepted processes. Its members campaigned for Eugene McCarthy in 1968 based largely on his promise to end the war in Vietnam.

Practically all these approaches failed. Factionalism within the VVAW followed after McCarthy's defeat and worsened when many members became caught up in riots at the Chicago Democratic Convention. As 1968 came to an end, the entire VVAW comprised approximately 500 members.[146] The group became what one author described as "a useful case study of the dynamics of a traditionally ignored protest movement."[147]

The VVAW did not die, but it morphed into far more confrontational and unconventional approaches to activism. VVAW founders Jan Barry and Carl Rogers became actively involved in the Serviceman's Link to the Peace Movement (or LINK). LINK differed from the Korean War–era Veterans Against the War in that it did not wait for service members to become veterans in order to proselytize to them about the inherent dangers of war and military service. LINK reached directly into the active-duty military. Moreover, it went far beyond generalities to address specific, controversial issues such as the fairness of the draft and the consequences of American military intervention in Vietnam.[148]

Although LINK gradually faded from the scene, it corresponded with a surge in underground newspapers within the military, numbering about 300 by the end of the sixties.[149] These publications differed significantly from *Stars & Stripes* and other divisional newspapers of World War II. They drastically varied in quality and overall readership. Most were produced on mimeograph paper and distributed clandestinely on bases and installations scattered around the continental United States. Most of these GI newspapers expressed outrage over military discipline and perceived abuses of power. Many offered explicit advice about individual rights and responsibilities under military law and regulations. A number of publications included editorials on American war aims in Vietnam, imperialism, and broader commentary on social injustices in the United States. Underground GI newspapers also regularly reported on protests at military bases around the country, focusing especially on free-speech rights for GIs who engaged in public discussion of the war.[150]

The establishment of "GI coffeehouses" outside a number of major military bases corresponded with the rise of underground military newspapers. Gathering places like the Shelter Half in Tacoma, Washington; the Oleo Strut in Killeen, Texas; and Mad Anthony's Headquarters in Waynesville, Missouri, varied in style, but the owner of the Shelter Half defined their purpose as "a place for soldiers, not a place to use them. The Army does enough of that."[151] Despite efforts to make it clear that GI coffeehouses were a sanctuary from politics and military discipline, it proved a difficult principle to preserve. Counterculture art and memorabilia commonly served as decorations. Featured folk music in some places regularly veered into protest songs. According to one *New York Times* story, antiwar activists saw them as places "to make opposition to the war by draftees more articulate and to encourage servicemen to raise critical questions in the barracks."[152]

Both the underground newspaper movement and GI coffeehouses struck a nerve. The military establishment was unconvinced that they were benign gathering places and attempted to close coffeehouses down or place them off limits. An armed forces disciplinary control board described the Shelter Half as "inimical to good morale, order and discipline."[153] Local authorities had a different but still negative opinion of coffeehouses. Appalled by the "slouchy, beatnik crowd," as the police chief of Columbia, South Carolina, put it, they harassed owners by revoking their business licenses and encouraged police raids intent on exposing drug use and juvenile delinquency. These practices triggered litigation by the American Civil Liberties Union but were popular in local communities who had more sympathy for the military than the counterculture.[154]

The 1970 incarnation of VVAW was far more vested in the counterculture than traditional approaches to activism. This was evident in its first national protest: Operation RAW (Rapid American Withdrawal). In September, approximately 200 veterans marched between Morristown, New Jersey, and Valley Forge, Pennsylvania, with the intent of re-creating combat "as realistically as possible without actually shooting anyone," according to VVAW executive director Al Hubbard.[155] Along the route, which covered 86 foot-sore miles, the VVAW re-created search-and-destroy missions utilizing toy weapons and civilian actors as Vietnamese peasants. According to an article that later appeared in *Ramparts*, veterans handed "astonished tourists" a pink pamphlet that said:

> *We might have burned your house*
> *We might have shot your dog*
> *We might have shot you . . .*
> *We might have bombed out bridges you use every day*
> *We might have raped your wife and daughters*
> *We might have turned you over to your government for torture*
> *We might have taken souvenirs from your property*
> *We might have shot things up a bit . . .*
> *We might have done all these things to you and your neighbors*
> *If it doesn't bother you that American soldiers do these things every day to the Vietnamese simply because they are gooks, then picture YOURSELF as one of the silent victims.*
> *HELP US END THE WAR BEFORE THEY TURN YOUR SON INTO A BUTCHER OR A CORPSE.*[156]

When they reached Valley Forge, where they symbolically smashed their fake M-16 rifles, the marchers were treated to a welcoming speech by Jane Fonda and a counterdemonstration by VFW Douglas MacArthur Post 1507.[157]

As a publicity event, Operation RAW was fairly successful. The *New York Times* covered the march along with a number of Philadelphia area newspapers.[158] Writers were attracted to the "realism" offered by veterans and reenactors, which was a novelty among protests at the time. For the sake of balance, however, most articles also regularly included statements by World War II veterans who decried the march, saying its participants were "a disgrace to everything we stand for," according to a 48-year-old former paratrooper who had fought in the Battle of the Bulge.[159] VVAW organizers finished Operation RAW somewhat frustrated that it did not become a rallying cry against the Vietnam War. Although its membership increased to almost 8,500 by the end of 1970, it did not appear that VVAW influenced official American military policy in Vietnam to any degree.[160]

The VVAW followed Operation RAW with a far more ambitious project that pushed the boundaries of radical activism far beyond symbolism and street theater. In the months following the march to Valley Forge, the VVAW organized the Winter Soldier Investigation in concert with other antiwar groups such as the Citizens Commission of Inquiry and Clergy and Laymen Concerned about Vietnam, Yale psychiatrist Robert Jay Lifton, and a number of celebrities like Dick Gregory, Donald Sutherland, and Jane Fonda.[161] The main purpose of the Winter Soldier Investigation was to reveal US culpability for war crimes committed in Vietnam. Held in Detroit over three days in late January and early February 1971, more than a hundred veterans offered testimony on their personal experiences during the war. The resulting narratives were often graphic, wrenching, and sometimes poignant. Testimony chronicled a disturbing litany of murder, rape, and torture committed against the Viet Cong and innocent civilians caught in American military operations. Taken as a whole, the Winter Soldier Investigation was far more damning than Donald Duncan's earlier *Ramparts* article. Behavior limited to US Special Forces advisers and the South Vietnamese military in 1966 now appeared normal within the US military establishment. The systemic callousness and indifference to the Vietnamese people that pervaded the testimony was chilling.[162]

Most mainstream media sources ignored the Winter Soldier Investigation. Unlike what occurred during Operation RAW, few journalists traveled to Detroit to cover the proceedings. Detracting further from its impact were claims that some of the eyewitness testimony had been exaggerated or falsified. Mark Lane, one of the earlier organizers of the meeting, came under particular fire from *New York Times* journalist Neil Sheehan before Winter Soldier testimony even began. Sheehan, who certainly was no friend of the Pentagon, had spent three years in Vietnam by 1970. When he turned his own investigative skills to corroborate claims made by Mark Lane, he found a clear pattern of inaccurate and uncorroborated information. Sheehan believed that "the country desperately needs a sane and honest inquiry into the question of war crimes and atrocities in Vietnam by a body of knowledgeable and responsible men who are not beholden to the current military establishment."[163] Unfortunately for the VVAW, Sheehan illuminated the risks of placing antiwar motives above basic due diligence. Fairly or not, the Winter Soldier Investigation was tainted by this apparent lapse.

The high-water mark of VVAW protests was in April 1971 when the organization sponsored Operation Dewey Canyon III.[164] According to internal documents, the VVAW intended to launch a "full division of Vietnam veterans" made up of "combat veterans, wounded and decorated, maimed in body and spirit," on a "limited incursion" to Washington. They would hold protests and meetings with Congress to "override Nixon's blood lust" and end the war.[165]

The actual Dewey Canyon III protests were an interesting study in divergent forms. The first revolved around angry public spectacle. Approximately 1,000 veterans marched to Arlington Cemetery and the Supreme Court building when the Justice Department requested an injunction against their encampment on the Mall. Many booed antiwar Democrats like Bella Abzug (Democrat, New York) and Pete McCloskey (Democrat, California) when they met with protesters and asked for patience with troop withdrawals. VVAW members who managed to see legislators often exploded with impatience when representatives refused to engage in meaningful discussions on the war. One of the most celebrated moments came when hundreds of Vietnam veterans threw their medals over a barrier on the west steps of the Capitol Building. Jan Crumb, one of the VVAW's original founders, stated, "At a minimum we showed that the Supreme Court, the executive branch and the Congress are irrelevant."[166]

A second component of Operation Dewey Canyon III was far more sober and moderate. It came when John Kerry, a decorated navy veteran who served in South Vietnam between 1968 and 1969, testified before the Senate Foreign Relations Committee on 22 April 1971. The transcript of his testimony reveals much of the same passion that inhabited other VVAW protesters in Washington then. Kerry spoke to the hypocrisy of needlessly sacrificing American lives in Vietnam for the "mystical war against communism."[167] He spoke of the anger and frustration at bearing the mental and physical burdens of the war while being derided by public officials like Spiro Agnew for joining the antiwar movement. Although Kerry used pointed language when he addressed the Senate Foreign Relations Committee, the video taken of his testimony reveals a different story. His tone was measured and respectful. Unlike many of the 1,000 veterans outside on the Mall, he appeared well groomed and calm, intent on acknowledging the solemnity of the proceedings. Most of all, it is clear that he was willing to observe the protocols of authority rather than alienate sympathetic political leaders like J. William Fulbright. Kerry's moderation cost him support with the VVAW. Many members resented his sudden media fame. Others suspected that Kerry had political ambitions beyond the antiwar movement.[168]

This criticism was unfair, but it illustrated the fine line traveled by the VVAW between expressing its profound distrust of the establishment and appealing to a broader constituency. Leaders like Jan Crumb believed that the diversity of approaches within the VVAW was a strength. He saw the VVAW breaking new ground in the antiwar movement, insisting that they "were neither the trashers, passive marchers, nor the usual non-violent civil disobedience types. We followed our own instincts and did things our own way. There was a great deal of humor and a great deal of seriousness about what we did."[169] The VVAW never endorsed violence against authority. In the aftermath of the Kent State shooting, when campuses around the country seethed, veterans provided "strike marshals" to mitigate clashes between protesters and local authorities.[170]

Perhaps one of the best examples of these efforts had to do with veterans' mental health. A common complaint among Vietnam-era veterans with war-related stress was the lack of bed space or treatment because older indigent veterans with non-service-related disabilities filled the VA hospital system. The problem of inadequate access was also made worse by a general distrust of the VA, which lacked treatment protocols for PTSD and tended to medicate veterans rather than offer them individual therapy.[171]

Without a real or perceived alternative, many Vietnam veterans began to meet in informal "rap groups" where they could discuss their experiences. At the end of 1970, VVAW eventually invited psychiatrists Robert Jay Lifton and Chaim Shatan to guide some of these discussions.[172] Mental health professionals from the New York University Postdoctoral Psychoanalytic Training Program, the New York Psychoanalytic Institute, and the Columbia University Psychoanalytic Clinic later joined in these sessions.[173]

The primary purpose of these rap groups, according to Shatan, was to allow veterans a chance to express the "unconsummated grief" resulting from combat trauma and ignored by traditional medical treatment.[174] In some respects, the approach was similar to the group therapy method adopted by the Menninger Clinic in Topeka, Kansas, to treat World War II veterans after 1945.[175] The resemblance was superficial, however. Both Lifton and Shatan, for example, directly challenged existing professional standards that emphasized clinical detachment from patients. Both were advocates of therapists becoming directly involved with their patients as an integral part of therapy. Another doctor described abandoning clinical objectivity in favor of a "therapeutic alliance." Similarly, Shatan saw "the end of our professional pseudo-neutrality" as a simple recognition of reality in the medical community.[176]

Taking the nontraditional approach a step further, both Lifton and Shatan also maintained that public activism was a critical means of personal therapy for veterans. Referring to Vietnam veterans in his book *Home from the War*, Lifton contended, "For a number of them, and at varying intervals, political activities become inseparable from psychological need."[177] In other words, individual anger over bad acts committed for authority could be resolved by actively challenging that authority. Shatan stressed the need for action:

> *To men who have been steeped in death and evil beyond imagination, a "talking cure" alone is worthless. And merely sharing their grief and outrage with comrades in the same dilemma is similarly unsatisfying. Active participation in the public arena was essential. By throwing onto the steps of Congress the medals with which they were rewarded for murder in a war they had come to abhor, the veterans symbolically shed some of their guilt.*[178]

It is not surprising that Lifton, Shatan, and like-minded professionals found a ready audience in the VVAW. Both groups were in a sense a product of their times, distrustful of institutions that had squandered their authority by virtue of their hubris. For Lifton, the medical community deserved contempt for failing to acknowledge the posttraumatic stress that was crippling veterans. For many VVAW members, all of the agencies responsible for wasting countless American and Vietnamese lives lay beyond contempt.

Unfortunately, the qualities that drew these two groups together also handicapped them as activists. Lifton may have been correct about the ongoing need to treat veterans' mental ailments, but flaunting professional practices hurt his campaign in the long run. The medical community would not recognize PTSD until 1980.[179] Despite whatever good intentions it may have had to reshape the antiwar movement and stir a complacent public, and despite a rise in membership to 25,000 by the early seventies, the VVAW lost too many potential constituents with rhetoric that reduced military service to being a "BUTCHER OR A CORPSE."[180] This type of dogmatism did not help, especially when it began to extend collective responsibility for Vietnam beyond veterans, the Congress, the White House, and the Pentagon. Shortly after Operation Dewey Canyon III, Jan Barry editorialized that the type of military service in Vietnam essentially was irrelevant: "One cannot participate in the Vietnam war without being at least in complicity in committing war crimes." He did not stop there. Barry maintained that the problem extended to baby boomers as a whole: "America's Vietnam generation isn't up against the wall: it's bricked in. Going to Vietnam is a war crime, refusing to go is a domestic crime and just sitting still, somewhere or somehow in exile or limbo, is a moral crime. It is a terrible time today to be American and young. In fact, it apparently is a crime."[181] In the end, "moderates" within the VVAW lost the day. John Kerry departed the organization's leadership by the end of 1971. In the years to come, the VVAW declined under the weight of ideological conflict and rivalries between regional offices.

Outside actors also played an important part in marginalizing the VVAW. As was the case with the Deacons for Defense and Justice, when veterans pushed the establishment, the establishment pushed back. This was especially true of the federal government during the Nixon years. Once it became clear that the VVAW was emerging as a leading light within the antiwar movement, it increasingly drew official fire. Some of it was rhetorical. In 1969, Vice President Spiro Agnew entered the antiwar fray with a speech denouncing organizers of the Vietnam Moratorium protest as "an effete corps of impudent snobs" and "hardcore dissidents and professional anarchists."[182] The administration's intent was not only to tar activists with terminology familiar to the McCarthy purges of the fifties but also to drive a wedge between protesting veterans and the "loyal" majority of veterans in mainstream society.[183]

While Agnew added to his catalogue of derisive terminology, other federal agencies moved against the VVAW behind the scenes. The Justice Department began a campaign of sustained legal prosecution, not for the sake of crimes committed by veterans but simply to tie up VVAW time and funding.[184] Like the Deacons for Defense and Justice and the Black Panther Party, the VVAW also found itself subject to COINTELPRO. Declassified files indicate years of constant FBI surveillance as well as attempts to infiltrate the organization to collect intelligence and provoke illegal actions. The FBI also reported the possibility of Communist infiltration of a number of VVAW chapters.[185] Despite the administration's best efforts, COINTELPRO and Justice Department harassment did not accomplish their desired goals. Allegations of Communist influence failed to resonate in the new era of détente. Ironically, as Stephen Ambrose observed, Nixon's own policy of withdrawal from Vietnam undercut his own credibility with more conservative sectors of American society, in some cases groups represented by the American Legion and the VFW.[186]

Conclusion

The modern history of veterans' activism offers an important study in the contrast between image and reality. Millions of veterans were certainly active in thousands of social projects around the country after World War II. History tends to remember not the mundane work that went into communities but instances of high-profile dissent that captured the public imagination with their audacity. Volunteerism for American Legion baseball, with its relentless schedule of carpooling, practices, and games, faded into the background noise of postwar American normalcy. There were moments when instances of visceral action shocked veterans and their communities out of the routine, a point driven home by the navy veteran who immolated himself in 1967 to protest the Vietnam War.[187]

It is fairly clear that veterans who pursued more radical methodologies were the outliers in the postwar history of activism. In the case of the civil rights movement, circumstances explained by ingrained racism, placed reasonable people demanding basic elements of citizenship on the fringe of society. Other groups like the Deacons for Defense and the VVAW deliberately flaunted accepted conventions and social fears. They succeeded in making their causes part of a public spectacle but almost inevitably alienated their larger audience and invited a backlash. As the VVAW found, striking a productive line between redefining a protest movement and enlarging a constituency proved extremely difficult.

Radicalism failed to resonate with the vast majority of Americans. Veterans were no different. After 1945, most appeared intent on engaging the political, religious, and civic aspects of life through traditional venues. In fact, veterans' outlooks on what needed attention rarely diverged from that of the mainstream. With the exception of some military topics (e.g., military spending), research indicates that veterans' opinions were remarkably consistent with those of civilians and were, in some cases, notable for more tolerance in some areas. Surveys conducted after Korea and Vietnam indicate little difference between veterans and nonveterans with respect to trust in government, crime and violence, and international affairs. Interestingly, it appears that veterans in the fifties and the seventies actually appeared to be more tolerant of Communists than their civilian counterparts.[188]

Positive factors account for part of this continuity. The veterans' lobby, comprising primarily the American Legion and the VFW, was consistently successful in shaping law to the benefit of its constituency. Only very late in the story, when it became apparent that the 1966 version of the GI Bill was not keeping pace with veterans' needs, did this consensus start to break down. In the meantime, veterans contributed their time and energy to traditional community activism after World War II. They did so guided by the belief in continued service for the country and in the spirit of reciprocity for benefits bestowed by a grateful nation.

Finally, there are darker elements to the story of veterans' activism that deserve some consideration. One of the most common themes surrounding Vietnam-era veterans was their sense of alienation from mainstream American society. A 1972 AVC report noted the "indifference, even hostility, of a society weary of the war" that increased the "sense of isolation" felt by men returning from Vietnam.[189] A 1968 edition of the *Nation* reported that one navy veteran was referred to as "the resident fascist pig" of his Harvard dormitory.[190] The result was the increasing tendency in a generation of veterans to be "non-heroes" who did "not wish to be identified as veterans; indeed, many regard their service as a badge of infamy."[191]

It is clear that this reticence was not limited to Vietnam veterans. Over the course of the period after World War II, alienation came from many sources. For minority veterans, challenging the status quo carried with it considerable risks. For members of the AVC, attacking Joseph McCarthy at the height of his influence offered similar difficulties. It is interesting that although surveys indicate that veterans were not as zealous about communism as nonveterans, they did not flock to the AVC. Rather than contest the conventional wisdom, many chose silence and conformity as the best means of self-preservation.

CONCLUSION

I was acting out the same dream that gripped hundreds of thousands of returning servicemen across America. Get a loan. Build. Put down roots. Establish a little kingdom for the family. Get a job. Be normal. Be average. Get the noise out of your head, if you could—the engines, the gunfire, the screams. Build a house that would withstand the furies of that war, a house that would keep the future connected to the innocent past; that would seal shut that raw gap of four and a half years and keep it shut forever.

—World War II pilot Robert Morgan, 2001[1]

As I noted at the start of the book, what defines a veteran goes far beyond labels like "hero" or "victim." The same is true with respect to the number of parties actively attempting to determine what the term "veteran" means. To state the obvious, veterans are not a monolithic group. Membership is defined by preconceptions in place before enlistment or conscription, by the particular branch of service and occupational specialty, and by actual wartime experience. It may be refined further by gender and race, class, age, education, and region. These distinctions defined individual veterans and the collective membership of veterans' organizations from the American Legion to the Deacons for Defense and Justice.

History also plays an important part in defining a veteran. Looking back on the history of World War II, Korea, and Vietnam veterans, it is clear that the context of the times defined both service and the environment awaiting returning veterans. Wars served as rallying points for Americans, although the passage of time had an impact on the durability of consensus.[2] Peacetime histories are also contextually important but equally fluid. The post-1945 consensus celebrated by Tom Brokaw and a generation of historians is a misnomer. It began in the difficult transition to peace and remained transitory and very fragile in the years afterward. It was buffeted by Cold War crises, the many stages of the baby boom, the emerging and diversifying "rights revolution," the sexual revolution, and creeping economic uncertainty, all of which defined American "normalcy" for veterans who came home.

Like history, the context provided by general civil society is critical to understanding the veteran after 1945. Colin Gray asserts that the military institution is inseparable from its parent culture.[3] This is important to consider when shaping any narrative considering the veteran and his or her life after war. Social context is the foundation of the life course theory.[4] It established the limits of tolerance for veterans' service, defining the boundaries of both opportunities and taboos. Most veterans sought out social norms in the pursuit of work, family, and social activism. For the most part, the majority determined the metrics of reassimilation. The standard was not an absolute, however. In many cases, veterans fought the majority social consensus when it became an obstacle to their own progress. This was the case with respect to minority veterans who joined the postwar civil rights movement to obtain what the good war promised.

Points of Separation between Veterans

There are points in the modern history of veterans where the separate parts of this story coalesce into a coherent whole. Some of the evidence suggests that there were significant distinctions separating veterans of World War II, Korea, and Vietnam. When men and women joined the military, it was clear that circumstances affecting that decision differed substantially over time. Service in World War II was driven by a sense of urgency over national survival that outweighed concerns regarding the terms of military service or its duration. In this case, Tom Brokaw's argument is partly correct. The generation raised in the wake of the Great Depression was more willing to make sacrifices for the sake of the greater good. That changed after 1945 with the advent of the GI Bill and onset of the Cold War. The 16 million new veterans who exited the good war won two victories that influenced subsequent generations of volunteers and draftees. They prevailed against global fascism and won a massive extension of the American welfare state. Taken together, these two achievements raised the prestige of military service, while concurrently increasing expectations that the country would reward it. Subsequently, when their sons and daughters entered the military, personal expectations about benefits began to accompany and crowd out the increasingly abstract imperatives of Cold War national security. Policy reflected this tendency in fixed tours of duty, first introduced in Korea and later reinstated during Vietnam. The consistent expansion of military deferment policies after 1945 is an even better example of individual prerogatives winning out over institutional needs.

The number of combat veterans present in American society clearly declined from World War II to the conclusion of the Vietnam War. One explanation is institutional. As the American military became increasingly complex, driven by modern technological breakthroughs, it became ever more dependent on logistics. Personnel assignments followed suit. Consequently, participation in the combat arms dropped significantly in the 30 years following World War II. By the time the United States began escalating deployments to Vietnam, a very small percentage of men actually engaged in direct combat operations.

Selective Service further refined the percentage of men assigned to combat. The prevalence of draftees in combat units during Vietnam reflected deliberate military personnel policy. Rather than spend resources on men with a two-year service commitment or whose aptitude scores fell below the minimum for technical occupations, the Pentagon force-fed draftees into infantry, armor, and field artillery specialties. Casualty figures indicate a definite divergence between risks posed to conscripts and volunteers during the war.

Doctrine sharpened this distinction further. The military took S. L. A Marshall's critique of individual American combat effectiveness seriously after World War II. Resulting training techniques like the Trainfire system were dedicated to improving accuracy under combat conditions as well as overall participation. When American combat forces deployed to Vietnam, they were the beneficiaries of improved training. The result of doctrine, the Selective Service System, and institutional priorities point out a wide gap between the mass of veterans exposed to combat and the substantially smaller numbers of Vietnam veterans at the sharp edge of the spear.

The relationship between veterans and work also exhibited a number of clear distinctions over time. Despite the chronic problems of inflation, shortages, and strikes that plagued the United States in the immediate aftermath of World War II, the national economy recovered within a few years and began a period of sustained growth. The postwar boom presented a broad range of economic opportunities for veterans in an array of skills, educational levels, and industries. The Korean War interrupted this momentum, forcing hundreds of thousands of World War II "retreads," National Guard, and reservists back into uniform just as their civilian careers began to prosper. When Korea veterans came back, the American economy lacked the same open-ended opportunities of the previous decade. Throughout the remainder of the fifties, recurring economic recessions and spiking unemployment rates indicated that the great boom was beginning to lose momentum. By the time the Vietnam War ended, it was clear that the economy was beginning to come apart at the seams. In the early seventies, mismanaged federal programs, war spending, an aging industrial base that could no longer effectively compete in the global market, high labor costs, and a host of other factors combined to make the seventies the worst economic period in American history since the Great Depression.

Veterans of each war did enjoy federal benefits to encourage their economic readjustment, but these varied in quality, especially the 1966 Cold War GI Bill. World War II veterans enjoyed unprecedented training and education benefits. Their passage through higher education and technical schools built skill sets that facilitated veterans' transition to a job market hungry for intellectual capital. Unfortunately, these benefit programs stagnated after the Korean War when Congress attempted to control costs by freezing the amount veterans received for tuition and school costs. By the time Vietnam veterans claimed their readjustment benefits under the 1966 law, inflation had seriously eroded actual payments. Transitional programs started by the Johnson and Nixon administrations failed to alleviate this problem, as did attempts to win voluntary cooperation from the private sector to hire discharged Vietnam veterans. In the tightening economy of the seventies, the bottom line spoke more strongly than patriotism or personal sympathy.

On its face, sharp distinctions separate veteran activists in the forties from protesters who dominated the news 20 years later. Toy drives and American Legion baseball stood in sharp contrast to the loud, visceral, confrontational approaches adopted by the Deacons for Defense and Justice and the Vietnam Veterans against the War. It appeared that the quiet, collective constructiveness of the greatest generation had given way to individuals intent on pursuing personal agendas—as Robert Jay Lifton and other therapists actually encouraged them—in place of contributing to the greater good. However, as the next two sections indicate, appearances could be deceptive. Additional analysis reveals a more accurate history and dispels many of the myths fostered by superficial assumptions.

Commonalities Binding Three Generations of Veterans

Veterans of World War II, Korea, and Vietnam shared far more commonalities in their transition to civilian life than differences. The evidence suggests that although America changed dramatically in the decades following 1945, there were permanent qualities of war and the veteran's experience that persisted despite the passage of time.[5] When men and women entered the military, for example, they did so for reasons that remained remarkably consistent over three decades. Simple patriotism motivated them, a sincere desire to protect the country in time of crisis. Family history mattered as well. Young men signed up because they were inspired by sacrifices of past generations and determined to make their own mark. Many of the personal reasons cited by veterans were purely subjective but remarkably consistent in World War II, Korea, and Vietnam. Curiosity about the benefits offered by the service, boredom with their lives, confidence in their ability, and a general ignorance about all things military unified successive generations of volunteers.

The relationship between veterans and combat offers another example of consistency. Measuring the total percentage of individuals assigned to combat units to gauge its effects is a crude metric. It ignores the fact that military personnel at war are all exposed to death and destruction whether or not they are direct participants in it. It was not until the Vietnam War that the medical community began to differentiate between degrees of "light" or "heavy" combat to understand its impact on individual veterans.

Similarly, modern medicine lacked the tools to measure the long-term impact of traumatic stress on veterans until very late in this story. Military health care developed excellent protocols to identify and treat battlefield mental disorders, but these were intended "to conserve the fighting strength" during war, not in its aftermath.[6] Vietnam combat veterans appeared to suffer a higher incidence of PTSD largely because by the time they returned home, the medical establishment had finally developed a conceptual framework to identify their problems.

With this framework in place, it became increasingly apparent that Vietnam veterans shared an array of PTSD symptoms with their predecessors. As research on veterans and PTSD proceeds, it is becoming more inclusive. Veterans of all three wars appear to share similar difficulties with depression and alcoholism. Female veterans of World War II, Korea, and Vietnam, whom both clinicians and policy makers assumed were far removed from combat, are now receiving long-awaited attention.[7] The same is true of World War II veterans in general. Advanced age has become an inevitable chapter in life course theory and, with it, the onset of problems associated with younger men home from Korea and Vietnam.

With respect to work, the economy awaiting returning veterans did shift and worsen throughout the extended post–World War II period. Essentially, the economic boom that began in 1945 was built on an unsustainable foundation. As the American manufacturing base aged and labor costs escalated, European and Asian reconstruction returned foreign competition to the global marketplace. The unplanned and poorly managed costs of the Vietnam War, followed by the 1973 energy crisis, left the era of American economic dominance in tatters.

Despite the increasingly difficult economic landscape, veterans of all three wars successfully negotiated the transition to work. The primary variable defining their success was time. Veterans of World War II reentered the economy relatively quickly, briefly delayed by reconversion troubles in the first years after the war but also by time spent in school and training. Korean War veterans returned to stable employment placed on hold when they were mobilized or found work in a labor market that continued to grow in the fifties despite short-term reversals. Vietnam veterans took the most amount of time. The poor job market accounted for part of the delay. Perhaps equally important was the relative youth of Vietnam veterans, who left the service in their early 20s. Lacking educational credentials or union seniority, and handicapped by race in some circumstances, these individuals found the process of economic reassimilation comparatively more difficult than their predecessors did after World War II and Korea. Yet they did succeed over the long term.

Although the mind's eye is drawn to images of bitter men hurling their medals onto the Capitol steps in 1971, other veterans courted controversy as activists throughout the post–World War II period. Veterans who flocked to the NAACP in the forties battled entrenched racism around the country. It is both sad and ironic that the more they adopted the benchmarks of normalcy and universal rights—work, housing, voting—the more they provoked a backlash from segregationists. Yet African American civil rights leaders, including many veterans, continued their campaign, winning incomplete victories against continuing resistance. Similarly, the risks associated with nonconformity during the height of the postwar Red Scare did not deter the American Veterans Committee from attacking Joseph McCarthy or his confederates in the American Legion.

Basic principles both guided and unified veteran activists after World War II. African American veterans in the civil rights movement, the AVC, and the VVAW all shared a sense of outrage at the failure of their country to live up to the basic standards they fought to defend. The AVC motto, "citizens first, veterans second," spoke to the desire for equality of opportunity and, perhaps more important, accountability from the American system for its decisions and their consequences. African American veterans wanted the country held accountable to the GI Bill and the Fourteenth Amendment for a start. The AVC paralleled and intersected with civil rights activists in its search for social justice.[8] The VVAW desired accountability from the civilian and military authorities to justify their sacrifices in Vietnam. Taken as a whole, activists wanted to close the gap between promise and reality.

The Distance between Myth, History, and Veterans

One of the great temptations of writing history is generalizing the topic at hand. When historians teach or write, we tend to compress complex issues for the sake of manageability and narrative flow. While this has an obvious value for the audience and speaker, it carries the risk of oversimplification. The lay public sometimes follows a similar process by allowing imagery to coalesce into accepted conventional wisdom. Both approaches produce assumptions that often fail to separate poorly understood history from outright myth.

One of these assumptions pertains to the basic nature of military service. The common understanding that most of the men who served during the Vietnam era were draftees is simply false on the facts. As it turned out, far more men entered the military as draftees during World War II. In the Vietnam era, nearly three-quarters of the men entering the military were volunteers.[9] What muddles our current perspective is the proportion of draftees assigned to combat units during the Vietnam War. However, it is equally likely that men with poor aptitude scores in World War II also found themselves in the infantry.

The evidence also indicates that combat trauma was not particularly unique to Vietnam veterans. Hospital records demonstrate that the Veterans Administration psychiatric caseload remained large and fairly consistent from World War II through the Vietnam War. Although the health-care system could identify and house these individuals, treatment lagged behind need. Medical studies conducted as early as the Korean War did not develop into a basic treatment protocol for PTSD until the post-Vietnam period. Given the current problems faced by Iraq and Afghanistan veterans, it is arguable that treatment still lags behind need.

Finally, it does not appear that Vietnam veterans in particular or veterans as a group were a threat to civil society after 1945. Although veterans were a popular media trope with respect to crime reporting, national crime statistics reveal a decline in most types of crime after World War II. When rates in the United States and most Western industrial nations did increase during the sixties, the actual source was more likely youthful offenders, not veterans.

These topics, and a host of others, deserve additional study. When I began this project, I wanted to approach veterans' reassimilation with a relatively broad brush, covering some of the basic elements of their experience. New research will no doubt further refine our understanding of motives for enlisting in the military, the legacy of combat, the importance of the work environment, and veterans' social activism. Perhaps more important, as research on veterans expands and diversifies, it will improve our overall understanding of the American society of which they are a large and important part.

NOTES

Introduction

1. "Seven Veterans and Their Town," *New York Times*, 8 September 1946, SM6.

2. Ronald J. Glasser, *365 Days* (New York: George Braziller, 1971), 5.

3. There is an extensive literature on the topic in European history: Niall Barr, *The Lion and the Poppy: British Veterans, Politics, and Society, 1921–1939* (Westport, CT: Praeger, 2005); James M. Diehl, *The Thanks of the Fatherland: German Veterans after the Second World War* (Chapel Hill: University of North Carolina Press, 1993); Mark Edele, *Soviet Veterans of the Second World War: A Popular Movement in an Authoritarian Society, 1941–1991* (New York: Oxford University Press, 2008); Robert Wheldon Whalen, *Bitter Wounds: German Victims of the Great War, 1914–1939* (Ithaca, NY: Cornell University Press, 1984).

4. See David A. Gerber, "Disabled Veterans, the State, and the Experience of Disability in Western Societies, 1914–1950," *Journal of Social History* 36 (Summer 2003): 899–916; Deborah Cohen, *The War Come Home: Disabled Veterans in Britain and Germany, 1914–1939* (Berkeley: University of California Press, 2001).

5. See, for example, Patrick J. Kelly, *Creating a National Home: Building the Veterans' Welfare State, 1860–1900* (Cambridge, MA: Harvard University Press, 1997); Michael Gambone, *Greatest Generation Comes Home: The Veteran in American Society* (College Station: Texas A&M University Press, 2005).

6. There is an enormous body of scholarship on the GI Bill, its precursors, and legacy. For more recent examples, see Stephen R. Ortiz, *Beyond the Bonus March and the GI Bill: How Veterans Politics Shaped the New Deal Era* (New York: New York University Press, 2010); Meredith Hindley, "A New Deal for Veterans: How the G.I. Bill Was Passed," *Humanities* 35 (July–August 2014): 16–19, 50–52.

7. For a recent example of scholarship examining this issue, see Andrew J. Huebner, *The Warrior Image: Soldiers in American Culture from the Second World War to the Vietnam Era* (Chapel Hill: University of North Carolina Press, 2008).

8. Michael D. Gambone, "Iraq War Veterans: For the Troops, but against the War," in *Encyclopedia of the Veteran in America*, ed. William Pencak (Santa Barbara, CA: ABC-CLIO, 2009), 2:237–46.

9. Tom Brokaw, *The Greatest Generation* (New York: Random House, 1998), xviii.

10. Ibid., 3.

11. Studs Terkel, *"The Good War": An Oral History of World War II* (New York: Pantheon Books, 1984).

12. Scholarship addressing consensus history and revisionism stretches back for decades. For a brief representative sample, see Sean Wilentz, "American Political Histories," *OAH Magazine of History* 21 (April 2007): 23–27; Leo P. Ribuffo, "What Is Still Living in 'Consensus' History and Pluralist Social Theory," *American Studies International* 38 (February 2000): 42–60; Andrew Hunt, "Why Did the Sixties Happen? Searching for New Directions," *Journal of Social History* 33 (Autumn 1999): 147–61; Neil A. Wynn, "The 'Good War': The Second World War and Postwar American Society," *Journal of Contemporary History* 31 (July 1996): 463–82; John Higham, "Changing Paradigms: The Collapse of Consensus History," *Journal of American History* 76 (September 1989): 460–66; Alan Brinkley, "Writing the History of Contemporary America: Dilemmas and Challenges," *Daedalus* 113 (Summer 1984): 121–41.

13. Warren W. Hassler, *With Shield and Sword: American Military Affairs, Colonial Times to the Present* (Iowa City: University of Iowa Press, 1982), 304.

14. Samuel Eliot Morison, Henry Steele Commager, and William E. Leuchtenberg, *The Growth of the American Republic* (New York: Oxford University Press, 1969), 2:619.

15. Robert Timberg, *The Nightingale's Song* (New York: Simon and Schuster, 1995), 86.

16. Robert Jay Lifton, *Home from War: Vietnam Veterans: Neither Victims nor Executioners* (New York: Simon and Schuster, 1973), 137.

17. American Battle Monuments Commission, Korean War Memorial, accessed January 11, 2017, https://www.abmc.gov/about-us/history/korean-war-memorial.

18. Bruce Cumings, *The Origins of the Korean War: The Roaring of the Cataract, 1947–1950*, vol. 2 (Princeton, NJ: Princeton University Press, 1990); Alan R. Millett, *The War for Korea, 1950–1951: They Came from the North* (Lawrence: University Press of Kansas, 2010).

19. David M. Kennedy, *Freedom from Fear: The American People in Depression and War, 1929–1945* (New York: Oxford University Press, 1999), 857.

20. Fintan Walsh, *Male Trouble: Masculinity and Performance of Crisis*

(New York: Palgrave Macmillan, 2010); Elaine Tyler May, *Homeward Bound: American Families in the Cold War Era*, 3rd ed. (New York: Basic Books, 2008); James Gilbert, *Men in the Middle: Searching for Masculinity in the 1950's* (Chicago: University of Chicago Press, 2005); John Horne, "Masculinity in Politics and War in the Age of Nation-States and World Wars, 1850–1950," in *Masculinities in Politics and War: Gendering Modern History*, eds. Stefan Dudink, Karen Hagemann, and John Tosh (New York: Manchester University Press, 2004), 22–34.

21. Melinda L. Pash, *In The Shadow of the Greatest Generation: The Americans Who Fought the Korean War* (New York: New York University Press, 2012).

22. Andy Rooney, *My War*, 2nd ed. (New York: PublicAffairs, 2000), 310.

23. Jerry Lembcke, *The Spitting Image: Myth, Memory, and the Legacy of Vietnam* (New York: New York University Press, 1998).

24. Russell W. Glenn, *Reading Athena's Dance Card: Men against Fire in Vietnam* (Annapolis, MD: Naval Institute Press, 2000), 124.

25. Eric T. Dean, "The Myth of the Troubled and Scorned Vietnam Veteran," *Journal of American Studies* 26 (April 1992): 60. See also Robert F. Saxe, *Settling Down: World War II Veterans' Challenge to the Postwar Consensus* (New York: Palgrave Macmillan, 2007).

Chapter 1

1. Tim O'Brien, *If I Die in a Combat Zone: Box Me Up and Ship Me Home* (New York: Dell, 1987), 20.

2. Allan R. Millett and Peter Maslowski, *For the Common Defense: A Military History of the United States of America* (New York: Free Press, 1994), 3.

3. The foundation of US manpower policy for more than a century was the Uniform Militia Act of 1792. See Ibid., 94–95.

4. Franklin D. Roosevelt, "Radio Address on Registration Day," 16 October 1940, in *Public Papers of the Presidents: Franklin Roosevelt*, ed. Samuel I. Rosenman (Washington, DC: Government Printing Office, 1941), 9:473.

5. "Offers Bill to Draft Single Women," *New York Times*, 2 June 1944, 10; George Gallup, "Voters Back Draft of Single Women," *New York Times*, 10 March 1944, 32.

6. See, for example, Gary C. Jacobson, "A Tale of Two Wars: Public Opinion on the US Military Interventions in Afghanistan and Iraq," *Presidential Studies Quarterly* 40 (December 2010): 585–610; Adam J. Berinsky, *In Time of War: Understanding American Public Opinion from World War II to Iraq*

(Chicago: University of Chicago Press, 2009); Christopher Gelpi, Peter D. Feaver, and Jason Reifer, *Paying the Human Costs of War: American Public Opinion and Casualties in Military Conflicts* (Princeton, NJ: Princeton University Press, 2009).

7. Ortiz, *Beyond the Bonus March and the GI Bill.*

8. A 1981 survey of Vietnam veterans found that 54% had fathers with prior military service, with 36% of these men seeing combat. See Arthur Egendorf, Charles Kadushin, Robert S. Laufer, Lee Sloan, and George Rothbart, *Legacies of Vietnam: Comparative Adjustment of Veterans and Their Peers: A Study Conducted for the Veterans Administration* (New York: Center for Policy Research, 1981), 117.

9. James Bradley, with Ron Powers, *Flags of Our Fathers* (New York: Bantam Books, 2000), 62. See also Berinsky, *In Time of War*, 33.

10. Brokaw, *The Greatest Generation*, 9.

11. Ibid., 14.

12. Louis Harris and Associates, Inc., *A Study of the Problems Facing Vietnam Era Veterans: Their Readjustment to Civilian Life* (New York: Louis Harris and Associates, 1971), 10.

13. See Helmuth C. Engelbrecht and Frank C. Hanighen, *Merchants of Death: A Study of the International Armament Industry* (New York: Dodd, Mead, 1934), 6.

14. Paul Fussell, *Wartime: Understanding and Behavior in the Second World War* (New York: Oxford University Press, 1989), 130.

15. Kennedy, *Freedom from Fear*, 386–88.

16. Charles A. Lindbergh, “Our Drift toward War: No People Ever Had a Greater Decision to Make,” *Vital Speeches of the Day* 18 (July 1940): 550. See also Frank L. Kluckhohn, “Morris Says Draft Would Lead Nation into Dictatorship,” *New York Times*, 13 August 1940.

17. American Legion, Summary of Proceedings, *Twenty-Second Annual National Convention of the American Legion, 23–26 September 1940*, 44, American Legion Library (AL), Manuscript Collection.

18. American Legion, National Publicity Division, “Suggested Address for American Legion before Legion Groups on Universal Service,” 4 November 1942, AL, Universal Draft File.

19. Hassler, *With Shield and Sword*, 297–99.

20. Fussell, *Wartime*, 138.

21. Franklin Delano Roosevelt, “The ‘Four Freedoms’ Speech,” in *Documents of American History*, ed. Henry Steele Commager (Englewood Cliffs, NJ: Prentice Hall, 1973), 2:446–49.

22. Mark Harris, *Five Came Back: A Story of Hollywood and the Second World War* (New York: Penguin Press, 2014), 217–19.

23. George Q. Flynn, *The Draft, 1940–1973* (Lawrence: University Press of Kansas, 1993), 11–12.

24. "City Youth Stages a Motley Parade," *New York Times*, 16 October 1940, 1.

25. US Senate, *An Act to Provide for the Common Defense by Increasing the Personnel of the Armed Forces of the United States and Provide for Its Training*, 76th Cong., 3rd sess., 16 September 1940, S. 4164, 886.

26. Richard W. Stewart, ed., *American Military History: The United States Army in a Global Era, 1917–2003* (Washington, DC: Center of Military History, 2005), 73.

27. Flynn, *The Draft*, 51.

28. Ibid., 85. See also "Report on Conditions of Military Service for the President's Commission on Veterans' Pensions: Section 1, Selection Process," n.d., iv, Dwight D. Eisenhower (DDE) Library, US President's Commission on Veterans' Pensions (Bradley Commission): Records, 1954–1958, Box 58.

29. Bradley, *Flags of Our Fathers*, 17–54, 75–98. Mike Strank was the only flag raiser on active duty at the time of the Pearl Harbor attack. Ira Hayes enlisted in August 1942.

30. Flynn, *The Draft*, 170–71. Flynn notes that in Korea, the monthly average was 80,000 men. In Vietnam, inductions peaked at 343,000 for all of 1966.

31. Millett and Maslowski, *For the Common Defense*, 653.

32. Bradley, *Flags of Our Fathers*, 282.

33. Max Hastings, *Inferno: The World at War, 1939–1945* (New York: Alfred A. Knopf, 2011), 614, 622. Okinawa also produced 34,000 "non-battle" casualties.

34. D. M. Giangreco, "Casualty Projections for the US Invasions of Japan, 1945–1946: Planning and Policy Implications," *Journal of Military History* 61 (July 1997): 521–81.

35. Pash, *In The Shadow of the Greatest Generation*, 13.

36. James Webb, *Fields of Fire* (New York: Bantam Books, 1978), 34.

37. Philip Caputo, *A Rumor of War* (New York: Holt, Rinehart and Winston, 1977), 5.

38. See also Richard Stacewicz, *Winter Soldiers: An Oral History of the Vietnam Veterans against the War* (Chicago: Haymarket Books, 1997), 43–46.

39. Rick Worland, "The Other Living-Room War: Prime Time Combat Series, 1962–1975," *Journal of Film and Video* 50 (Fall 1998): 3–23.

40. Ron Kovic, *Born on the Fourth of July* (New York: McGraw-Hill, 1976), 42–45; Caputo, *A Rumor of War*, 6.

41. Frank Ninkovich, *The Wilsonian Century: US Foreign Policy since 1900* (Chicago: University of Chicago Press, 1999), 178; John Lewis Gaddis, *The Cold War: A New History* (New York: Penguin Books, 2005), 40–47, 58–60.

42. Hanson W. Baldwin, "US Lacks Aim in Korea," *New York Times*, 13 April 1951, 7; "Peace Talks Cause Confusion in Army," *New York Times*, 26 June 1951, 7.

43. Gene Gilmore, "I'm Bitter," *American Legion Magazine*, November 1952, 24 (emphasis in original).

44. James C. Jones, "All's Quiet on the Home Front," *American Legion Magazine*, February 1952, 20, 60.

45. "Rotation Quota Raised," *New York Times*, 30 December 1952, 3.

46. "Program Outlined on Troop Rotation," *New York Times*, 11 October 1951, 24. The navy limited the term of service to 17 months for World War II veterans. The air force set the commitment for organized reserves called into service before June 1951 at 21 months. Marine reservists recalled before June 1951 were obligated to 12 additional months of service.

47. "Morale of the G.I. Is High but He Wants to Go Home," *New York Times*, 20 May 1951, E4.

48. John P. Monks, "College Men at War," *Memoirs of the American Academy of Arts and Sciences* 24 (1957): 291.

49. US President's Commission on Veterans' Pensions, Memorandum for the Assistant Secretary of Defense (Manpower and Personnel), "Final Report—Ad Hoc Committee on the Future of Military Service as a Career That Will Attract and Retain Capable Career Personnel," 30 October 1953, 2, DDE, Bradley Commission, Box 2.

50. Doris Kearns, *Lyndon Johnson and the American Dream* (New York: Harper and Row, 1976), 251.

51. Leslie H. Gelb, *The Irony of Vietnam: The System Worked* (Washington, DC: Brookings Institution, 1979), 25, 129.

52. John E. Mueller, *War, Presidents and Public Opinion* (New York: John Wiley and Sons, 1973), 70–71; George H. Gallup, *The Gallup Poll: Public Opinion, 1935–1971* (New York: Random House, 1972), 3:1951, 1993, 2052.

53. Marilyn B. Young, *The Vietnam Wars, 1945–1990* (New York: Harper Perennial, 1991), 210–11.

54. Gelb, *The Irony of Vietnam*, 160.

55. James T. Patterson, *Grand Expectations: The United States, 1945–1973* (New York: Oxford University Press, 1996), 613; William Beecher, "Most Reserves Will Stay in Reserve," *New York Times*, 26 February 1967, E4.

56. Guenter Lewy, *America in Vietnam* (New York: Oxford University Press, 1978), 31, 42, 147.

57. Flynn, *The Draft*, 171, 212; "302,000 Men Face Draft during '68, a 72,000 Increase," *New York Times*, 20 January 1968, 3.

58. US Selective Service System, accessed 23 June 2014, www.sss.gov/About/History-And-Records/Induction-Statistics. According to the Selective Service System, 1,857,304 men were drafted during the Vietnam War. Vietnam figures are from August 1964 to February 1973.

59. Ibid. Korea figures are from June 1950 to June 1953; Flynn, *The Draft*, 85, 119, 123, 136. The Korean War involved 3.9 million enlisted men. This number also included 243,000 reservists, 138,597 National Guard, and 640,000 World War II veterans. A total of 1,529,539 were drafted into service.

60. Flynn, *The Draft*, 200–201.

61. Egendorf et al., *Legacies of Vietnam*, 150.

62. Peter B. Levy, "Blacks and the Vietnam War," in *The Legacy: The Vietnam War in the American Imagination*, ed. Michael D. Shafer (Boston: Beacon Press, 1990), 211.

63. Victoria I. Young, *Evolution of the US Army Force Structure* (McLean, VA: Science Applications International, 1989), 1:ES-16.

64. See Mueller, *War, Presidents and Public Opinion*, 54–55; Gelb, *The Irony of Vietnam*, 218–20.

65. Louis Harris and Associates, Inc., *The Harris Survey Yearbook of Public Opinion, 1971* (New York: Louis Harris and Associates, 1975), 101.

66. Press Release, American Veterans Committee, "Education and the Returning Vietnam Veterans," n.d., Gelman Library, American Veterans Committee (AVC Papers), Box 4.

67. Bradley, *Flags of Our Fathers*, 17–54, 75–98.

68. Flynn, *The Draft*, 117–18.

69. Ibid., 16–17, 85.

70. "Army Set-Up Ready for Service Law," *New York Times*, 25 July 1940, 1.

71. Charles C. Moskos, "The American Dilemma in Uniform: Race in the Armed Forces," *Annals of the American Academy of Political and Social Science* 406 (March 1973): 99. A 1961 government study of minority participation in the military reflected similar proportions. See President's Committee on Equal Opportunity in the Armed Forces, *Equality of Treatment and Opportunity for Negro Military Personnel Stationed within the United States*, 13 June 1963, Library of Congress (LOC), National Urban League Records, 1900–1988, Part II: A, Administration Department File, 1953–1966, Whitney M. Young Papers, 1961–1965, Box II, A92.

72. "College Athlete Loses Draft Plea," *New York Times*, 14 December 1941, 59.

73. Memorandum, Colonel Frank A. Mezur (Joint Working Group) to Brigadier General L. V. Warner (OSD), "Report on Conditions of Military Service for the President's Commission on Veterans' Pensions relating to Question 11, *Mortality and Combat Service*," n.d., 8, DDE, Bradley Commission, Box 61.

74. "Draft in February to Call Up 53,000; All for Army," *New York Times*, 28 December 1952, 1.

75. Flynn, *The Draft*, 30.

76. George Q. Flynn, "Conscription and Equity in Western Democracies, 1940–1975," *Journal of Contemporary History* 33 (January 1998): 8.

77. "385,000 Will Lose Draft Deferment," *New York Times*, 13 June 1951, 16; "New Draft Rules Take in Husbands," *New York Times*, 30 August 1951, 14.

78. Flynn, *The Draft*, 169.

79. Ibid., 81. See also "Civilian Occupational Back Ground of Army and Naval Personnel," n.d., 46, DDE, Bradley Commission, Box 58.

80. "Exempts Cheese Makers," *New York Times*, 23 April 1944, 30.

81. Kennedy, *Freedom from Fear*, 637–44.

82. "Tennessee, Alabama Tell Miners to Work or Fight," *New York Times*, 4 June 1943, 1.

83. "The Reply to Mister Lewis," *New York Times*, 25 June 1943, 16.

84. For an overall examination of this topic, see Diane B. Kunz, *Butter and Guns: America's Cold War Economic Diplomacy* (New York: Free Press, 1997). For the specific impact of Vietnam on the US economy, see Robert W. Stevens, *Vain Hopes, Grim Realities: The Economic Consequences of the Vietnam War* (New York: Franklin Watt, 1976), 1–26.

85. "Lower Draft Held Blow to Colleges," *New York Times*, 16 October 1942, 10.

86. Gambone, *The Greatest Generation Comes Home*, 65.

87. Hanson W. Baldwin, "Reserve Program: Arguments Weighed," *New York Times*, 19 June 1955, E7.

88. Flynn, "Conscription and Equity in Western Democracies," 7.

89. Flynn, *The Draft*, 141.

90. Ibid., 153.

91. US Congressional Budget Office, *The All-Volunteer Military: Issues and Performance*, Pub. No. 2960 (Washington, DC: Congressional Budget Office, July 2007), 5.

92. Paul Starr, *The Discarded Army: Veterans after Vietnam: The Nader Report on Vietnam Veterans and the Veterans Administration* (New York: Charterhouse, 1973), 190.

93. "Report on Training: Prepared for the President's Commission on Veterans' Pensions by a Joint Working Group Representing the Army, Navy, Marine Corps, and Air Force," December 1955, 28, DDE, Bradley Commission, Box 58.

94. Starr, *The Discarded Army*, 190.

95. Neil Sheehan, "Military Ready to Absorb Influx of Former 'Rejects,'" *New York Times*, 16 October 1966, 9.

96. Starr, *The Discarded Army*, 194.

97. Ibid., 192.

98. "Rights Leaders Deplore Plan to 'Salvage' Military Rejects," *New York Times*, 26 August 1966, 3.

99. US Senate, *Selective Training and Service Act*, 16 September 1940, S. 4164, 889; Kennedy, *Freedom from Fear*, 633.

100. Ronald H. Bailey, *The Home Front: USA* (New York: Time-Life Books, 1977), 45–46.

101. Scott A. Merriman, *Religion and Law in America: An Encyclopedia of Personal Belief and Public Policy* (Santa Barbara, CA: ABC-CLIO, 2007), 1:77–78.

102. Flynn, *The Draft*, 179.

103. Ibid., 181.

104. Monks, "College Men at War," 76. Overall, 1,850,000 of 16 million men examined (12%) for service were rejected as mentally unfit. See also Michael M. Davis, "How Healthy Are We?," *New York Times*, 22 February 1942, SM11.

105. Memorandum for General L. V. Warner (OSD), "Report on Conditions of Military Service for the President's Commission on Veterans' Pensions relating to Section 2, Enlistment Procedure," n.d., 15–16; "Results of Preinduction Examinations (July 1950 through July 1953)," n.d., 51, DDE, Bradley Commission, Box 58.

106. David E. Rosenbaum, "More Youths Look for a Medical 'Out' to Avoid the Draft," *New York Times*, 11 October 1970, 1, 66.

107. Ibid.

108. Michael D. Shafer, "The Vietnam-Era Draft: Who Went, Who Didn't, and Why It Matters," in Shafer, *The Legacy*, 69.

109. Millett and Maslowski point out that the middle class provided the bulk of junior combat officers through ROTC. This contingent accounted for

5,000 deaths during the war, proportionally one of the highest rates among those who served in Vietnam. See Millett and Maslowski, *For the Common Defense*, 587–88.

110. Ibid. See also John Willis, "Variations in State Casualty Rates in World War II and the Vietnam War," *Social Problems* 22 (April 1975): 558.

111. Jerome Johnston and Jerald G. Bachman, *Young Men Look at Military Service: A Preliminary Report* (Ann Arbor, MI: Institute for Social Research, 1971), 12–13.

112. Willis, "Variations in State Casualty Rates," 565.

113. Timberg, *The Nightingale's Song*, 88.

114. See Swarthmore College Peace Collection, Central Committee for Conscientious Objectors Records, 1948–2010, Collection DG075.

115. "To Do the Job—How Much Mobilization?," *New York Times*, 9 July 1950, E1; "Services Rebuked on Reserve Calls," *New York Times*, 15 June 1951, 25.

116. "Hostility Is Found to Draft Lottery," *New York Times*, 13 November 1966, 3.

117. Flynn, *The Draft*, 219.

118. Morris Janowitz, "The All-Volunteer Military as a 'Sociopolitical' Problem," *Social Problems* 22 (February 1975): 433.

119. American Legion, Committee on National Defense, *Summary of Proceedings: Twenty-Fourth Annual National Convention of the American Legion*, 19–21 September 1942, 90, 92, AL, Manuscripts Collection.

120. "The Selective Service," *Yale Law Journal* 76 (November 1966): 164.

121. Gambone, *Greatest Generation Comes Home*, 45, 82.

122. Clay Blair, *The Forgotten War: America in Korea, 1950–1953* (New York: Random House, 1987), 8.

123. "To Do the Job," E1.

124. Michael D. Gambone, *Eisenhower, Somoza, and the Cold War in Nicaragua, 1953–1961* (Westport, CT: Praeger, 1997), 15–17, 80–81, 184–89.

125. Mark R. Grandstaff, "Making the Military American: Advertising, Reform, and the Demise of an Antistanding Military Tradition," *Journal of Military History* 60 (April 1996): 303.

126. Memorandum for the Assistant Secretary of Defense (Manpower and Personnel), "Final Report—Ad Hoc Committee on the Future of Military Service as a Career That Will Attract and Retain Capable Career Personnel," 30 October 1953, 2.

127. Public Opinion Surveys, Inc., *Attitudes of Adult Civilians toward the Military Service as a Career: Part I of a Study for the Office of Armed Forces*

Information and Education, Department of Defense (Princeton, NJ: Public Opinion Surveys, 1955), 2.

128. Public Opinion Surveys, Inc., *Attitudes of 16 to 20 Year Old Males toward the Military Service as a Career: Part II of a Study for the Office of Armed Forces Information and Education, Department of Defense* (Princeton, NJ: Public Opinion Surveys, 1955), i.

129. William M. McClenahan and William H. Becker, *Eisenhower and the Cold War Economy* (Baltimore: Johns Hopkins University Press, 2011), 23–29, 36; Gambone, *Eisenhower, Somoza*, 81.

130. Dwight D. Eisenhower, "Peace in the World: Acts, Not Rhetoric Needed," *Vital Speeches* 19 (May 1953): 418–19.

131. Janowitz, "The All-Volunteer Military as a 'Sociopolitical' Problem," 435.

132. Bowsley Crowther, "Screen: Shameful Incident of War," *New York Times*, 27 December 1957, 23.

133. Colin Young, "The Old Dependables," *Film Quarterly* 13 (Autumn 1959): 12–13. See also Marilyn B. Young, "Now Playing: Vietnam," *OAH Magazine of History*18 (October 2004): 22–26.

134. Hassler, *With Shield and Sword*, 299; Gambone, *Eisenhower, Somoza*, 187.

135. Eugene S. Uyeki, "Draftee Behavior in the Cold-War Army," *Social Problems* 8 (Autumn 1960): 153–54.

136. David A. Hackworth, *About Face: The Odyssey of an American Warrior* (New York: Simon and Schuster, 1989), 316–17.

137. US Department of Labor, "Trends in Military and Civilian Compensation," 20 February 1956, 3, DDE, Bradley Commission, Box 62.

138. Grandstaff, "Making the Military American," 310–11.

139. E. James Lieberman, "American Families and the Vietnam War," *Journal of Marriage and Family* 33 (November 1971): 712.

140. Edward Shils and Morris Janowitz, "Cohesion and Disintegration in the Wehrmacht in World War II," *Public Opinion Quarterly* 12 (Summer 1948): 281–84.

141. Uyeki, "Draftee Behavior in the Cold-War Army," 153–54.

142. Doug McAdam, *Freedom Summer* (New York: Oxford University Press, 1988), 17.

143. Gambone, *Greatest Generation Comes Home*, 115.

144. Moskos, "The American Dilemma in Uniform," 99. The army had the highest percentage of African Americans in 1949 at 8.6%, while the Marine Corps was the lowest at 1.9%.

145. Peter B. Levy, "Blacks and the Vietnam War," in Shafer, *The Legacy*, 211.

146. Angelita Garcia-Cabrera, "The Hispanic Veteran of the Armed Services and in the Veterans Administration" (PhD diss., Brandeis University, 1978), 30, 35; US Department of Veterans Affairs, National Center for Veterans Analysis and Statistics, *Minority Veterans: 2011* (Washington, DC: Department of Veterans Affairs, May 2013), 11. Latinos made up 4% of the military enlisted ranks by 1972. See Aline O. Quester and Curtis L. Gilroy, *America's Military: A Coat of Many Colors*, CRM D0004368.A1/Final (Alexandria, VA: CAN, July 2001), 4.

147. Wallace Terry, *Bloods: An Oral History of the Vietnam War by Black Veterans* (New York: Random House, 1984), 6.

148. Interview, Joseph Lopez, n.d., LOC, Veterans History Project.

149. Moskos, *The American Enlisted Man*, 219. Some 37.2% of respondents cited this reason. In contrast, the primary (39.1%) reason for white respondents was the draft.

150. Egendorf et al., *Legacies of Vietnam*, 324, 386. See also Louis Harris and Associates, *A Study of the Problems Facing Vietnam Era Veterans*, 86, 146.

151. Moskos, "The American Dilemma in Uniform," 100, 102–3.

152. Henry A. J. Ramos, *The American G.I. Forum: In Pursuit of the Dream, 1948–1983* (Houston: Arte Publico Press, 1998), 2–6; Jennifer Brooks, "From Hitler and Tojo to Talmadge and Jim Crow: World War Two Veterans and the Remaking of Southern Political Tradition" (PhD diss., University of Tennessee, Knoxville, 1997); Manfred Berg, "Civil Rights and Liberal Anticommunism: The NAACP in the Early Cold War," *Journal of American History* 96 (June 2007): 75–96.

153. William Arce, "Nation in Uniform: Chicano/Latino War Narratives and the Construction of Nation in the Korean War and the Vietnam War" (PhD diss., University of Southern California, 2009), 11.

154. Flynn, *The Draft*, 206.

155. Thomas A. Johnson, "Negro Veteran Is Confused and Bitter," *New York Times*, 29 July 1968, 1.

156. Terry, *Bloods*, 20.

157. Kathryn Marshall, *In the Combat Zone: An Oral History of American Women in Vietnam, 1966–1975* (Boston: Little, Brown, 1987), 36.

158. Steven Rosales, "Soldados Razos: Chicano Politics, Identity, and Masculinity in the US Military, 1945–1975" (PhD diss., University of California, Irvine, 2007), 34. See also Lynn Marie Getz, "Lost Momentum: World War II and the Education of Hispanos in New Mexico," in *Mexican Americans &*

World War II, ed. Maggie Rivas-Rodriguez (Austin: University of Texas Press, 2005), 93–113.

159. Levy, "Blacks and the Vietnam War," 211; Lieberman, "American Families and the Vietnam War," 711.

160. Thomas A. Johnson, "Armed Forces: Racial Violence Mars the Integration Record," *New York Times*, 17 August 1969, E6.

161. Sol Stern, "When the Black G.I. Comes Back from Vietnam," *New York Times*, 24 March 1968, SM27; Johnson, "The Negro Veteran Is Confused and Bitter," 1.

162. Quester and Gilroy, *America's Military*, 3–4; Congressional Budget Office, *The All-Volunteer Military*, 23.

163. William E. Leuchtenburg, *A Troubled Feast: American Society since 1945* (Boston: Little, Brown, 1983), 50.

164. "May Register Women Eventually," *New York Times*, 4 February 1942, 14.

165. Gallup, *The Gallup Poll*, 2:972.

166. Ibid., 3:2051, 2180.

167. "Draft Law of 1967, Exempting Women, Challenged in Court," *New York Times*, 15 November 1970, 5.

168. US Department of Veterans Affairs, National Center for Veterans Analysis and Statistics, *America's Women Veterans: Military Service History and VA Benefit Utilization Statistics* (Washington, DC: Department of Veterans Affairs, November, 2011), 3.

169. Janann Sherman, "They Either Need These Women or They Do Not: Margaret Chase Smith and the Fight for Regular Status for Women in the Military," *Journal of Military History* 54 (January 1990): 58–59; D'Ann Campbell, *Women at War with America: Private Lives in a Patriotic Era* (Cambridge, MA: Harvard University Press, 1984), 22–26.

170. Kate A. Arbogast, "The Procurement of Women for the Armed Forces: An Analysis of Occupational Choice" (PhD diss., George Washington University, 1974), 48–49.

171. "Woman War Worker Opposed by Dr. Rusk," *New York Times*, 17 November 1950, 32. See also Evelyn M. Monahan and Rosemary Neidel-Greenlee, *A Few Good Women: America's Military Women from World War I to the Wars in Iraq and Afghanistan* (New York: Alfred A. Knopf, 2010), 217.

172. US Department of Veterans Affairs, *America's Women Veterans*, 5.

173. Ibid., 1.

174. "US to Send Vietnam Women Military Aides," *New York Times*, 4 December 1964, 16.

175. Marshall, *In the Combat Zone*, 4. Judy Klemesrud, "For Women in the Military, New Attractions," *New York Times*, 2 August 1971, 28. The number of women serving, according to these sources, was between 7,500 and 11,000.

176. Interview, Georgia Jane Ford, 27 March 2004, LOC, Veterans History Project.

177. Marshall, *In the Combat Zone*, 92, 103.

178. Interview, Constance Anderson, n.d., LOC, Veterans History Project.

179. Interview, Mary E. Chatfield, n.d., LOC, Veterans History Project.

180. Arbogast, "The Procurement of Women for the Armed Forces," 128, 175.

181. Louis Harris and Associates, Inc., *Survey of Female Veterans: A Study of the Needs, Attitudes, and Experiences of Women Veterans*, Study No. 843002 (New York: Louis Harris and Associates, 1985), 29.

182. US Department of Defense, Office of the Assistant Secretary of Defense (Manpower and Reserve Affairs), Directorate for Manpower Research, *Recruiting of Women for the Military: Assessment of the Mental and Medical Standards and Their Present and Potential Effects on Recruiting Needs*, Report No. MR 75–4 (Alexandria, VA: Human Resources Research Organization, 1975), 30. The study identified 9% women and 4.2% men in Category I and 76.5% women and 30.4% men in Category II.

183. Rodney R. Baker, Shirley W. Menard, and Louis A. Johns, "The Military Nurse Experience in Vietnam: Stress and Impact," *Journal of Clinical Psychology* 45 (September 1989): 738; Gambone, *Greatest Generation Comes Home*, 94.

184. Shelley Saywell, *Women in War* (New York: Viking Penguin, 1985), 251.

185. "First Lady Hails Women in Service," *New York Times*, 20 October 1943, 23.

186. Gambone, *Greatest Generation Comes Home*, 91–92.

187. Marshall, *In the Combat Zone*, 116–17.

188. "First Lady Hails Women in Service," 23. See also Jean Dunlavy, "A Band of Sisters: Womens Veterans' Organization for Rights and Recognition, 1965–1995" (PhD diss., Boston University, 2007), 11; Charlotte A. Power, "A Quiet Revolution: American Women and the Vietnam War, 1964–1975" (PhD diss., University of Memphis, 2001), 35–36.

189. Klemesrud, "For Women in the Military," 28.

190. US Department of Defense, *Recruiting of Women for the Military*, 1–8.

191. Arbogast, "The Procurement of Women for the Armed Forces," 134.

192. US Department of Veterans Affairs, *America's Women Veterans*, 3.

193. It would be an understatement to describe scholarship on this topic as large. See, for example, David J. Armor, "Race and Gender in the US Military," *Armed Forces and Society* 23 (Fall 1996): 7–27; Thomas Owens Mackubin, "It's Time to Face the Gender Paradox, " *US Naval Institute Proceedings* 124 (July 1998): 43–50; O. M. Kuzovchikova, "Army Feminization: Its Essence, Evolution, and Basic Trends," *Military Thought* 15 (2006): 167–77.

194. US Administrator of Veterans Affairs, *Annual Report, 1973* (Washington, DC: Veterans Administration, 1973), 2, National Archives and Records Administration (NARA), Records Group (RG) 15, Entry 53, Box 1.

195. Louis Harris and Associates, *Survey of Female Veterans*, 144–45, 183.

196. American Legion, *Summary of Proceedings: Thirty-Fourth Annual National Convention of the American Legion*, 25–28 August 1952, 92–93, AL, Manuscripts Collection.

197. US President's Commission on Veterans' Pensions, *Veterans' Benefits in the United States: A Report to the President by the President's Commission on Veterans' Pensions* (Washington, DC: Government Printing Office, 1956), 10.

198. Similar concerns have reappeared with respect to private military contractors. See Lindy Heinecken, "Outsourcing Public Security: The Unforeseen Consequences for the Military Profession," *Armed Forces & Society* 40 (2014): 637–38; David Isenberg, *Private Military Contractors and US Grand Strategy* (Oslo: International Peace Research Institute, 2009), 23.

199. Lieberman, "American Families and the Vietnam War," 709.

200. Shafer, "The Vietnam-Era Draft," 67.

201. Ibid.

Chapter 2

1. William Manchester, *Goodbye Darkness: A Memoir of the Pacific War* (Boston: Little, Brown, 1979), 380.

2. Glasser, *365 Days*, 111.

3. Edgar Jones, "Historical Approaches to Post-combat Disorders," *Philosophical Transactions: Biological Sciences* 361 (April 2006): 535.

4. Gerald Nicosia, *Home to War: A History of the Vietnam Veterans' Movement* (New York: Crown Publishers, 2001), 159.

5. Chaim F. Shatan, "The Grief of Soldiers: Vietnam Combat Veterans' Self-Help Movement," *American Journal of Orthopsychiatry* 43 (July 1973): 640–53; Sarah A. Haley, "When the Patient Reports Atrocities: Specific Treat-

ment Considerations of the Vietnam Veteran," *Archives of General Psychiatry* 30 (February 1974): 191–96.

6. Robert S. Laufer, M. S. Gallops, and Ellen Frey-Wouters, "War Stress and Trauma: The Vietnam Veteran Experience," *Journal of Health and Social Behavior* 25 (March 1984): 65–85.

7. Lifton, *Home from War*, 25.

8. Melvyn P. Leffler, "9/11 and American Foreign Policy," *Diplomatic History* 29 (June 2005): 395–413. For exposition on a much older standard, see Donald J. Kagay, "The Theory and Practice of Just War in the Late-Medieval Crown of Aragon," *Catholic Historical Review* 91 (October 2005): 591–610.

9. For a more recent example, see Berinsky, *In Time of War*.

10. Walter Millis, *Arms and Men: A Study of American Military History* (New York: Putnam, 1956), 13–71.

11. Gambone, *Greatest Generation Comes Home*, 83.

12. Robert A. Caro, *Means of Ascent: The Years of Lyndon Johnson* (New York: Knopf, 1991), 2:46–53.

13. Jeremi Suri, *Power and Protest: Global Revolution and the Rise of Détente* (Cambridge, MA: Harvard University Press, 2003), 7–17. See also John Lewis Gaddis, *Strategies of Containment: A Critical Appraisal of Postwar American Security Policy* (New York: Oxford University Press, 1982), 54–88.

14. David Halberstam, *The Best and the Brightest* (Greenwich, CT: Fawcett, 1969), 77.

15. Hassler, *With Shield and Sword*, 297, 356.

16. US Administrator of Veterans Affairs, *Annual Report, 1960* (Washington, DC: Government Printing Office, 1961), 7; Millett and Maslowski, *For the Common Defense*, 653.

17. John Morton Blum, *V Was for Victory: Politics and American Culture during World War II* (New York: Harcourt Brace, 1976), 53–64.

18. Audie Murphy, *To Hell and Back* (New York: Holt, Rinehart and Winston, 1949), 5, 8.

19. Bill Mauldin, *Up Front* (New York: Henry Holt, 1945), 18.

20. Robert Sherrod, *Tarawa: The Story of a Battle* (New York: Duell, Sloan and Pearce, 1944), 31.

21. Ernie Pyle, *Brave Men* (New York: Henry Holt, 1944), 34.

22. Demaree Bess, "The Army's Favorite General," *Saturday Evening Post*, 3 October 1942, 19.

23. Ibid., 109.

24. Sherrod, *Tarawa*, 35.

25. Guerric DeBona, "Masculinity on the Front: John Huston's *The Red*

Badge of Courage (1951) Revisited," in *The War Film*, ed. Robert Eberwein (New Brunswick, NJ: Rutgers University Press, 2005), 118, 120–21.

26. John Toland, *Battle: The Story of the Bulge* (New York: Random House, 1959), 328–29.

27. Janet G. Valentine, "The American Combat Soldier in the Korean War" (PhD diss., University of Alabama, 2002), 25.

28. Gallup, *The Gallup Poll*, 2:928, 960, 933.

29. John Osborne, "Report from the Orient: Guns Are Not Enough," *Life*, 21 August 1950, 77.

30. Freda Kirchwey, "Liberation by Death," *The Nation*, 10 March 1951, 215.

31. Ibid., 215–16.

32. Andrew J. Huebner, "The Embattled Americans: A Cultural History of Soldiers and Veterans, 1941–1982 (PhD diss., Brown University, 2004), 148 (emphasis added).

33. "Fighting Chance," *Time*, 18 June 1951, 26.

34. Gallup, *The Gallup Poll*, 2:928, 960.

35. "Legion Head Urges Home-Town Welcomes," *New York Times*, 19 August 1951, 2.

36. Hackworth, *About Face*, 288–89 (emphasis in original).

37. "Jungle Faculty," *Newsweek*, 6 March 1961, 33.

38. Young, *The Vietnam Wars*, 210–11.

39. Flynn, *The Draft*, 168–256.

40. Gelb, *The Irony of Vietnam: The System Worked*, 218–20.

41. Lewy, *America in Vietnam*, 83–84.

42. Stanley Karnow, *Vietnam: A History* (New York: Viking Press, 1983), 546–47.

43. For a detailed discussion of specific attributes, see Colin S. Gray, "The American Way of War: Critique and Implications," in *Rethinking the Principles of War*, ed. Anthony D. McIvor (Annapolis, MD: Naval Institute Press, 2005), 13–40.

44. Rafael Steinberg, *Island Fighting* (Alexandria, VA: Time-Life Books, 1978), 108.

45. Conrad C. Crane, "Raiding the Beggar's Pantry: The Search for Airpower Strategy in the Korean War," *Journal of Military History* 63 (October 1999): 891–93.

46. Blair, *The Forgotten War*, 876–77; "Men at War: A Bridge for Andong," *Time*, 18 June 1951, 30.

47. Gray, "The American Way of War," 31; Lewy, *America in Vietnam*, 57–58.

48. Glasser, *365 Days*, 53.

49. Shils and Janowitz, "Cohesion and Disintegration in the Wehrmacht," 281–84.

50. David G. Mandelbaum, *Group Dynamics of Military Units* (Washington, DC: Department of Defense, Research and Development Board, 1951), 3, Army Heritage and Education Center (AHEC), Manuscripts Collection.

51. J. Glenn Gray, *The Warriors: Reflections on Men in Battle* (New York: Harcourt, Brace, 1959), 26.

52. Ibid., 64, 80, 85.

53. Ibid., 85.

54. Harry G. Summers Jr., *On Strategy: A Critical Analysis of the Vietnam War* (New York: Dell, 1982).

55. Caputo, *A Rumor of War*, 73–74 (emphasis in original).

56. Ibid., 74.

57. O'Brien, *If I Die in a Combat Zone*, 127.

58. Lewy, *America in Vietnam*, 83.

59. Charles C. Moskos, "Why Men Fight: American Combat Soldiers in Vietnam," in *The Vietnam Veteran in Contemporary Society: Collected Materials Pertaining to the Young Veterans*, by US Department of Veterans Affairs, Department of Medicine and Surgery (Washington, DC: Veterans Administration, 1972), III-11.

60. Michael D. Shafer, "The Vietnam Combat Experience: The Human Legacy," in Shafer, *The Legacy*, 83.

61. Peter G. Bourne, *Men, Stress, and Vietnam* (Boston: Little, Brown, 1970), 41–42.

62. Michael Maclear, *The Ten Thousand Day War: Vietnam, 1945–1975* (New York: St. Martin's Press, 1981), 195.

63. US Department of the Army, General Staff, G-1, *Army Rotation Study*, 23 March 1953, i, Tab E, Tab F, AHEC, Manuscripts Collection.

64. William M. Donnelly, "The Best Army That Can Be Put in the Field in the Circumstances: The US Army July 1951–July 1953," *Journal of Military History* 71 (July 2007): 809–47; Bill Mauldin, *Bill Mauldin in Korea* (New York: W. W. Norton, 1952), 41.

65. Glenn, *Reading Athena's Dance Card*, 89–90; "Army Rotation Details Disclosed," *Pacific Stars & Stripes*, 5 August 1951, 2.

66. Samuel A. Stouffer, Arthur A. Lumsdaine, Marion Harper Lumsdaine, Robin McWilliams, M. Brewster Smith, Irving L. Janis, Shirley A. Star, and Leonard S. Cottrell, *The American Soldier: Combat and Its Aftermath* (Princeton, NJ: Princeton University Press, 1949), 2:457.

67. Ibid., 458–59.

68. See 82nd Airborne Division, War Memorial Museum, www.82ndairborne-divisionmuseum. The official assigned strength of the division was 12,921.

69. Stouffer, *The American Soldier*, 8–9.

70. Young, *Evolution of the US Army Force Structure*, 1:ES-16. A study conducted by the Pentagon in 1955 placed the percentage of combatants at 38.8%. See "Enlisted Occupational Groupings for President's Commission on Veterans' Pensions," n.d., 7, DDE, Bradley Commission, Box 59.

71. Gambone, *Greatest Generation Comes Home*, 183.

72. John J. McGrath, *The Other End of the Spear: The Tooth-to-Tail Ratio (T3R) in Modern Military Operations*, The Long War Series Occasional Paper No. 23 (Fort Leavenworth, KS: Combat Studies Institute Press, 2007), 65.

73. US Veterans Administration, Office of Information Management and Statistics, *Data on Vietnam Era Veterans* (Washington, DC: Veterans Administration, April 1985), 9.

74. S. L. A. Marshall, *Men against Fire: The Problem of Battle Command in Future War*, 2nd ed. (New York: William Morrow, 1977), 9–10.

75. Glenn, *Reading Athena's Dance Card*, 1–6.

76. Stouffer, *American Soldier*, 229.

77. Howard H. McFann, John A. Hammes, and John E. Taylor, *TRAINFIRE I: A New Course in Basic Rifle Marksmanship*, Technical Report 22 (Washington, DC: Department of the Army, Human Resources Research Office, 1955), 4, AHEC, Manuscripts Collection.

78. James C. Fry, *Assault Battle Drill* (Harrisburg, PA: Military Service Publishing, 1955), 13, AHEC, Manuscripts Collection.

79. Marshall, *Men Against Fire*, 66.

80. Stouffer, *American Soldier*, 222.

81. Neil E. Miller, *Fear and Courage in Training and Combat* (Washington, DC: Department of Defense, Research and Development Board, 1951), 1, AHEC, Manuscripts Collection.

82. Ibid., 2. See also Gwynne Dyer, *War* (New York: Crown Publishers, 1985), 125.

83. Fry, *Assault Battle Drill*, 6.

84. US Department of the Army, *TRAINFIRE*, DA Pamphlet No. 355–14 (Washington, DC: Government Printing Office, July 1958), 8–14, AHEC, Manuscripts Collection.

85. Marshall, *Men against Fire*, 9.

86. Dave Grossman, *On Killing: The Psychological Cost of Learning to Kill in War and Society*, 3rd ed. (New York: Little, Brown, 2009), 36.

87. Glenn, *Reading Athena's Dance Card*, 37.

88. Carri-Ann Gibson, "Review of Posttraumatic Stress Disorder and Chronic Pain: The Path to Integrated Care," *Journal of Rehabilitation Research and Development* 49 (2012): 554.

89. US Veterans Administration, Reports & Statistics Service, Office of the Controller, *Data on Vietnam Era Veterans* (Washington, DC: Veterans Administration, 1977), 42.

90. Stouffer, *American Soldier*, 599.

91. Ibid., 646.

92. Ibid., 633.

93. Egendorf et al., *Legacies of Vietnam*, 324, 386.

94. Mandelbaum, *Group Dynamics of Military Units*, 58.

95. William Ruger, Sven E. Wilson, and Shawn L. Waddoups, "Warfare and Welfare: Military Service, Combat, and Marital Dissolution," *Armed Forces and Society* 29 (Fall 2002): 85–107. This survey included 3,800 men.

96. Ibid., 98.

97. For an excellent examination of this topic, see John Costello, *Virtue under Fire: How World War II Changed Our Social and Sexual Attitudes* (Boston: Little, Brown, 1985).

98. James Jones, *WWII* (New York: Ballantine Books, 1976), 256.

99. Glen H. Elder and Elizabeth C. Clipp, "Wartime Losses and Social Bonding: Influences across 40 Years of Men's Lives," *Psychiatry* 51 (May 1988): 185–91.

100. Gambone, *Greatest Generation Comes Home*, 53–54. See also National Committee on Service to Veterans, *The Home Town Job: A Report on Community Services for Veterans* (New York: National Social Work Council, 1945), AL, Miscellaneous Employment File; US Veterans Administration, VA Pamphlet 6–2, *Your Job as a Volunteer* (Washington, DC: Veterans Administration, September 1949), NARA, RG 15, Box 1, Entry 38.

101. Monks, "College Men at War," 76.

102. Brian H. Chermol, "Wounds without Scars: Treatment of Battle Fatigue in the US Armed Forces in the Second World War," *Military Affairs* 49 (January 1985): 9.

103. Ibid., 11.

104. Elspeth Cameron Ritchie, "Psychiatry in the Korean War: Perils, PIES, and Prisoners of War," *Military Medicine* 167 (November 2002): 898.

105. Ibid., 899–900.

106. Douglas R. Bey and Walter E. Smith, "Organizational Consultation in a Combat Unit," *American Journal of Psychiatry* 128 (October 1971): 401–6;

Sandra L. Huppenbauer, "A Portrait of a Problem," *American Journal of Nursing* 82 (November 1982): 1700; Edward M. Colbach and Matthew D. Parrish, "Army Mental Health Activities in Vietnam, 1965–1970," in US Department of Veterans Affairs, *The Vietnam Veterans in Contemporary Society*, III-39.

107. Administrator of Veterans Affairs, *Annual Report, 1958* (Washington, DC: Government Printing Office, 1959), 9. See also Veterans Administration, Department of Medicine and Surgery, Information Bulletin, "Psychiatry, Neurology, and Psychology in the Veterans Administration, A Profile: 1952," 9 May 1952, 6–11, DDE, Bradley Commission, Box 38.

108. Administrator of Veterans Affairs, *Annual Report, 1967* (Washington, DC: Government Printing Office, 1968), 12. This percentage was virtually unchanged by 1972 at 47.4%. See Administrator of Veterans Affairs, *Annual Report, 1973* (Washington, DC: Government Printing Office, 1974), 16, NARA, RG 15, Box 1, Entry 53.

109. F. Gentry Harris, Joseph Mayer, and Herman A. Becker, *Experiences in the Study of Combat in the Korean Theater: Report on Psychiatric and Psychological Data* (Washington, DC: Walter Reed Army Institute of Research, 1955), 33, 69, AHEC, Manuscripts Collection. See also Bourne, *Men, Stress, and Vietnam*, 18–19.

110. Egendorf et al., *Legacies of Vietnam*, 347.

111. Ibid., 315, 335–39.

112. Wilbur J. Scott, "PTSD in DSM-III: A Case in the Politics of Diagnosis and Disease," *Social Problems* 37 (August 1990): 298.

113. Lifton, *Home from War*, 29.

114. Ibid., 100.

115. Ibid., 167.

116. Nicosia, *Home to War*, 158–209.

117. For the initial definition of PTSD, see Robert L. Spitzer, ed., *DSM-III: Diagnostic and Statistical Manual of Mental Disorders*, 3rd ed. (Washington, DC: American Psychiatric Press, 1980), 236.

118. Ibid., 236–37.

119. Kathryn H. Andersen and Jean M. Mitchell, "Effects of Military Experience on Mental Health Problems and Work Behavior," *Medical Care* 30 (June 1992): 554. Interestingly, the percentage corresponds almost exactly with estimates of Vietnam-era combatants. See Flynn, *The Draft*, 227; Bourne, *Men, Stress, and Vietnam*, 43.

120. Andersen and Mitchell, "Effects of Military Experience," 557.

121. Gibson, "Review of Posttraumatic Stress Disorder and Chronic Pain," 756.

122. H. Stuart Hughes, "Emotional Disturbance and American Social Change," in US Department of Veterans Affairs, *The Vietnam Veterans in Contemporary Society*, II-2.

123. Edward W. McCranie and Leon A. Hyer, "Posttraumatic Stress Disorder Symptoms in Korean Conflict and World War II Combat Veterans Seeking Outpatient Treatment," *Journal of Traumatic Stress* 13 (2000): 437.

124. Huppenbauer, "A Portrait of a Problem," 1700.

125. McCranie and Hyer, "Posttraumatic Stress Disorder Symptoms," 428–30.

126. Charles Kaiman, "PTSD in the World War II Combat Veteran," *American Journal of Nursing* 103 (November 2003): 34–35. Recent research has also begun to examine PTSD and ethnicity. See Michele R. Spoont, James Hodges, Maureen Murdoch, and Sean Nugent, "Race and Ethnicity as Factors in Mental Health Service Use among Veterans with PTSD," *Journal of Traumatic Stress* 22 (December 2009): 648–53.

127. Saywell, *Women in War*, 225.

128. Baker, Menard, and Johns, "The Military Nurse Experience in Vietnam," 737; Gina M. Scuteri, "Casualties of War and Research: A Case Study of US Women Veterans of Vietnam" (PhD diss., Purdue University, 1993), 38.

129. Memorandum, P. H. Springsteen (Editorial Division) to Chief Medical Director, 1 August 1946, NARA, RG 15, Entry 33, Box 3.

130. Louis Harris and Associates, *Survey of Female Veterans*, 5.

131. Scuteri, "Casualties of War and Research," 52.

132. Dixon Wecter, *When Johnny Comes Marching Home* (Boston: Houghton Mifflin, 1944), 5.

133. "The New Public Enemy No. 1," *Time*, 28 June 1971, 30–31.

134. Michael Hakeem, "Service in the Armed Forces and Criminality," *Journal of Criminal Law and Criminology* 37 (July–August 1946): 121.

135. Dane Archer and Rosemary Gartner, "Violent Acts and Violent Times: A Comparative Approach to Postwar Homicide Rates," *American Sociological Review* 41 (December 1976): 941–44.

136. Willard Waller, *The Veteran Comes Back* (New York: Dryden Press, 1944), 124.

137. Hakeem," Service in the Armed Forces and Criminality,"127–31.

138. Harry Willbach, "Crimes and Veterans," *Journal of Criminal Law and Criminology* 38 (January–February 1948): 501–8.

139. Ted R. Gurr, "Historical Trends in Violent Crime: A Critical Review of the Evidence," *Crime and Justice* 3 (1981): 321. There was a brief surge of serious crime, specifically murder, robbery, and manslaughter, in the first

year after the war. See US Federal Bureau of Investigation, *Uniform Crime Reports for the United States and Its Possessions*, vol. 17, no. 2 (Washington, DC: Government Printing Office, 1946), 1.

140. For example, the number of murders per 100,000 population decreased from 5.49 in 1945 to 4.8 in 1959. Rapes declined from 11.54 in 1945 to 8.3 per 100,000 in 1959. Aggravated assault actually increased from 59.8 instances per 100,000 population in 1945 to 67.3 instances per 100,000 in 1959. See US Federal Bureau of Investigation, *Uniform Crime Reports for the United States and Its Possessions*, vol. 16, no. 2 (Washington, DC: Government Printing Office, 1946), 78; US Federal Bureau of Investigation, *Crime in the United States: Uniform Crime Reports—1959* (Washington, DC: Government Printing Office, 1960), 33.

141. Gurr, "Historical Trends in Violent Crime," 323; Archer and Gartner, "Violent Acts and Violent Times," 937; US Bureau of the Census, *The Statistical History of the United States: From Colonial Times to the Present* (New York: Basic Books, 1976), 413.

142. Egendorf et al., *Legacies of Vietnam*, 373–78, 430. The study surveyed 1,380 veterans across the country.

143. FBI, *Crime in the United States*, 16.

144. Gurr, "Historical Trends in Violent Crime," 337–40.

145. Herbert Marcuse, *One-Dimensional Man: Studies in the Ideology of Advanced Industrialized Society* (Boston: Beacon Press, 1964), 257.

146. Jeremy Kuzmarov, "The Myth of the Addicted Army: Vietnam and the Modern War on Drugs" (PhD diss., Brandeis University, 2006), 1; see also Felix Belair, "Pentagon Unit Finds Drugs 'Military Problem' in Asia," *New York Times*, 4 January 1971, 1.

147. Kuzmarov, "The Myth of the Addicted Army," 4.

148. "A Debate on Current Care for Veteran Drug Addicts," *American Legion Magazine*, October 1972, 28. The 100,000 figure was generally accepted by a number of organizations, including the American Veterans Committee. See June A. Willenz, "The Returning Vietnam Veterans: A Challenge to the Nation's Conscience," *Vital Issues* 22 (October 1972): 3, Gelman Library, American Veterans Committee Papers, Box 15.

149. Jeremy Kuzmarov, "From Counter-insurgency to Narco-insurgency: Vietnam and the International War on Drugs," *Journal of Public Policy* 20 (2008): 348.

150. See Nicholas Rasmussen, "Medical Science and the Military: The Allies' Use of Amphetamine during World War II," *Journal of Interdisciplinary History* 42 (Autumn 2011): 207, 212–17; Akihiko Sato, "Methamphetamine

Use in Japan after the Second World War: Transformation of Narratives," *Contemporary Drug Problems* 35 (Winter 2008): 718–20.

151. Nicholas Rasmussen, *On Speed: The Many Lives of Amphetamine* (New York: New York University Press, 2008), 84.

152. Nicholas Rasmussen, "Making the First Anti-depressant: Amphetamine in American Medicine, 1929–1950," *Journal of the History of Medicine and Allied Sciences* 61 (2006): 319.

153. Lester Grinspoon and Peter Hedblom, *The Speed Culture: Methamphetamine Use and Abuse in America* (Cambridge, MA: Harvard University Press, 1975), 20.

154. US House of Representatives, Select Committee on Crime, *Amphetamines: Fourth Report by the Select Committee on Crime* (Washington, DC: Government Printing Office, 1971), 2.

155. Ibid., 7–8.

156. US Department of the Treasury, Bureau of Narcotics, *Comments on Narcotic Drugs: Interim Report of the Joint Committee of the American Bar Association and the American Medical Association on Narcotic Drugs* (Washington, DC: Bureau of Narcotics, 1958), 63.

157. US Department of the Treasury, Bureau of Narcotics, *Traffic in Opium and Other Dangerous Drugs for the Year Ended December 31, 1957* (Washington, DC: Government Printing Office, 1958), 14; US Department of the Treasury, Bureau of Narcotics, *Traffic in Opium and Other Dangerous Drugs for the Year Ended December 31, 1964* (Washington, DC: Government Printing Office, 1965), 19.

158. US Department of the Treasury, Bureau of Narcotics, *Traffic in Opium and Other Dangerous Drugs for the year ended December 31, 1967* (Washington, DC: Government Printing Office, 1968), 1.

159. Andersen and Mitchell, "Effects of Military Experience," 557. Reported instances of depression were equal for Korea and Vietnam combat veterans at 4%. World War II veterans experienced a lower rate of 2%.

160. Gayle K. Lumry and Gordon Braatz, "The Vietnam Era Veteran and Psychiatric Implications," in US Department of Veterans Affairs, *The Vietnam Veterans in Contemporary Society*, IV-99–IV-102.

161. Patrick A. Boudewyns, M. Gail Woods, Lee Hyer, and J. William Albrecht, "Chronic Combat-Related PTSD and Concurrent Substance Abuse: Implications for Treatment of This Frequent 'Dual Diagnosis,'" *Journal of Traumatic Stress* 4 (1991): 550–51.

162. Egendorf et al., *Legacies of Vietnam*, 370–72, 424.

163. Ibid., 408. For white combat veterans, drug use declined by 0.1% and alcohol use increased by 1.0%. For African American combat veterans, drug problems declined by 0.7% and alcohol problems by 0.2%.

164. Andersen and Mitchell, "Effects of Military Experience," 557. See also L. Branchy, W. Davis, and C. S. Lieber, "Alcoholism in Vietnam and Korea Veterans: A Long-Term Follow-Up," *Alcoholism: Clinical and Experimental Research* 8 (November–December 1984): 572.

165. Kuzmarov, "The Myth of the Addicted Army," 30.

166. Lumry and Braatz, "The Vietnam Era Veteran and Psychiatric Implications," IV-101.

167. Blum, *V Was for Victory*, 53.

Chapter 3

1. "Returning Heroes Get the Cold Shoulder," *Business Week*, 31 July 1971, 46.

2. For a history of military benefits, see US President's Commission on Veterans' Pensions, *Veterans' Benefits in the United States*, 33–61.

3. Alex Abella, *Soldiers of Reason: The RAND Corporation and the Rise of the American Empire* (New York: Harcourt, 2008), 11–17.

4. Wecter, *When Johnny Comes Marching Home*, 535.

5. Robert J. Donovan, *Conflict and Crisis: The Presidency of Harry S. Truman, 1945–1948* (New York: W. W. Norton, 1977), 108.

6. David McCullough, *Truman* (New York: Simon and Schuster, 1992), 469.

7. "Fact Book on Veterans' Readjustment Benefits and Related Problems," 24 October 1955, 1, DDE, Bradley Commission, Box 12. See also US Department of Labor, *Thirty-Fourth Annual Report of the Secretary of Labor for the Fiscal Year Ended June 30, 1946* (Washington, DC: Government Printing Office, 1947), 5, 211.

8. US Bureau of the Census, *Statistical History of the United States*, 135; US Department of Labor, Bureau of Labor Statistics, "The Employment Situation during the Period of Demobilization after Five Wars, and in 1955," 20 January 1956, 4, DDE, Bradley Commission, Box 62.

9. Gambone, *Greatest Generation Comes Home*, 24.

10. US Bureau of the Census, *Statistical History of the United States*, 199.

11. Patterson, *Grand Expectations*, 43.

12. Center for Strategic Studies, *Economic Impact of the Vietnam War*,

Special Report Series No. 5 (Washington, DC: Center for Strategic Studies, 1967), 19.

13. Judith Stein, *Pivotal Decade: How the United States Traded Factories for Finance in the Seventies* (New Haven, CT: Yale University Press, 2010), 5–6. See also Paul Kennedy, *The Rise and Fall of the Great Powers: Economic Change and Military Conflict from 1500 to 2000* (New York: Random House, 1987), 436.

14. Patterson, *Grand Expectations*, 738. As foreign competition improved, the American economy suffered from declining productivity, averaging 3% annually from 1947 to 1965, 2.4% from 1965 to 1970, and 1.2% from 1973 to 1979. See James T. Patterson, *Restless Giant: The United States from Watergate to* Bush v. Gore (New York: Oxford University Press, 2005), 62.

15. Kearns, *Lyndon Johnson and the American Dream*, 219–20, 288.

16. David Milne, "'Our Equivalent of Guerrilla Warfare': Walt Rostow and the Bombing of North Vietnam, 1961–1968," *Journal of Military History* 71 (January 2007): 169–203.

17. US Bureau of the Census, *Statistical History of the United States*, 340.

18. Stevens, *Vain Hopes*, 25. Stevens estimated the cost of social programs between 1964 and 1972 to be $199 billion (in 1973 dollars).

19. Arthur M. Okun, *The Political Economy of Prosperity* (Washington, DC: Brookings Institution, 1970), 97; Stein, *Pivotal Decade*, 1.

20. US Bureau of the Census, *Statistical History of the United States*, 199.

21. Okun, *The Political Economy of Prosperity*, 91.

22. Allen J. Matusow, *Nixon's Economy: Booms, Busts, Dollars, and Votes* (Lawrence: University Press of Kansas, 1998), 39.

23. US Bureau of the Census, *Statistical History of the United States*, 135.

24. Ibid., 382.

25. Ibid., 1,114; Leuchtenberg, *A Troubled Feast*, 39.

26. Center for Strategic Studies, *Economic Impact of the Vietnam War*, 18.

27. Stephen E. Ambrose, *Eisenhower* (New York: Simon and Schuster, 1984), 2:158.

28. Millis, *Arms and Men*, 13–71; Theodore Ropp, *War in the Modern World*, 2nd ed. (New York: Macmillan, 1962), 19–59.

29. Michael D. Gambone, "Veterans," in *Twentieth-Century War and Conflict*, ed. Gordon Martel (Chichester, UK: John Wiley and Sons, 2015), 212–15.

30. See Ortiz, *Beyond the Bonus March and the GI Bill*, 13–31.

31. Christopher P. Loss, "'The Most Wonderful Thing Happened to Me in the Army': Psychology, Citizenship, and American Higher Education in World War II," *Journal of American History* 92 (December 2005): 887.

32. Waller, *The Veteran Comes Back*, 92, 143.

33. Henry F. Pringle, "Are We Making a Bum out of G.I. Joe?," *Ladies' Home Journal*, September 1946, 48. See also Renwick C. Kennedy, "The G.I. Gravy Train," *Christian Century*, 6 August 1947, 944–45.

34. Thomas M. Johnson, "How Veterans Are Creating New Business Ideas," *Readers' Digest*, August 1947, 117–19.

35. "Now Maybe We'll Get Courtesy," *Saturday Evening Post*, 9 February 1946, 124.

36. Veterans Administration, *Occupational Outlook Information Series: Mississippi: Employment by Industry and Occupation* (Washington, DC: Veterans Administration, 1947), 2, NARA, RG 15, Entry 38, Box 1.The number of manufacturing workers increased from 53,000 in 1939 to 95,000 by mid-1943. In June 1946, it remained at 86,000; Veterans Administration, *Occupational Outlook Information Series: Alabama: Employment by Industry and Occupation* (Washington, DC: Veterans Administration, 1947), 3, NARA, RG 15, Entry 38, Box 1. In mid-1943, there were 240,000 manufacturing workers in Alabama.

37. Veterans Administration, *Occupational Outlook Information Series: California: Employment by Industry and Occupation* (Washington, DC: Veterans Administration, 1947), 4, NARA, RG 15, Entry 38, Box 1.

38. William Thomas, "The Heuristics of War: Scientific Method and the Founders of Operations Research," *British Journal for the History of Science* 40 (June 2009): 251–74.

39. Jack J. Honomichl, "Decision Making in a New Dimension," *Challenge* 12 (January 1964): 29–32.

40. Channing E. Dooley, "The Training within Industry Report, 1940–1945," *Developing Human Resources* 3 (May 2001): 157, 160; US Department of Labor, Women's Bureau, *Effective Industrial Use of Women in the Defense Program* (Washington, DC: Government Printing Office, 1940), 2–8. See also William J. Breen, "Social Science and State Policy in World War II: Human Relations, Pedagogy, and Industrial Training, 1940–1945," *Business History Review* 76 (Summer 2002): 238–47.

41. "Trends and Developments in Military Training," n.d., Tab E-1, DDE, Bradley Commission, Box 58.

42. Veterans Administration, Office of Vocational Rehabilitation and Education, *Educational Opportunities for Veterans in Approved Institutions of Higher Education* (Washington, DC: Veterans Administration, 1946), 3, NARA, RG 15, Entry 38, Box 1.

43. Gambone, *Greatest Generation Comes Home*, 69.

44. A few of these men were waiting for the author when he attended university: Robert K. Murray at Penn State and Arthur Mann at the University of Chicago.

45. US Department of Commerce, *Historical Statistics of the United States: Colonial Times to 1970* (Washington, DC: Government Printing Office, 1975), 140.

46. *Jones & Laughlin Steel Corporation: A Study of the Company's Changes and Prospects* (New York: Reynolds, 1949), 3, 5; *Twenty-Fourth Annual Report of the Jones & Laughlin Steel Corporation and Subsidiary Companies for the Fiscal Year Ended December 31, 1946* (Pittsburgh: Jones & Laughlin Steel Corporation, 1947), 8, both in Jones & Loughlin Corporation Records, Hagley Museum and Library, Imprints.

47. Gambone, *Greatest Generation Comes Home*, 74–76.

48. Sam Stavisky, "Jobs for Unemployed Veterans," *American Legion Magazine*, September 1956, 22–23.

49. Ibid., 23. States with 400,000 or fewer people received one VES field officer. States with between 400,000 and one million people received two. Larger states with more than one million population received three.

50. Ibid., 61.

51. *Twenty-Fourth Annual Report of the Jones & Laughlin Steel Corporation*, 8.

52. Jack Sher, "Why Hire Disabled Vets?," *American Legion Magazine*, October 1947, 22–23; Veterans Administration, Administration Order No. 41-A, "Organization of the Vocational Rehabilitation Division at Those Field Stations Having Regional Office Activities," 16 June 1943, AL, Veterans' Welfare Classification, Vocational Rehabilitation.

53. Veterans Administration, Department of Veterans Benefits, Office of Vocational Rehabilitation and Education, "Training Benefits Utilized by Disabled Veterans of World War II," 20 October 1955, 1, DDE, Bradley Commission, Box 12.

54. *Shell . . . Soldier and Civilian* (New York: Shell Union Oil Corporation, 1945), 3, Shell Corporation Records, Hagley Museum and Library, Imprints.

55. Labor, "The Employment Situation during the Period of Demobilization after Five Wars, and in 1955," 20 January 1956, 3–4, DDE, Bradley Commission, Box 62.

56. Patterson, *Grand Expectations*, 65.

57. "The Labor Force in the First Year of Peace," *Monthly Labor Review* 63 (November 1946): 670.

58. Dionicio Valdés, "The Mexican American Dream and World War II," in *Mexican Americans & World War II*, ed. Maggie Rivas-Rodriguez (Austin: University of Texas Press, 2005), 121.

59. "Comparative Situation: Veterans and Non-veterans," 12 April 1956 (Draft), 4, DDE, Bradley Commission, Box 63.

60. White veterans born between 1920 and 1929 consistently averaged 11.3 years of education at the conclusion of their military service. African American veterans' education was less consistent, from a low of 7.5 years for men born in 1920 to a high of 10.4 years for the 1927 cohort. Overall, African Americans averaged 9.4 years of education after completing their service. See Sarah Turner and John Bound, "Closing the Gap or Widening the Divide: The Effects of the G.I. Bill and World War II on the Educational Outcomes of Black Americans," *Journal of Economic History* 63 (March 2003): 150.

61. Ibid., 145–77.

62. Loss, "The Most Wonderful Thing Happened to Me in the Army," 889.

63. National Urban League, "Adjustment of Negro Veterans: A Report of the Adjustment Problems of Negro Veterans in 50 Cities," March 1946, 1–3, LOC, NAACP Papers, Box II, A397.

64. Charles G. Bolté and Louis Harris, *Our Negro Veterans*, Public Affairs Pamphlet No. 128 (New York: Public Affairs Committee, 1947), 4–5, 9–10.

65. American Veterans Committee (AVC), "Report on Negro Veterans in the South," 15 March 1956, 3, DDE, Bradley Commission, Box 9. See also Jessie Parkhurst Guzman, *Negro Year Book: A Review of Events Affecting Negro Life, 1941–1946* (Tuskegee, AL: Tuskegee Institute, 1947), 151–52.

66. US Bureau of the Census, *Statistical History of the United States*, 64; Richard Polenberg, *War and Society: The United States, 1941–1945* (New York: J. P. Lippincott, 1972), 151–53. In 1946, 17.9 per 1,000 married females were divorced, the highest rate between 1920 and 1970.

67. Sherna Berger Gluck, *Rosie the Riveter Revisited: Women, War and Social Change* (Boston: Twayne, 1987), 16. Between July and December 1945, approximately four million women left the labor force. See US Department of Labor, *Thirty-Fifth Annual Report of the Secretary of Labor for the Fiscal Year Ended June 30, 1947* (Washington, DC: Government Printing Office, 1948), 104.

68. D'Ann Campbell, "Servicewomen of World War II," *Armed Forces and Society* 16 (Winter 1990): 257–58; Nancy McInerny, "The Woman Vet Has Her Problems Too," *New York Times Magazine*, 30 June 1946, 18; Lou Harris and Associates, *Survey of Female Veterans*, 98–108.

69. Doris Weatherford, *American Women in World War II* (New York: Facts on File, 1990), 64.

70. Eleanor Lake, "A Smarter GI Jane Comes Home," *Readers' Digest*, September 1946, 35.

71. According to historian D'Ann Campbell, 45% of nurses and 27% of women in other military fields never married, but only 5% of women overall in their generation never married. See Campbell, "Servicewomen of World War II," 257–58.

72. US Department of Commerce, Department of the Census, *Seventeenth Census of the United States: Characteristics of the Population, U.S. Summary* (Washington, DC: Government Printing Office, 1953), 1–253–1–273.

73. Leuchtenberg, *A Troubled Feast*, 38.

74. US Defense Finance and Accounting Service, "Military Pay Charts—1949 to 2016," Defense Finance and Accounting Service, updated 30 December 2016, http://www.dfas.mil/militarymembers/payentitlements/military-pay-charts.html.

75. Bill Mauldin, "The Manpower Problem in the Air Force," *Collier's*, 22 July 1955, 34.

76. Ibid., 35.

77. Barrett, "Portrait of the Korean War Veteran," SM12.

78. Ibid.

79. Gilmore, "I'm Bitter," *American Legion Magazine*, November 1952, 24.

80. Patterson, *Grand Expectations*, 271.

81. American Legion, *Summary of Proceedings: Thirty-Fourth Annual National Convention*, 92–93; "We've Been Asked: Veterans' Help—Still On?," *US News & World Report*, 30 April 1954, 52.

82. American Legion, *Summary of Proceedings: Thirty-Sixth Annual National Convention of the American Legion*, 30 August to 2 September 1954, 53, AL, Manuscripts Collection. See also US Department of Labor, *Thirty-Sixth Annual Report of the Secretary of Labor for the Fiscal Year Ended June 30, 1948* (Washington, DC: Government Printing Office, 1949), 82–83.

83. The 1944 version of the GI Bill provided a monthly stipend of $75 for individuals, $105 for veterans with one dependent, and $120 for veterans with two or more dependents. See President's Commission on Veterans' Pensions, *Veterans' Benefits in the United States*, 54–55; "Public Law 550, the 'Korean G.I. Bill,'" n.d., 122–23, DDE, Bradley Commission, Box 42; Benjamin Fine, "Veterans of Korea Flock to Colleges under US Grants," *New York Times*, 14 September 1953, 1.

84. Benjamin Fine, "Educators Back Korean Veterans," *New York Times*, 15 January 1954, 2.

85. "Statement by John R. Holden, National Legislative Director of AM-

VETS before the Committee on Veterans' Affairs on the Report of the President's Commission on Veterans' Pensions," 10 May 1956, 3, DDE, Bradley Commission, Box 104.

86. Letter, Thurlow E. Hargreaves to H. V. Higley (VA), 15 October 1956, DDE, White House Central File (WHCF), General File, Box 448; Letter, Florence P. Dwyer to Dwight D. Eisenhower, 25 April 1958, DDE, WHCF, General File, Box 443.

87. Memorandum for Bernard M. Shanley (Special Counsel to the President), "Proposed VA Hospital in Brecksville, Ohio," 6 August 1954, DDE, WHCF, General File, Box 448.

88. Benjamin Fine, "Korean War Veterans Are Not Flocking to Colleges as They Were Expected," *New York Times*, 24 October 1954, E9.

89. McClenahan and Becker, *Eisenhower and the Cold War Economy*, 43–47, 85–96, 102–3, 94.

90. US Department of Labor, "At Press Time," *Employment Security Review* 22 (June 1955): 1, DDE, Bradley Commission, Box 12.

91. "Fewer Ex-G.I.'s Train," *New York Times*, 29 November 1958, 9.

92. Between 1955 and 1961, American GDP grew 2.3%. See Stein, *Pivotal Decade*, 12.

93. McClenahan and Becker, *Eisenhower and the Cold War Economy*, 94–95.

94. "Comparative Situation," 12 April 1956 (Draft), 4, DDE, Bradley Commission, Box 63.

95. Veterans Administration, Reports & Statistics Service, Office of the Controller, *Data on Vietnam Era Veterans*, 20.

96. Michelotti Kopp and Kathryn R. Gover, "The Employment Situation of Vietnam Era Veterans," *Monthly Labor Review* 95 (December 1972): 9.

97. Donald E. Johnson, "An Unforgivable Gamble," *American Legion Magazine*, August 1965, 7.

98. Starr, *The Discarded Army*, 134.

99. Willenz, "The Returning Vietnam Veterans," 3; Starr, *The Discarded Army*, 134–36. These accounted for 88,408 discharges.

100. Public Law 89–358, The Veterans Readjustment Benefits Act of 1966, 3 March 1966, Chapter 34, Section 1652, 13.

101. Statement of Dr. F. J. Pepper, National Vice Chairman, American Veterans Committee before the Subcommittee on Health and Hospitals of the Committee on Veterans Affairs and Subcommittee on Alcoholism and Narcotics of the Committee on Labor and Public Welfare—Meeting Jointly, 23 June 1971, LOC, NAACP Records, Box V, 2839.

102. Veterans Administration, *Two Years of Outreach, 1968–1970: A Report from the Administrator of Veterans Affairs*, n.d., 2–5, NARA, RG 15, Entry 69, Box 4. See also Vernon Louviere, "What We're Doing for Vietnam Vets," *American Legion Magazine*, March 1968, 24.

103. Administrator of Veterans Affairs, *1970 Annual Report* (Washington, DC: Government Printing Office, 1971), NARA, RG 15, Entry 53, Box 1.

104. Starr, *The Discarded Army*, 214.

105. Letter, June A. Willenz (Director, AVC) to IBM, Director of Public Relations, 17 September 1968, Gelman Library, AVC Papers, Box 7.

106. "The Plight of Viet Nam Era Vets," *Time*, 27 December 1971, 57.

107. Letter, Headquarters, First United States Army, to Charles Eason (Acting Director, Eastern Regional Office, National Urban League), 13 June 1972, LOC, National Urban League Records, 1900–1988, Part III: Economic Development, 1961–1977, Military and Veterans Affairs Division, 1967–1976, Box III, 156.

108. Veterans Administration, *Two Years of Outreach, 1968–1970*, 14–15.

109. Ibid., 29. Memorandum, Henry A. Talbert (Army Officers' Procurement) to Thomas Brady (Acting Director, Economic Development), "Monthly Report—March 1972, 1, LOC, National Urban League Records, 1900–1988, Part III: Economic Development, 1961–1977, Military and Veterans Affairs Division, 1967–1976, Box III, 156.

110. Starr, *The Discarded Army*, 211.

111. Ibid., 210.

112. Louis Harris and Associates, *A Study of the Problems Facing Vietnam Era Veterans*, 72. "Word of mouth" (48%), "From family" (35%), and "Newspaper ads" (16%) accounted for the vast majority of placement, according to the poll. "Public employment service" (13%) and "Job Marts/Job Fairs for veterans" (1%) were very last on the list.

113. Willenz, "The Returning Vietnam Veterans," 3; Starr, *The Discarded Army*, 201.

114. Memorandum, William H. Edward to Thomas Brady (Director, Military and Veterans Affairs Division) to George Northcroft, 22 May 1974, 4, LOC, National Urban League Papers, Part III: Economic Development, 1961–1977, Military and Veterans Affairs Division, 1967–1976, Box III, 157.

115. "Testimony of Lewis C. Olive Jr., Director of Military and Veterans Affairs, National Urban League, on Unemployment Problems of Returning Minority Veterans, before the Committee on Veterans Affairs, the United States Senate, 28 April 1972, LOC, NAACP Papers, Box V, 2716.

116. Starr, *The Discarded Army*, 210.

117. "Returning Heroes Get the Cold Shoulder," 47.

118. Michelotti and Gover, "The Employment Situation of Vietnam Era Veterans," 7–8.

119. Starr, *The Discarded Army*, 37.

120. Michelotti and Gover, "The Employment Situation of Vietnam Era Veterans," 8.

121. "A Close Look at the Cold War GI Bill," *American Legion Magazine*, September 1966, 24–28.

122. Ibid., 26, 28. The number of months of funding was based on "one month of aid for each month, or fraction, of service on active duty after January 31, 1955."

123. Administrator of Veterans Affairs, *Annual Report, 1966* (Washington, DC: Government Printing Office, 1967), 2.

124. US Veterans Administration, Reports & Statistics Service, Office of the Controller, *Data on Vietnam Era Veterans*, 13.

125. Willenz, "The Returning Vietnam Veterans," 1.

126. Memorandum, James D. Tschirgi (Bureau of the Budget) to Rufus Wilson (VA), 1 July 1969, NARA, RG 15, Entry 69, Box 3.

127. See "Enrollments 1888 to Present," University of Wisconsin–Madison, updated 7 January 2017, http://registrar.wisc.edu/enrollments_1888_to_present.htm.

128. Tschirgi to Wilson, 1 July 1969.

129. Public Law 91–219, Veterans Training and Education Amendments Act, 26 March 1970, Chapter 1, Section 101, 76–77.

130. Administrator of Veterans Affairs, *1970 Annual Report*, 3.

131. Administrator of Veterans Affairs, *Annual Report: VA 73* (Washington, DC: Government Printing Office, 1974), 67–68, NARA, RG 15, Entry 53, Box 1.

132. Robert L. Eaton, "The Sorry State of Vietnam Vets' Education," *American Legion Magazine*, June 1974, 8.

133. Memorandum for the AVC National Office, "GI Bill in Trouble—Veto Promised," 22 November 1974, Gelman Library, AVC Papers, Box 7; Mark Boulton, *Failing Our Veterans: The G.I. Bill and the Vietnam Generation* (New York: New York University Press, 2014), 190–95.

134. "Returning Heroes Get the Cold Shoulder," 47. See also Letter, Lewis H. Olive (Director, Military and Veterans Affairs) to Ruby B. McZier (Special Assistant, Department of Housing and Urban Development), LOC, Part III: Economic Development, 1961–1977, Military and Veterans Affairs Division, National Urban League Papers, 1967–1976, Box III, 158.

135. Egendorf et al., *Legacies of Vietnam*, 197, 199.

136. US Department of Labor, *Thirty-Fifth Annual Report of the Secretary of Labor for the Fiscal Year Ended June 30, 1947*, 104.

137. Scuteri, "Casualties of War and Research," 81.

138. Mark C. Berger and Barry T. Hirsch, "The Civilian Earnings Experience of Vietnam-Era Veterans," *Journal of Human Resources* 18 (Autumn 1983): 461.

139. Saul Schwartz, "The Relative Earnings of Vietnam and Korea-Era Veterans," *Industrial and Labor Relations Review* 39 (July 1986): 568. Family income for Korea veterans was $10,020 and $9,930 for civilians. Family income for Vietnam veterans was $23,030 and $23,170 for civilians, according to the author. See also Berger and Hirsch, "The Civilian Earnings Experience of Vietnam-Era Veterans," 477.

140. Barry T. Hirsch and Stephen L. Mehay, "Evaluating the Labor Market Performance of Veterans Using a Matched Group Design," *Journal of Human Resources* 38 (Summer 2003): 693–95.

141. Russell Baker, "Twelve Men Close to Kennedy," *New York Times*, 22 January 1961, SM6. For more recent scholarship on the topic, see Milne, "'Our Equivalent of Guerrilla Warfare,'" 169–203; George Friedman and Meredith Friedman, *The Future of War: Power, Technology, and American World Dominance in the 21st Century* (New York: Crown Publishers, 1996), 55–59.

142. Summary Technical Report of the Applied Psychology Panel, *Human Factors in Military Efficiency: Aptitude and Classification* (Washington, DC: Office of Scientific Research and Development, 1946), 1:v, Hagley Museum and Library, Imprints.

143. Ibid.

144. Tufts College, Institute for Applied Experimental Psychology. *Handbook of Human Engineering Data* (Port Washington, NY: US Naval Training Device Center, 1960), 1–2, Hagley Museum and Library, Imprints.

145. Summary Technical Report of the Applied Psychology Panel, *Human Factors in Military Efficiency: Aptitude and Classification*, viii–ix; Jack W. Dunlap, "Bio-mechanics," in *Handbook of Applied Psychology*, eds. Douglas H. Fryer and Edwin Henry (New York: Rinehart, 1950), 1:311–22.

146. Tufts College, *Handbook of Human Engineering Data*, i.

147. National Defense Research Committee, *Summary Technical Report of Division 7, Gunfire Control* (Washington, DC: Office of Scientific Research and Development, 1946), 1:3, NARA, RG 227, Entry 23, Box 1.

148. Ibid., 4 (emphasis in original).

149. Branden Hookway, "Cockpit," in *Cold War Hothouses: Inventing Postwar Culture from Cockpit to Playboy*, eds. Beatriz Colomina, Annmarie Bren-

nan, and Jeannie Kim (Princeton, NJ: Princeton Architectural Press, 2004), 22–53.

150. *Shell . . . Soldier and Civilian*, 1–2.

151. Stephen Phillips, "Plastics," in Colomina, Brennan, and Kim, *Cold War Hothouses*, 96–97.

152. Hookway, "Cockpit," 255–56. Other examples include James Doolittle as vice president of Shell Oil, Albert C. Wedemeyer as vice president of AVCO, and Leslie Groves as vice president of Remington Rand. The original list is contained in C. Wright Mills, *The Power Elite* (New York: Oxford University Press, 1956), 214.

153. Stephen R. Patnode, "Labor's Lost Love: The Influence of Gender, Race, and Class on the Workplace in Postwar America" (PhD diss., SUNY Stonybrook, 2008), 98, 105.

154. National Association of Manufacturers, "Probationary Employee Rating Sheet—Non-exempt Employees," 1959, Hagley Museum and Library, National Association of Manufacturers Records, Box 101.

155. *Will the War Veterans Be Super-salesmen*? (Pittsburgh: Ketchum, MacLeod & Grove, 1944), Hagley Museum and Library, Imprints.

156. Deborah Shapely, *Promise and Power*: *The Life and Times of Robert McNamara* (Boston: Little, Brown, 1993), 41; George M. Watson, "'Whiz Kid': Robert S. McNamara's World War II Service," *Air Power History* 50 (Winter 2003): 6.

157. Remington Rand, *Remington Rand Presents*: *The Electronic Era for Business with UNIVAC Fact-Troller*: *The First Universal Electronic System Designed for Both Management and Science* (New York: Remington Rand Accounting-Tabulating Management Controls Division, 1950), 2. See also Emil D. Schell, "The Role of Automatic Programming for UNIVAC," *The Programmer* (July 1956): 8–15, Hagley Museum and Library, Imprints.

158. Sperry Rand, *Introducing the New Sperry Rand Research Center* (Sudbury, MA: Sperry Rand, 1961), 2, Hagley Museum and Library, Imprints.

159. See, for example, Arthur C. Clarke, *Man and Space* (New York: Time, 1964), 178–90.

160. Hookway, "Cockpit," 43; see also "New Atlanta Headquarters," *Focus on Remington Rand Office Systems Division* 1 (1967): 11, Hagley Museum and Library, Imprints. Robert Moses has attracted significant academic attention over the past 40 years. For a recent example of scholarship, see Peter R. Eisenstadt, *Rochdale Village*: *Robert Moses, 6,000 Families and New York City's Great Experiment in Integrated Housing* (Ithaca, NY: Cornell University Press, 2010).

161. L. P. Herrington, "Industrial Ventilation," in Fryer and Henry, *Handbook of Applied Psychology*, 1:288–97.

162. Auren Uris, *Developing Your Executive Skills* (New York: McGraw-Hill, 1955), 42. See also Charles J. Hitch, "Management Problems of Large Organizations," *Operations Research* 44 (March–April 1996): 257–64.

163. Shapely, *Promise and Power*, 67–68.

164. Ibid., 50–51.

165. Betty Friedan, *The Feminine Mystique* (New York: W. W. Norton, 1963), 293.

166. May, *Homeward Bound*, 169–70. See also Thomas Childers, *Soldier from the War Returning: The Greatest Generation's Troubled Homecoming from World War II* (New York: Houghton Mifflin, 2009), 242–47.

167. Organization Development Program Group, Industrial Relations Committee, *What's Wrong with Work? How to Release Human Potential and Improve Production* (New York: National Association of Manufacturers, 1967), 5, Hagley Museum and Library, Imprints.

168. Ibid., 9.

169. C. Wright Mills, *White Collar: The American Middle Classes* (New York: Oxford University Press, 1951), 227.

170. David Riesman, *The Lonely Crowd: A Study of the Changing American Character* (New Haven, CT: Yale University Press, 1950), 132–35.

171. Patterson, *Restless Giant*, 62–66. Moreell retired as president in 1952 but remained as chairman and chief executive officer until 1958.

172. Veterans frequently referred to both in postwar interviews. See the Rutgers Oral History Archives of World War II and the World War II Veterans Survey Project, AHEC.

173. Ron Zemke, Claire Raines, and Bob Filiczak, *Generations at Work: Managing the Clash of Veterans, Boomers, Xers, and Nexters in Your Workplace* (New York: American Management Association, 1999), 37.

174. Students for a Democratic Society, *The Port Huron Statement*, 2nd ptg. (New York: Students for a Democratic Society, 1964), 3, 6.

175. For the initial definition of PTSD, see Spitzer, *DSM-III*, 236–39.

176. Kaiman, "PTSD in the World War II Combat Veteran," 35. See also Kelly Bedard and Oliver Deschenes, "The Long-Term Impact of Military Service on Health: Evidence from World War II and Korean War Veterans," *American Economic Review* 96 (March 2006): 176–94.

177. Hugh Gusterson, "The McNamara Complex," *Anthropological Quarterly* 75 (Winter 2001): 170–77.

Chapter 4

1. Nicholas M. McKnight, "They Know What They Want," *School and Society* 63 (June 1946): 452.

2. Whitney M. Young, "When the Negroes in Vietnam Come Home," *Harper's Magazine*, June 1967, 63.

3. Andrew E. Hunt, "The Turning: Vietnam Veterans against the War, 1967 to the Present" (PhD diss., University of Utah, 1997), 188.

4. Alexis de Tocqueville, *Democracy in America* (New York: Library of America, 2004), 513–17.

5. Robert D. Putnam, *Bowling Alone: The Collapse and Revival of American Community* (New York: Simon and Schuster, 2000), 53–54.

6. Ibid., 438. By his account, they made up 388 out of every 1,000 veterans in 1945.

7. E. M. Schreiber, "Enduring Effects of Military Service? Opinion Differences between US Veterans and Nonveterans," *Social Forces* 57 (March 1979): 824–26.

8. M. Kent Jennings and Gregory B. Markus, "The Effects of Military Service on Political Attitudes: A Panel Study," *American Political Science Review* 71 (March 1977): 133.

9. For an excellent example of recent scholarship, see Ortiz, *Beyond the Bonus March and the GI Bill.*

10. American Legion, National Rehabilitation Committee, "A Statement on the Servicemen's Readjustment Act of 1944," 9 May 1945, AL, Veterans Welfare Classification, GI Bill, Folder 9.

11. David Cameron, "I Saw the GI Bill Written," *American Legion Magazine*, November 1949, 18–20, 43–48.

12. *The Budget of the United States for the Fiscal Year Ending June 30, 1947* (Washington, DC: Government Printing Office, 1946), 114–16.

13. Ibid.

14. American Legion, National Headquarters, "Progress Report on Serviceman's Readjustment Act of 1944," 25 June 1947, AL, Veterans Welfare Classification, GI Bill, Folder 10.

15. American Legion, *Summary of Proceedings: Thirty-Sixth Annual National Convention*, 53. See also US Department of Labor, *Thirty-Sixth Annual Report of the Secretary of Labor for the Fiscal Year Ended June 30, 1948*, 82–83. See President's Commission on Veterans' Pensions, *Veterans' Benefits in the United States*, 54–55; "Public Law 550, the 'Korean G.I. Bill,'" 122–23; Fine, "Veterans of Korea Flock to Colleges under US Grants," 1.

16. Elmo Roper, *A Study of Veterans' Attitudes toward Veterans' Benefits Prepared for the National Civil Service League*, October 1954, DDE, Bradley Commission, Box 63.

17. President's Commission on Veterans' Pensions, *Veterans' Benefits in the United States*, 112–13.

18. "Excerpts from President Eisenhower's 1956 Budget Message," n.d., DDE, Bradley Commission, Box 3.

19. President's Commission on Veterans' Pensions, *Veterans' Benefits in the United States*, 4.

20. Ibid., 24.

21. Letter, George J. Pickett to General Paul Hawley, 3 January 1956, DDE, Bradley Commission, Box 9.

22. Memorandum, "Reaction to the Commission's Report, 10 May 1956, 1, DDE, Bradley Commission, Box 7.

23. "Statement of Omar B. Ketchum, Director, National Legislative Service, Veterans of Foreign Wars of the US before the House Committee on Veterans Affairs," 11 May 1956, 2, DDE, Bradley Commission, Box 104.

24. Letter, Philip E. Richards (Chairman, Legislative Committee, Disabled Americans Chapter 87) to General Omar N. Bradley, 20 August 1955, DDE, Bradley Commission, Box 9.

25. "Analysis of Comments Submitted by Veterans' Organizations and Other Groups in Answer to General Bradley's Letter of March 29, 1955," 21 July 1955, DDE, Bradley Commission, Box 8.

26. US Bureau of the Census, *Statistical History of the United States*, 1146.

27. President's Commission, *Veterans' Benefits in the United States*, 23.

28. Starr, *The Discarded Army*, 41.

29. Robert B. Pitkin, "The Legion Fights Disaster," *American Legion Magazine*, February 1950, 24–25.

30. American Legion, Press Release, 3 August 1949, AL, Subject Files.

31. Robert B. Pitkin, "The American Legion in Louisiana," *American Legion Magazine*, June 1959, 19, 40–42.

32. "How You Made 3,000,000 Kids Happy," *American Legion Magazine*, August 1950, 26–27.

33. Letter, Abbott Washburn (USIA) to Sherman Adams (Assistant to the President), 24 January 1957, DDE, WHCF, General File, Box 713.

34. Robert B. Pitkin, "The American Legion's Youth Programs," *American Legion Magazine*, January 1960, 20.

35. American Legion, Child Welfare Foundation Annual Report, 1975, 1, n.d., AL, Child Welfare Foundation File.

36. See Kennedy, *Freedom from Fear*, 776–82. See also Costello, *Virtue under Fire*.

37. Pitkin, "The American Legion's Youth Programs," 20–21.

38. Steven R. Bullock, "Vital Connections: Baseball and the American Military during World War II" (PhD diss., University of Nebraska, 2001), 1.

39. Wanda Ellen Wakefield, *Playing to Win: Sports and the American Military, 1898–1945* (Albany: State University of New York Press, 1997), 95.

40. Ibid., 103–4.

41. Ibid., 7, 13.

42. "Legion Baseball," *New York Times*, 6 July 1945, 15; Ty Cobb, "Batting Out Better Boys, *Rotarian*, July 1947, 11.

43. Wakefield, *Playing to Win*, 137.

44. Christopher C. Nehls, "A Grand and Glorious Feeling: The American Legion and American Nationalism between the World Wars" (PhD diss., University of Virginia, 2007), 155.

45. Ibid., 156–57.

46. American Legion, National Americanism Commission, *Americanism Manual* (Indianapolis, IN: American Legion, October 1943), 34.

47. Ibid.

48. See, for example, Cathy D. Knepper, *Greenbelt, Maryland: A Living Legacy of the New Deal* (Baltimore: Johns Hopkins University Press, 2001).

49. Kent M. Krause, "From Americanism to Athleticism: A History of the American Junior League Baseball Program" (PhD diss., University of Nebraska, 1998), 122–23.

50. See, for example, "Pro Clubs May Sign Legion Ball Players," *New York Times*, 21 January 1945, 53; "State Legion Nine Wins: Beats Connecticut Youths, 8–1, at Polo Grounds," *New York Times*, 11 August 1946, 85.

51. Krause, "From Americanism to Athleticism," 127–48.

52. For an excellent discussion of this topic, see Millis, *Arms and Men*.

53. Karen O. Dunivin, "Military Culture: Change and Continuity," *Armed Forces & Society* 20 (Summer 1994): 531–47.

54. Millett and Maslowski, *For the Common Defense*, 504–5.

55. Maxwell D. Taylor, *The Uncertain Trumpet* (New York: Harper and Brothers, 1959), 4, 17. See also Anthony Leviero, "Ridgeway Assails US Stress on Air and Atom," *New York Times*, 15 July 1955, 1.

56. Howard Jablon, "General David M. Shoup, USMC: Warrior and War Protestor," *Journal of Military History* 60 (July 1996): 513–38.

57. John W. Finney, "Shoup, Calling for Talks, Doubts Military Victory," *New York Times*, 21 March 1968, 12.

58. James M. Gavin, *Crisis Now* (New York: Random House, 1968), 55, 61–62.

59. John H. Fenton, “Gavin Quits Post with Democrats,” *New York Times*, 5 August 1967, 3; Anthony Ripley, “Gavin Is Pushed for Presidency,” *New York Times*, 1 October 1967, 36.

60. “Admiral True Tour Set,” *Veterans Stars & Stripes for Peace*, September 1967, 1.

61. “Veterans Plan a War Protest in Capital,” *New York Times*, 17 March 1971, 21.

62. Mauldin, *Up Front*, 24.

63. Ibid., 20–21.

64. Rooney, *My War*, 282.

65. Ralph Peterson, “Good Legions and Bad,” *Tomorrow* 4 (July 1945): 2, LOC, NAACP Papers, Box II, B3.

66. Bill Mauldin, *Back Home* (New York: Bantam, 1948), 68.

67. Ibid., 72–73.

68. Peterson, “Good Legions and Bad,” 3.

69. Saxe, *Settling Down*, 117–53.

70. Peter D. Hoefer, “A David against Goliath: The American Veterans Committee’s Challenge to the American Legion in the 50s” (PhD diss., University of Maryland, 2010), 76, 111.

71. “Veterans Protest College Fees,” *New York Times*, 3 December 1945, 19.

72. “37 Hurt, 13 Seized in Coast Movie Riot,” *New York Times*, October 1946, 3.

73. Wendy Plotkin, “‘Hemmed In’: The Struggle against Racial Restrictive Covenants and Deed Restrictions in Post–World War II Chicago,” *Journal of the Illinois State Historical Society* 94 (Spring 2001): 67; Robert L. Tyler, “The American Veterans Committee: Out of a Hot War and into the Cold,” *American Quarterly* 18 (Autumn 1966): 422.

74. Hoefer, “A David against Goliath,” 112.

75. Letter, June A. Willenz (AVC, Executive Director) to Director of Public Relations (IBM), 17 September 1968, Gelman Library, AVC Records, Box 7; American Veterans Committee, “A Sampling of Veterans’ Cases Assisted by the American Veterans Committee (AVC),” 9 November 1967, Gelman Library, AVC Records, Box 7.

76. Resolution, Veterans of Foreign Wars, Clark-Lyon Post No, 4731 of Indianola, Mississippi, 15 February 1954, DDE, WHCF, General File, Box 712.

77. American Veterans Committee, “A Petition for the Redress of Grievances,” 12 September 1955, LOC, NAACP Papers, Box II, A362. See also Let-

ter, Charles G. Bolté (AVC) to Omar Bradley, 3, DDE, Bradley Commission, Box 9.

78. US Department of Justice, Federal Bureau of Investigation, "American Veterans Committee," 25 May 1953, DDE, WHCF, Confidential File, Subject Series, Box 4.

79. Hoefer, "A David against Goliath," 78–93.

80. American Veterans Committee, "Statement of American Veterans Committee (AVC) on Suspension without Pay of Federal Employees under Executive Order 10450, Entitled Security Requirements for Government Employment," 24 June 1954, LOC, Bill Mauldin Papers, Box 2.

81. American Veterans Committee, National Office, Press Release, "Mauldin Reveals Response to Invitations to Veterans Leaders to Draft 'Code of Conduct,'" 22 February 1954, LOC, Bill Mauldin Papers, Box 2.

82. Ibid.

83. Hoefer, "A David against Goliath," 13, 29, 73. AVC membership remained at about 30,000 for the remainder of the fifties. In contrast, the American Legion had 2.8 million members in 1956. The Veterans of Foreign Wars could count 1.6 million members in 1955.

84. Roosevelt, "The 'Four Freedoms' Speech," 2:446–49.

85. War Department, Bureau of Public Relations, "Address by Mr. Truman K. Gibson, Jr., Civilian Aid to the Secretary of War, before the War Mothers, Gold Star Awards Committee," 13 May 1945, LOC, NAACP Papers, Branch Files, 1940–1955, Box A648.

86. Donovan, *Conflict and Crisis*, 244.

87. Guzman, *Negro Year Book*, 246.

88. Brooks, "From Hitler and Tojo to Talmadge and Jim Crow," 170.

89. Charles M. Payne, *I've Got the Light of Freedom: The Organizing Tradition and the Mississippi Freedom Struggle* (Berkeley: University of California Press, 1995), 57; Gambone, *Greatest Generation Comes Home*, 125.

90. Letter, Frank T. Hines to Jesse O. Dedmon, 9 April 1945, LOC, NAACP Papers, Microfilm Collection, Reel 7, Frames 180–181.

91. NAACP, Press Release, 5 December 1945, LOC, NAACP Files, Branch Files, 1940–1955, Box A657.

92. National Urban League, "Adjustment of Negro Veterans: A Report of the Adjustment Problems of Negro Veterans in 50 Cities," March 1946, 3, LOC, NAACP, Box II, A397.

93. Mickey Levine, National Chairman, American Veterans Committee (AVC), "Report on Negro Veterans in the South," 15 March 1956, 1, DDE, Bradley Commission Papers, Box 9.

94. Ibid., 3.

95. Ibid., 5.

96. Doug McAdam, *Political Process and the Development of Black Insurgency, 1930–1970* (Chicago: University of Chicago Press, 1982), 102–7; Howard Ball, *A Defiant Life: Thurgood Marshall and the Persistence of Racism in America* (New York: Crown, 1998), 92–93.

97. Brooks, "From Hitler and Tojo to Talmadge and Jim Crow," 13, 29, 55–60.

98. For an earlier dissection of the Great Society, see Kearns, *Lyndon Johnson and the American Dream*, 10–50.

99. Starr, *The Discarded Army*, 203–25; "A Close Look at the Cold War GI Bill," *American Legion Magazine*, September 1966, 48.

100. Louis Harris and Associates, *A Study of the Problems Facing Vietnam Era Veterans*, 48.

101. Ibid., 56.

102. Memorandum, Lewis C. Olive (Director, Military and Veterans Affairs) to Mahlon T. Puryear (Director Economic Development), 2 January 1973, 1, LOC, National Urban League Records, 1900–1988, Part III: Economic Development, 1961–1977, Military and Veterans Affairs Division, 1967–1976, Box III, 159.

103. Memorandum, Lewis C. Olive (Military and Veterans Affairs) to Mahlon T. Puryear (Director, Economic Development), "NUL Task Force on Concerns to the President," 2 January 1973, LOC, National Urban League Records, 1900–1988, Part III: Economic Development, 1961–1977, Box III, 159.

104. Memorandum, William H. Edward (Director) to Faith Williams (Communications), "National Urban League's Military Affairs Updated Fact Sheet," 19 May 1975, LOC, National Urban League Records, 1900–1988, Box III, 157.

105. Memorandum, Lewis C. Olive (Director, Veterans Affairs) to Regional National Urban League Offices, "Monthly Reports," 20 May 1971, LOC, National Urban League Records, 1900–1988, Box III, 159.

106. Memorandum, Henry A. Talbert (Army Officers' Procurement) to Thomas Brady (Acting Director, Economic Development), "Monthly Report—March 1972, LOC, National Urban League Records, 1900–1988, Box III, 156.

107. National Urban League, "Statement of Interest, Evaluation of the Implementation of Decentralized Manpower Programs: Project 7401," 6 February 1974, LOC, National Urban League Records, 1900–1988, Box III, 155.

108. Brooks, "From Hitler and Tojo to Talmadge and Jim Crow," 125.

109. Lance Hill, *The Deacons for Defense: Armed Resistance and the Civil Rights Movement* (Chapel Hill: University of North Carolina Press, 2004), 26, 42.

110. Interview Transcript, D'Army Bailey, 13 August 2013, 38, LOC, American Folklife Center, Civil Rights History Project.

111. Interview Transcript, Kathleen Neal Cleaver, 16 September 2011, 38, LOC, American Folklife Center, Civil Rights History Project.

112. Interview Transcript, Fletcher Anderson, 27 May 2011, 38, LOC, American Folklife Center, Civil Rights History Project.

113. Charles E. Cobb, *This Nonviolent Stuff'll Get You Killed: How Guns Made the Civil Rights Movement Possible* (New York: Basic Books, 2014), 203.

114. Jackie Robinson, "Deacons Here to Stay?," *Chicago Defender*, 31 July 1965, 10.

115. Thomas A. Johnson, "Negro in Vietnam Is Uneasy about US," *New York Times*, 1 May 1968, 14.

116. Thomas Corpora, "Negro Veterans Aren't Returning Home to Riot," *Chicago Daily Defender*, 27 June 1968, 20.

117. "Brothers in Arms," *The Nation*, 28 October 1968, 421–22.

118. Ibid.

119. Corpora, "Negro Veterans Aren't Returning Home to Riot," 20.

120. Young, "When the Negroes in Vietnam Come Home," 65.

121. Curtis Austin, "The Black Panthers and the Vietnam War," in *America and the War in Vietnam: Re-examining the Culture and History of a Generation*, eds. Andrew Wiest, Mary Kathryn Barbier, and Glenn Robins (New York: Routledge, 2010), 102, 104.

122. Cobb, *This Nonviolent Stuff'll Get You Killed*, 208.

123. Fred Powledge, "Armed Negroes Make Jonesboro Unusual Town," *New York Times*, 21 February 1965, 52.

124. Roy Reed, "Armed Negro Unit Spreads in South," *New York Times*, 6 June 1965, 1.

125. Hill, *The Deacons for Defense*, 53–57; Christopher B. Strain, "'We Walked like Men': The Deacons for Defense and Justice," *Louisiana History* 38 (Winter 1997): 48–50.

126. Roy Reed, "The Deacons, Too, Ride by Night," *New York Times*, 15 August 1965, SM 10; "Klan Is Warned by Negro Leader," *New York Times*, 29 January 1966, 9.

127. Sol Stern, "When the Black G.I. Comes Back from Vietnam," *New York Times*, 24 March 1968, SM38.

128. "Deacons Organize Chicago Chapter," *New York Times*, 6 April 1966, 29.

129. Stern, "When the Black G.I. Comes Back from Vietnam," SM37.

130. Thomas A. Johnson, "Negro Veteran Is Confused and Bitter," *New York Times*, 29 July 1968, 14.

131. John Skow, "The Flicker of Fear," *Saturday Evening Post*, 7 September 1968, 24.

132. Patterson, *Grand Expectations*, 663–67.

133. "Police Stockpiling Weapons for Riots," *New York Times*, 2 March 1968, 16.

134. Anthony Ripley, "Cleveland Police Bitter over Replacement by Negro Patrols," *New York Times*, 30 July 1968, 18.

135. Memo, Special Agent in Charge (Albany) to Director (FBI), Counterintelligence Program, Black Nationalist—Hate Groups, Internal Security," 25 August 1967, 3, 100-HQ-448006–01; Memo, Special Agent in Charge (Chicago) to the Director (FBI), "Counterintelligence Program, Black Nationalist—Hate Groups, Racial Intelligence," 29 October 1968, 179, 100-HQ-448006–02, FBI COINTELPRO—Black Extremism, both at https://archive.org/details/FBI-COINTELPRO-BLACK.

136. Memo, Special Agent in Charge (St. Louis) to the Director (FBI), "Counterintelligence Program, Black Nationalist—Hate Groups, Racial Intelligence," 29 October 1968, 179, 100-HQ-448006–04; Special Agent in Charge (Detroit) to the Director (FBI), "Counterintelligence Program, Black Nationalist—Hate Groups (Republic of New Africa)," 18 November 1969, 188, 100-HQ-448006–15, FBI COINTELPRO—Black Extremism, both at https://archive.org/details/FBI-COINTELPRO-BLACK.

137. Fussell, *Wartime*, 130–38.

138. "Legion Head Urges We Avoid Hysteria," *New York Times*, 21 May 1940, 18; "Holt, Van Zandt Talk Tomorrow at Peace Rally," *Chicago Tribune*, 19 December 1940, 2.

139. "Legion Yells Down a Neutrality Call," *New York Times*, 27 September 1940, 12.

140. Letter, Veterans against the War, n.d., Swarthmore College Peace Collection.

141. Veterans against the War, Newsletter #2, January 1953, 2, Swarthmore College Peace Collection.

142. M. S. Handler, "Vietcong Talks Urged by Ex G.I.," *New York Times*, 4 March 1966, 3.

143. Donald Duncan, "The Whole Thing Was a Lie!," *Ramparts* 4, no. 10 (February 1966): 23; Jack Raymond, "Veteran of Special Forces Denounces US Policy in Vietnam as a 'Lie,'" *New York Times*, 10 February 1966, 2.

144. Letter, Ad Hoc Committee of Veterans for Peace in Vietnam, 28 December 1965, Swarthmore College Peace Collection.

145. Hunt, "The Turning," 8–9.

146. Ibid., 30, 48–50.

147. Andrew Hunt, "'When Did the Sixties Happen?': Searching for New Directions," *Journal of Social History* 33 (Autumn 1999): 154–56.

148. Nicosia, *Home to War*, 41–44; Melvin Small, *Antiwarriors: The Vietnam War and the Battle for America's Hearts and Minds* (Lanham, MD: SR Books, 2004), 62.

149. John Ernst and Yvonne Baldwin, "The Not So Silent Majority: Louisville's Antiwar Movement, 1966–1975," *Journal of Southern History* 73 (February 2007): 113.

150. "Victory at Ft. Jackson," *Counterpoint* 2 (June 1969): 1–2; "Jane Fonda Banned from Fort," *Fed Up*! 1 (April 1970): 1–2; "How to Get Over," *Free Press* 2 (May 1971): supplement. There are numerous collections available for researchers. See, for example, the University of Washington Pacific Northwest Labor and Civil Rights Projects, 2008, http://depts.washington.edu/antiwar/gi_history.shtml.

151. Wallace Turner, "G.I. Coffeehouses under Coast Fire," *New York Times*, 16 February 1969, 80.

152. Donald Johnson, "Antiwar Coffeehouses Delight G.I.'s but Not Army," *New York Times*, 12 August 1968, 1.

153. Earl Caldwell, "Army Acts to Close Coffee House Where G.I.'s Relax Off Duty and Damn the War," *New York Times*, 22 January 1970, 13.

154. Johnson, "Antiwar Coffeehouses Delight G.I.'s," 41; Turner, "G.I. Coffeehouses Under Coast Fire," 80. See also Ernst and Baldwin, "The Not So Silent Majority," 105–42.

155. Ronald Sullivan, "Veterans for Peace Simulate the War," *New York Times*, 5 September 1970, 6.

156. Art Goldberg, "Vietnam Vets: The Anti-war Army," *Ramparts* 10 (July 1971): 12.

157. Stacewicz, *Winter Soldiers*, 229–31; Hunt, "The Turning," 82–90.

158. Sullivan, "Veterans for Peace Simulate War," 6.

159. Ibid.

160. Hunt, "The Turning," 106.

161. The Citizens Commission of Inquiry eventually left the Winter Soldier Investigation. Their main concern was the veracity of information being provided by journalist Mark Lane regarding war crimes in Vietnam.

162. See Vietnam Veterans against the War, *The Winter Soldier Investigation: An Inquiry into American War Crimes* (Boston: Beacon Press, 1972).

163. Neil Sheehan, "Conversations with Americans: Book Review," *New York Times*, 27 December 1970, 19.

164. Operation Dewey Canyon III was named after two previous military operations conducted in 1969 and 1971.

165. Vietnam Veterans against the War, "Vietnam Vets March on D.C.," n.d., Swarthmore College Peace Collection.

166. Goldberg, "Vietnam Vets," 14.

167. "Complete Testimony of Lt. John Kerry to Senate Foreign Relations Committee on Behalf of the Vietnam Veterans against the War," 92nd Cong., 1st sess., 22 April 1971, 182.

168. Ibid., 210–11.

169. Goldberg, "Vietnam Vets," 14.

170. Hunt, "The Turning," 76. Hunt uses the example of Ohio State University.

171. Haley, "When the Patient Reports Atrocities," 192.

172. Nicosia, *Home to War*, 59.

173. Shatan, "The Grief of Soldiers," 642.

174. Ibid., 648.

175. Gambone, *Greatest Generation Comes Home*, 48.

176. Shatan, "The Grief of Soldiers," 651; Haley, "When the Patient Reports Atrocities," 195. Haley's term was "therapeutic alliance."

177. Lifton, *Home from War*, 69. See also Robert Jay Lifton, *History and Human Survival* (New York: Random House, 1970), 214.

178. Shatan, "The Grief of Soldiers," 649.

179. Scott, "PTSD in DSM-III," 294–310.

180. Hunt, "The Turning," 3.

181. Jan Barry, "Why Veterans March against the War," *New York Times*, 23 April 1971, 37.

182. Marjorie Hunter, "Agnew Says 'Effete Snobs' Incited Moratorium," *New York Times*, 20 October 1969, 1.

183. Lembcke, *The Spitting Image*, 49–51.

184. Stephen E. Ambrose, *Nixon: The Triumph of a Politician, 1962–1972* (New York: Simon and Schuster, 1989), 2:265.

185. Memo, Special Agent in Charge (SAC), New York to Director, FBI, "Winter Soldier Investigation," 24 November 1970, www.wintersoldier.com/index.php?topc=UUAWFBI. See also *Hearings before the Select Committee to Study Governmental Operations with Respect to Intelligence Activities of the United States Senate, Ninety-Fourth Congress, First Session*, vol. 6 (Washington, DC: Government Printing Office, 1976).

186. Ambrose, *Nixon*, 302.

187. "Veteran Kills Himself to Protest the War," *New York Times*, 20 August 1967, 31.

188. Schreiber, "Enduring Effects of Military Service?," 830–37; Jennings and Markus, "The Effects of Military Service on Political Attitudes," 137–42.

189. Willenz, "The Returning Vietnam Veterans," 1.

190. Sandy Goodman, "Invisible Veterans," *The Nation*, 3 June 1968, 724.

191. June A. Willenz, "The Veterans Establishment—Outlook for the 70's," n.d., Gelman Library, AVC Records, Box 14.

Conclusion

1. Robert Morgan, with Ron Powers, *The Man Who Flew the* Memphis Belle: *Memoir of a WWII Bomber Pilot* (New York: Penguin, 2001), 345. See also Thomas M. Smock, "From Myth to Identity: Oral History, Popular Culture, and the Making of the Greatest Generation" (PhD diss., Drew University, 2006), 148.

2. For a recent study, see Berinsky, *In Time of War*.

3. Gray, "The American Way of War," 13–40.

4. H. Stuart Hughes, "Emotional Disturbance and American Social Change," in US Department of Veterans Affairs, *The Vietnam Veterans in Contemporary Society*, II-2.

5. Desmond P. Wilson and Jessie Horack, "Military Experience as a Determinant of Veterans' Attitudes," in US Department of Veterans Affairs, *The Vietnam Veterans in Contemporary Society*, IV-15–IV-17.

6. The term comes from the Army Medical Corps motto. See US Army Medical Department, Army Medical Department Regiment, last modified 2 February 2015, http://ameddregiment.amedd.army.mil/heraldic/distinct.html.

7. Research has also incorporated ethnicity. See Spoont et al., "Race and Ethnicity as Factors in Mental Health Service," 648–53; Alexander N. Ortega and Robert Rosenheck, "Posttraumatic Stress Disorder among Hispanic Vietnam Veterans," *American Journal of Psychiatry* 157 (April 2000): 615–19.

8. Saxe, *Settling Down*, 117–90.

9. Statistics are from the US Selective Service System website, www.sss.gov/old/old-site-hist.

SELECTED BIBLIOGRAPHY

ARCHIVES

American Legion Library and Museum, Indianapolis, IN
Child Welfare Foundation File
Manuscripts Collection
Miscellaneous Employment File
Subject File
Universal Draft File
Veterans Employment Committee File
Veterans' Welfare Classification
Army Heritage and Education Center (AHEC), Carlisle, PA
Manuscripts Collection, Dwight David Eisenhower Library (DDE), Abilene, KS
Records as President, White House Central File (WHCF), 1954–1961
US President's Commission on Veterans' Pensions (Bradley Commission): Records, 1954–1958
Gelman Library, George Washington University, Washington, DC
American Veterans Committee Records
Hagley Museum and Library, Wilmington, DE
Jones & Laughlin Steel Corporation Records
National Association of Manufacturers Records
Remington Rand Records
Shell Corporation Records
Library of Congress (LOC), Washington, DC
American Folklife Center
Bill Mauldin Papers
Civil Rights History Project
NAACP Records
National Urban League Records, 1900–1988
Veterans History Project
National Archives and Records Administration (NARA), College Park, MD
Records Group (RG) 15Veterans Administration

Records Group 65Federal Bureau of Investigation
Records Group 147Selective Service Administration
Records Group 227Office of Scientific Research and Development
Records Group 407Army-AG Decimal Files
Old National Archives, Washington, DC
Swarthmore College Peace Collection, Swarthmore, PA

Primary Sources

Bush, Vannevar, James B. Conant, and Charles W. Bray. *Human Factors in Military Efficiency*. Washington, DC: Office of Scientific Research and Development, National Defense Research Committee, Applied Psychology Panel, 1946.

Christie, Richard, and Stuart W. Cook. *Psychological Stresses in the Transition from Civilian to Military Life*. Washington, DC: Department of Defense, Research and Development Board, 1950.

Drake, Francis. *Readability of Military Communications*. Washington, DC: Department of Defense, Research and Development Board, 1950.

Harris, F. Gentry, Joseph Mayer, and Herman A. Becker. *Experiences in the Study of Combat in the Korean Theater: Report on Psychiatric and Psychological Data*. Washington, DC: Walter Reed Army Institute of Research, 1955.

Human Resources Research Institute, Air University. *Research on Combat Behavior*. Washington, DC: Department of Defense, Research and Development Board, 1951.

Mandelbaum, David G. *Group Dynamics of Military Units*. Washington, DC: Department of Defense, Research and Development Board, 1951.

McFann, Howard H., John A. Hammes, and John E. Taylor. *TRAINFIRE I: A New Course in Basic Rifle Marksmanship*. Technical Report 22. Washington, DC: Department of the Army, Human Resources Research Office, 1955.

Miller, Neal E. *Fear and Courage in Training and Combat*. Washington, DC: Department of Defense, Research and Development Board, 1951.

———. *Selection of Men Who Will Be Courageous in Combat*. Washington, DC: Department of Defense, Research and Development Board, 1951.

National Association of Manufacturers, Organizational Development Group, Industrial Relations Committee. *What's Wrong with Work?*

How to Release Human Potential and Improve Productivity. New York: National Association of Manufacturers, 1967.

Public Opinion Surveys, Inc. *Attitudes of Adult Civilians toward the Military Service as a Career: Part I of a Study for the Office of Armed Forces Information and Education, Department of Defense*. Princeton, NJ: Public Opinion Surveys, 1955.

———. *Attitudes of 16 to 20 Year Old Males toward the Military Service as a Career: Part II of a Study for the Office of Armed Forces Information and Education, Department of Defense*. Princeton, NJ: Public Opinion Surveys, 1955.

Savelli, Joel M., John C. Woelfel, and Barry Collins. *Attitudes concerning Job Appropriateness for Women in the Army*. Research Memorandum 75–3. Fort Belvoir, VA: Research Institute for the Behavioral Sciences, June 1975.

Shell Soldier and Civilian. New York: Shell Union Oil and Associate Companies, 1945.

Standard Oil Company, Employee Relations Department, Social Science Research Division. *Summary Report of the Early Identification of Management Potential Research Project in Standard Oil and Affiliated Companies*. New York: Standard Oil, 1961.

Tufts College, Institute for Applied Experimental Psychology. *Handbook of Human Engineering Data*. Port Washington, NY: US Naval Training Device Center, 1960.

US Administrator of Veterans Affairs. *Annual Report, 1959*. Washington, DC: Government Printing Office, 1960.

———. *Annual Report, 1960*. Washington, DC: Government Printing Office, 1961.

———. *Annual Report, 1967*. Washington, DC: Government Printing Office, 1968.

US Bureau of the Census. *The Statistical History of the United States: From Colonial Times to the Present*. New York: Basic Books, 1976.

US Chamber of Commerce. *Jobs for Veterans*. Washington, DC: Chamber of Commerce of the United States, 1970.

US Congress, Joint Economic Committee. *The 1974 Economic Report of the President*. Washington, DC: Government Printing Office, 1974.

US Congressional Budget Office. *The All-Volunteer Military: Issues and Performance*. Pub. No. 2960. Washington, DC: Congressional Budget Office, 2007.

US Defense Advisory Committee on Women in the Armed Forces.

Changing Roles of Women in the Armed Forces. Washington, DC: DACOWITS, 1978.

US Department of Defense, Office of the Assistant Secretary of Defense (Manpower and Reserve Affairs), Directorate for Manpower Research. *Recruiting of Women for the Military: Assessment of the Mental and Medical Standards and Their Present and Potential Effects on Recruiting Needs*. Report No. MR 75–4. Alexandria, VA: Human Resources Research Organization, July 1975.

US Department of Defense, Office of the Deputy Assistant Secretary of Defense for Military Manpower and Personnel Policy. *Hispanics in America's Defense*. Washington, DC: Government Printing Office, 1990.

US Department of Labor. *Thirty-Fourth Annual Report of the Secretary of Labor for the Fiscal Year Ended June 30, 1946*. Washington, DC: Government Printing Office, 1947.

———. *Thirty-Fifth Annual Report of the Secretary of Labor for the Fiscal Year Ended June 30, 1947*. Washington, DC: Government Printing Office, 1948.

———. *Thirty-Sixth Annual Report of the Secretary of Labor for the Fiscal Year Ended June 30, 1948*. Washington, DC: Government Printing Office, 1949.

US Department of the Army. *Evaluation of Women in the Army: Final Report*. Washington, DC: Department of the Army, 1978.

US Department of the Army, General Staff, Deputy Chief of Staff for Personnel. *The Final Report of the Women in the Army Study Group*. Washington, DC: Headquarters, Department of the Army, 1976.

US Department of the Army, General Staff, Office of the Assistant Chief of Staff, G-1, Plans Division. *Army Rotation Study*. Washington, DC: Department of the Army, 1953.

US Department of the Army. *TRAINFIRE*. DA Pamphlet No. 355–14. Washington, DC: Government Printing Office, July 1958.

US Department of the Treasury, Bureau of Narcotics. *Comments on Narcotic Drugs*: *Interim Report of the Joint Committee of the American Bar Association and the American Medical Association on Narcotic Drugs*. Washington, DC: Bureau of Narcotics, 1958.

———. *Traffic in Opium and Other Dangerous Drugs for the Year Ended December 1950*. Washington, DC: Government Printing Office, 1951.

———. *Traffic in Opium and Other Dangerous Drugs for the Year Ended December 31, 1957*. Washington, DC: Government Printing Office, 1958.

———. *Traffic in Opium and Other Dangerous Drugs for the Year Ended December 31, 1964*. Washington, DC: Government Printing Office, 1965.

———. *Traffic in Opium and Other Dangerous Drugs for the Year Ended December 31, 1967*. Washington, DC: Government Printing Office, 1968.

US Department of Veterans Affairs, Assistant Secretary for Planning and Analysis, Office of Program and Data Analysis. *Data on Veterans of the Korean War*. Washington, DC: Department of Veterans Affairs, 2000.

US Department of Veterans Affairs, Department of Medicine and Surgery. *The Vietnam Veterans in Contemporary Society: Collected Materials Pertaining to the Young Veterans*. Washington, DC: Veterans Administration, 1972.

US Department of Veterans Affairs, National Center for Veterans Analysis and Statistics. *America's Women Veterans: Military Service History and VA Benefit Utilization Statistics*. Washington, DC: Department of Veterans Affairs, 2011.

———. *Minority Veterans: 2011*. Washington, DC: Department of Veterans Affairs, 2013.

US Federal Bureau of Investigation. *Crime in the United States: Uniform Crime Reports—1959*. Washington, DC: Government Printing Office, 1960.

———. *Uniform Crime Reports for the United States and Its Possessions*. Vol. 15, no. 2. Washington, DC: Government Printing Office, 1945.

———. *Uniform Crime Reports for the United States and Its Possessions*. Vol. 16, no. 2. Washington, DC: Government Printing Office, 1946.

———. *Uniform Crime Reports for the United States and Its Possessions*. Vol. 17, no. 2. Washington, DC: Government Printing Office, 1947.

US House of Representatives, Select Committee on Crime. *Amphetamines: Fourth Report by the Select Committee on Crime*. Washington, DC: Government Printing Office, 1971.

US President's Commission on Veterans' Pensions. *The Historical Development of Veterans' Benefits in the United States: A Report on Veterans' Benefits in the United States: Staff Report No. 1*. Washington, DC: Government Printing Office, 1956.

———. *Veterans' Benefits in the United States: A Report to the President by the President's Commission on Veterans' Pensions*. Washington, DC: Government Printing Office, 1956.

US Senate, Committee on Veterans' Affairs. *A Study of the Problems Facing Vietnam Era Veterans*. Washington, DC: Government Printing Office, 1972.

US Veterans Administration, Office of Information Management and Statistics. *Data on Vietnam Era Veterans*. Washington, DC: Veterans Administration, 1985.

US Veterans Administration, Reports & Statistics Service, Office of the Controller. *Data on Vietnam Era Veterans*. Washington, DC: Veterans Administration, 1977.

US War Manpower Commission, Bureau of Training, Training within Industry Service. *Training within Industry Materials*. Washington, DC: Government Printing Office, 1945.

Secondary Sources

Abella, Alex. *Soldiers of Reason: The RAND Corporation and the Rise of the American Empire*. New York: Harcourt, 2008.

Ainspan, Nathan D., and Walter E. Penk. *When the Warrior Returns: Making the Transition at Home*. Annapolis, MD: Naval Institute Press, 2012.

Ambrose, Stephen E. *Eisenhower: The President*. Vol. 2. New York: Simon and Schuster, 1984.

———. *Nixon: The Triumph of a Politician, 1962–1972*. Vol. 2. New York: Simon and Schuster, 1989.

Andersen, Kathryn H., and Jean M. Mitchell. "Effects of Military Experience on Mental Health Problems and Work Behavior." *Medical Care* 30 (June 1992): 554–63.

Arbogast, Kate A. "The Procurement of Women for the Armed Forces: An Analysis of Occupational Choice." PhD diss., George Washington University, 1974.

Arce, William. "Nation in Uniform: Chicano/Latino War Narratives and the Construction of Nation in the Korean War and the Vietnam War." PhD diss., University of Southern California, 2009.

Archer, Dane, and Rosemary Gartner. "Violent Acts and Violent Times: A Comparative Approach to Postwar Homicide Rates." *American Sociological Review* 41 (December 1976): 937–63.

Baker, Rodney R., Shirley W. Menard, and Louis A. Johns. "The Military Nurse Experience in Vietnam: Stress and Impact." *Journal of Clinical Psychology* 45 (September 1989): 736–44.

Bedard, Kelly, and Oliver Deschenes. "The Long-Term Impact of Military Service on Health: Evidence from World War II and Korean War Veterans." *American Economic Review* 96 (March 2006): 176–94.

Berinsky, Adam J. *In Time of War: Understanding American Public Opinion from World War II to Iraq*. Chicago: University of Chicago Press, 2009.

Berrett, Jesse. "Feeding the Organization Man: Diet and Masculinity in Postwar America." *Journal of Social History* 30 (Summer 1997): 805–25.

Bey, Douglas R., and Walter E. Smith. "Organizational Consultation in a Combat Unit." *American Journal of Psychiatry* 128 (October 1971): 401–6.

Blair, Clay. *The Forgotten War: America in Korea, 1950–1953*. New York: Times Books, 1987.

Blum, John Morton. *V Was for Victory: Politics and American Culture during World War II*. New York: Harcourt Brace, 1976.

Boudewyns, Patrick A., M. Gail Woods, Lee Hyer, and J. William Albrecht. "Chronic Combat-Related PTSD and Concurrent Substance Abuse: Implications for Treatment of This Frequent 'Dual Diagnosis.'" *Journal of Traumatic Stress* 4 (1991): 549–60.

Bouffard, Leana A. "Examining the Relationship between Military Service and Criminal Behavior during the Vietnam Era: A Research Note." *Criminology* 41 (May 2003): 491–510.

Bourne, Peter G. *Men, Stress, and Vietnam*. Boston: Little, Brown, 1970.

Bradley, James, with Ron Powers. *Flags of Our Fathers*. New York: Bantam Books, 2000.

Branchy, L., W. Davis, and C. S. Lieber. "Alcoholism in Vietnam and Korea Veterans: A Long-Term Follow-Up." *Alcoholism: Clinical and Experimental Research* 8 (November–December 1984): 572–75.

Breen, William J. "Social Science and State Policy in World War II: Human Relations, Pedagogy, and Industrial Training, 1940–1945." *Business History Review* 76 (Summer 2002): 233–66.

Brokaw, Tom. *The Greatest Generation*. New York: Random House, 1998.

Brooks, Jennifer E. "From Hitler and Tojo to Talmadge and Jim Crow: World War Two Veterans and the Remaking of the Southern Political Tradition." PhD diss., University of Tennessee, 1997.

Campbell, D'Ann. "Servicewomen of World War II." *Armed Forces and Society* 16 (Winter 1990): 251–70.

———. *Women at War with America: Private Lives in a Patriotic Era*. Cambridge, MA: Harvard University Press, 1984.

Caputo, Philip. *A Rumor of War*. New York: Holt, Rinehart and Winston, 1977.

Center for Strategic Studies. *Economic Impact of the Vietnam War*. Special Report Series No. 5. Washington, DC: Center for Strategic Studies, 1967.

Chermol, Brian H. "Wounds without Scars: Treatment of Battle Fatigue in the US Armed Forces in the Second World War." *Military Affairs* 49 (January 1985): 9–12.

Childers, Thomas. *Soldier from the War Returning: The Greatest Generation's Troubled Homecoming from World War II*. New York: Houghton Mifflin, 2009.

Cobb, Charles E. *This Nonviolent Stuff'll Get You Killed: How Guns Made the Civil Rights Movement Possible*. New York: Basic Books, 2014.

Colomina, Beatriz, Annmarie Brennan, and Jeannie Kim, eds. *Cold War Hothouses: Inventing Postwar Culture from Cockpit to Playboy*. New York: Princeton Architectural Press, 2004.

Costello, John. *Virtue under Fire: How World War II Changed Our Social and Sexual Attitudes*. Boston: Little, Brown, 1985.

Davis, Gilbert. "An Ecological Study of the Mentally-Ill Veteran in Kansas City, Mo." *Midwest Sociologist* 12 (Fall 1949): 15.

Dean, Eric T. "The Myth of the Troubled and Scorned Vietnam Veteran." *Journal of American Studies* 26 (April 1992): 59–74.

Dewhurst and Associates, J. Frederic. *America's Needs and Resources: A New Survey*. New York: Twentieth Century Fund, 1955.

Dienstfrey, Stephen J., and Robert H. Feitz. *Chart Book of Black and Hispanic Veterans: Data from the 1980 Census of Population and Housing*. IM&S M 70–85–4. Washington, DC: Office of Information Management and Statistics, 1985.

Donnelly, William M. "The Best Army That Can Be Put in the Field in the Circumstances: The US Army July 1951–July 1953." *Journal of Military History* 71 (July 2007): 809–47.

Donovan, Beverly, Edgardo Padin-Rivera, and Sean Kowaliw. "Transcend: Initial Outcomes from a Posttraumatic Stress Disorder/Substance Abuse Treatment Program." *Journal of Traumatic Stress* 14 (2001): 757–72.

Donovan, Robert J. *Conflict and Crisis: The Presidency of Harry S. Truman, 1945–1948*. New York: W. W. Norton, 1977.

Dooley, Channing E. "The Training within Industry Report, 1940–1945." *Developing Human Resources* 3 (May 2001): 127–287.

Duncan, Donald. "The Whole Thing Was a Lie!" *Ramparts* 4 (February 1966): 12–24.

Dyer, Gwynne. *War*. New York: Crown Publishers, 1985.

Eagles, Charles W. *The Price of Defiance: James Meredith and the Integration of Ole Miss*. Chapel Hill: University of North Carolina Press, 2009.

Eaton, Walter H. "Research on Veterans' Adjustment." *American Journal of Sociology* 51 (March 1946): 483–87.

Eberwein, Robert, ed. *The War Film*. New Brunswick, NJ: Rutgers University Press, 2005.

Egendorf, Arthur, Charles Kadushin, Robert S. Laufer, Lee Sloan, and George Rothbart. *Legacies of Vietnam: Comparative Adjustment of Veterans and Their Peers: A Study Conducted for the Veterans Administration*. New York: Center for Policy Research, 1981.

Elder, Glen H., and Elizabeth C. Clipp. "Wartime Losses and Social Bonding: Influences across 40 Years of Men's Lives." *Psychiatry* 51 (May 1988): 177–98.

Engelbrecht, Helmuth C., and Frank C. Hanighen. *Merchants of Death: A Study of the International Armament Industry*. New York: Dodd, Mead, 1934.

Ernst, John, and Yvonne Baldwin. "The Not So Silent Majority: Louisville's Antiwar Movement, 1966–1975." *Journal of Southern History* 73 (February 2007): 105–42.

Fair, William R. "Analogue Computations of Business Decisions." *Journal of the Operations Research Society of America* 1 (August 1953): 208–19.

Flynn, George Q. *The Draft, 1940–1973*. Lawrence: University Press of Kansas, 1993.

Friedl, Vicki L. *Women in the United States Military, 1901–1995: A Research Guide and Annotated Bibliography*. Westport, CT: Greenwood Press, 1996.

Fry, James C. *Assault Battle Drill*. Harrisburg, PA: Military Service Publishing, 1955.

Fryer, Douglas H., and Edwin R. Henry, eds. *Handbook of Applied Psychology*. 2 vols. New York: Rinehart, 1950.

Galbraith, John Kenneth. *Economics and the Public Purpose*. Boston: Houghton Mifflin, 1973.

Gallagher, Henry T. *James Meredith and the Ole Mississippi Riot: A Soldier's Story*. Jackson: University of Mississippi Press, 2012.

Gallup, George H. *The Gallup Poll: Public Opinion, 1935–1971*. 3 vols. New York: Random House, 1972.

Gambone, Michael D. *The Greatest Generation Comes Home: The Veteran in American Society*. College Station: Texas A&M University Press, 2005.

Gavin, James M. *Crisis Now*. New York: Random House, 1968.

Gelb, Leslie H. *The Irony of Vietnam: The System Worked*. Washington, DC: Brookings Institution, 1979.

Gelpi, Christopher, and Peter D. Feaver. "Speak Softly and Carry a Big Stick? Veterans in the Political Elite and the American Use of Force." *American Political Science Review* 96 (December 2002): 779–93.

Gibson, Carri-Ann. "Review of Posttraumatic Stress Disorder and Chronic Pain: The Path to Integrated Care." *Journal of Rehabilitation Research and Development* 49 (2012): 553–76.

Glanz, Aaron. *The War Comes Home: Washington's Battle against America's Veterans*. Berkeley: University of California Press, 2009.

Glasser, Ronald J. *365 Days*. New York: George Braziller, 1971.

Glenn, Russell W. *Reading Athena's Dance Card: Men against Fire in Vietnam*. Annapolis, MD: Naval Institute Press, 2000.

Grandstaff, Mark R. "Making the Military American: Advertising, Reform, and the Demise of an Antistanding Military Tradition." *Journal of Military History* 60 (April 1996): 299–323.

Grinspoon, Lester, and Peter Hedblom. *The Speed Culture: Methamphetamine Use and Abuse in America*. Cambridge, MA: Harvard University Press, 1975.

Gross, Harriet Engel. "Micro and Macro Level Implications for a Sociology of Virtue: The Case of Draft Protestors to the Vietnam War." *Sociological Quarterly* 18 (Summer 1977): 319–39.

Grossman, Dave. *On Killing: The Psychological Cost of Learning to Kill in War and Society*. 3rd ed. New York: Little, Brown, 2009.

Gurr, Ted R. "Historical Trends in Violent Crime: A Critical Review of the Evidence." *Crime and Justice* 3 (1981): 295–353.

Gusterson, Hugh. "The McNamara Complex." *Anthropological Quarterly* 75 (Winter 2001): 170–77.

Guzman, Jessie Parkhurst. *Negro Year Book: A Review of Events Affecting Negro Life, 1941–1946*. Tuskegee, AL: Tuskegee Institute, 1947.

Hackworth, David A. *About Face: The Odyssey of an American Warrior*. New York: Simon and Schuster, 1989.

Hakeem, Michael. "Service in the Armed Forces and Criminality." *Journal of Criminal Law and Criminology* 37 (July–August 1946): 120–31.

Haley, Sarah A. "When the Patient Reports Atrocities: Specific Treatment Considerations of the Vietnam Veteran." *Archives of General Psychiatry* 30 (February 1974): 191–96.

Hall, Simon. *Peace and Freedom: The Civil Rights and Antiwar Movements in the 1960s.* Philadelphia: University of Pennsylvania Press, 2005.

Harris, Mark. *Five Came Back: A Story of Hollywood and the Second World War.* New York: Penguin Press, 2014.

Hassler, Warren W. *With Shield and Sword: American Military Affairs, Colonial Times to the Present.* Ames: Iowa State University Press, 1982.

Hill, Lance. *The Deacons for Defense: Armed Resistance and the Civil Rights Movement.* Chapel Hill: University of North Carolina Press, 2004.

Hirsch, Barry T., and Stephen L. Mehay. "Evaluating the Labor Market Performance of Veterans Using a Matched Group Design." *Journal of Human Resources* 38 (Summer 2003): 673–700.

Hitch, Charles J. "Management Problems of Large Organizations." *Operations Research* 44 (March–April 1996): 257–64.

Honomichl, Jack J. "Decision Making in a New Dimension." *Challenge* 12 (January 1964): 29–32.

Huebner, Andrew J. *The Warrior Image: Soldiers in American Culture from the Second World War to the Vietnam Era.* Chapel Hill: University of North Carolina Press, 2008.

Hunt, Andrew E. "The Turning: Vietnam Veterans against the War, 1967 to the Present." PhD diss., University of Utah, 1997.

———. "'When Did the Sixties Happen?' Searching for New Directions." *Journal of Social History* 33 (Autumn 1999): 147–61.

Huppenbauer, Sandra L. "A Portrait of a Problem." *American Journal of Nursing* 82 (November 1982): 1699–1703.

Isaac, Joel. "Tangled Loops: Theory, History, and the Human Sciences in Modern America." *Modern Intellectual History* 9 (2009): 397–424.

Jablon, Howard. "General David M. Shoup, USMC: Warrior and War Protestor." *Journal of Military History* 60 (July 1996): 513–38.

Jacobs, Marianne Scherer. "The Best of Times, the Worst of Times: The Vietnam Experiences and Posttraumatic Stress Disorder among Female Nurse Veterans." PhD diss., University of Washington, 1990.

Janowitz, Morris. "The All-Volunteer Military as a 'Sociopolitical' Problem." *Social Problems* 22 (February 1975): 432–49.

Jennings, M. Kent, and Gregory B. Markus. "The Effects of Military Service on Political Attitudes: A Panel Study." *American Political Science Review* 71 (March 1977): 131–47.

Johnston, Jerome, and Jerald G. Bachman. *Young Men Look at Military Service: A Preliminary Report.* Ann Arbor, MI: Institute for Social Research, 1971.

Kaiman, Charles. "PTSD in the World War II Combat Veteran." *American Journal of Nursing* 103 (November 2003): 32–42.

Karner, Tracy. "Fathers, Sons, and Vietnam: Masculinity and Betrayal in the Life Narrations of Vietnam Veterans with Post Traumatic Stress Disorder." *American Studies* 37 (Spring 1996): 63–94.

Karnow, Stanley. *Vietnam: A History.* New York: Viking Press, 1983.

Kearns, Doris. *Lyndon Johnson and the American Dream.* New York: Harper and Row, 1976.

Korb, Lawrence J. "The Budget Process in the Department of Defense, 1947–1977: The Strengths and Weaknesses of Three Systems." *Public Administration Review* 9 (July–August 1977): 334–47.

Kuzmarov, Jeremy. "The Myth of the Addicted Army: Vietnam and the Modern War on Drugs." PhD diss., Brandeis University, 2006.

Larsen, Sarah A., and Jennifer M. Miller. "Wisconsin Korean War Stories: Veterans Tell Their Stories from the Forgotten War." *Wisconsin Magazine of History* 91 (Spring 2008): 24–27.

Laufer, Robert S., M. S. Gallops, and Ellen Frey-Wouters. "War Stress and Trauma: The Vietnam Veteran Experience." *Journal of Health and Social Behavior* 25 (March 1984): 65–85.

Leavitt, Harold J. *Managerial Psychology: An Introduction to Individuals, Pairs, and Groups in Organizations.* Chicago: University of Chicago Press, 1958.

Leland, Anne, and Mari-Jana Oboroceanu. *American War and Military Operations Casualties: Lists and Statistics.* CRS Report RL32492. Washington, DC: Congressional Research Service, 2010.

Lembcke, Jerry. *The Spitting Image: Myth, Memory, and the Legacy of Vietnam.* New York: New York University Press, 1998.

Leuchtenburg, William E. *A Troubled Feast: American Society since 1945.* Boston: Little, Brown, 1983.

Lewy, Guenter. *America in Vietnam.* New York: Oxford University Press, 1978.

Lieberman, E. James. "American Families and the Vietnam War." *Journal of Marriage and Family* 33 (November 1971): 709–21.

Lifton, Robert Jay. "From Analysis to Form: Towards a Shift in Psychological Paradigm." *Salmagundi* 28 (Winter 1975): 43–78.

———. *History and Human Survival.* New York: Random House, 1970.

———. *Home from War: Vietnam Veterans: Neither Victims nor Executioners*. New York: Simon and Schuster, 1973.

Loss, Christopher P. "'The Most Wonderful Thing Happened to Me in the Army': Psychology, Citizenship, and American Higher Education in World War II." *Journal of American History* 92 (December 2005): 864–91.

Louis Harris and Associates, Inc. *The Harris Survey Yearbook of Public Opinion, 1971*. New York: Louis Harris and Associates, 1975.

———. *A Study of the Problems Facing Vietnam Era Veterans: Their Readjustment to Civilian Life*. New York: Louis Harris and Associates, 1971.

———. *Survey of Female Veterans: A Study of the Needs, Attitudes, and Experiences of Women Veterans*. Study No. 843002. New York: Louis Harris and Associates, 1985.

Ludlow, Herbert Glenn. "Trends and Issues in Standardized Testing." *Journal of Educational Research* 47 (December 1953): 279–84.

Mann, Arthur. *The One and the Many: Reflections on the American Identity*. Chicago: University of Chicago Press, 1979.

Mariscal, George, ed. *Aztlán and Viet Nam: Chicano and Chicana Experiences of the War*. Berkeley: University of California Press, 1999.

Marshall, Kathryn. *In the Combat Zone: An Oral History of American Women in Vietnam, 1966–1975*. Boston: Little, Brown, 1987.

Marshall, S. L. A. *Men against Fire: The Problem of Battle Command in Future War*. New York: William Morrow, 1947.

Matusow, Allen J. *Nixon's Economy: Booms, Busts, Dollars, and Votes*. Lawrence: University Press of Kansas, 1998.

Mauldin, Bill. *Back Home*. New York: Bantam Books, 1948.

———. *Bill Mauldin in Korea*. New York: W. W. Norton, 1952.

May, Elaine Tyler. *Homeward Bound: American Families in the Cold War Era*. 3rd ed. New York: Basic Books, 2008.

McClenahan, William M., and William H. Becker. *Eisenhower and the Cold War Economy*. Baltimore: Johns Hopkins University Press, 2011.

McCranie, Edward W., and Leon A. Hyer. "Posttraumatic Stress Disorder Symptoms in Korean Conflict and World War II Combat Veterans Seeking Outpatient Treatment." *Journal of Traumatic Stress* 13 (2000): 427–39.

McGrath, John J. *The Other End of the Spear: The Tooth-to-Tail Ratio (T3R) in Modern Military Operations*. Long War Series Occasional Paper No. 23. Fort Leavenworth, KS: Combat Studies Institute Press, 2007.

McIvor, Anthony D, ed. *Rethinking the Principles of War*. Annapolis, MD: Naval Institute Press, 2005.

Meese, Michael J. "Defense Decision Making under Budget Stringency: Explaining Downsizing in the United States Army." PhD diss., Princeton University, 2000.

Millis, Walter. *Arms and Men: A Study in American Military History*. NewBrunswick, NJ: Rutgers University Press, 1984.

Mills, C. Wright. *The Power Elite*. New York: Oxford University Press, 1956.

———. *White Collar: The American Middle Class*. New York: Oxford University Press, 1951.

Milne, David. "'Our Equivalent of Guerrilla Warfare': Walt Rostow and the Bombing of North Vietnam, 1961–1968." *Journal of Military History* 71 (January 2007): 169–203.

Monahan, Evelyn M., and Rosemary Neidel-Greenlee. *A Few Good Women: America's Military Women from World War I to the Wars in Iraq and Afghanistan*. New York: Alfred A. Knopf, 2010.

Monks, John P. "College Men at War." *Memoirs of the American Academy of Arts and Sciences* 24 (1957): 1–310.

Moon, Nathan W. "The Amphetamine Years: A Study of the Medical Applications and Extramedical Consumption of Psychostimulant Drugs in the Postwar United States, 1945–1980." PhD diss., Georgia Institute of Technology, 2009.

Morin, Raul R. *Among the Valiant: Mexican-Americans in WWII and Korea*. Los Angeles: Borden Publishing, 1963.

Moskos, Charles C. "The American Dilemma in Uniform: Race in the Armed Forces." *Annals of the American Academy of Political and Social Science* 406 (March 1973): 94–106.

Mosse, George L. "Two World Wars and the Myth of the War Experience." *Journal of Contemporary History* 21 (October 1986): 491–513.

Mueller, John E. *War, Presidents and Public Opinion*. New York: John Wiley, 1973.

Murphy, Audie. *To Hell and Back*. New York: Holt, Rinehart and Winston, 1949.

"New Atlanta Headquarters." *Focus on Remington Rand Office Systems Division* 1, no. 2 (1967): 10–11.

Nicosia, Gerald. *Home to War: A History of the Vietnam Veterans' Movement*. New York: Crown Publishers, 2001.

Okun, Arthur M. *The Political Economy of Prosperity*. Washington, DC: Brookings Institution, 1970.

Olson, Keith W. "The G.I. Bill and Higher Education: Success and Surprise." *American Quarterly* 25 (December 1973): 596–610.

Ortiz, Stephen R. *Beyond the Bonus March and the GI Bill: How Veterans Politics Shaped the New Deal Era*. New York: New York University Press, 2010.

Parker, Christopher S. *Fighting for Democracy: Black Veterans and the Struggle against White Supremacy in the Postwar South*. Princeton, NJ: Princeton University Press, 2009.

Pash, Melinda L. *In The Shadow of the Greatest Generation: The Americans Who Fought the Korean War*. New York: New York University Press, 2012.

Patten, Thomas H. "Health and Behavior in Homes for Veterans: Some Old and New Patterns." *Journal of Health and Human Behavior* 2 (Spring 1961): 47–58.

Prados, John, ed. *In Country: Remembering the Vietnam War*. New York: Ivan R. Dee, 2011.

Putnam, Robert D. *Bowling Alone: The Collapse and Revival of American Community*. New York: Simon and Schuster, 2000.

Pyle, Ernie. *Brave Men*. New York: Henry Holt, 1944.

Quester, Aline O., and Curtis L. Gilroy. *America's Military: A Coat of Many Colors*. CRM D0004368.A1/Final. Alexandria, VA: CAN, July 2001.

Rasmussen, Nicholas. "Making the First Anti-depressant: Amphetamine in American Medicine, 1929–1950." *Journal of the History of Medicine and Allied Sciences* 61 (2006): 288–323.

———. "Medical Science and the Military: The Allies' Use of Amphetamine during World War II." *Journal of Interdisciplinary History* 42 (Autumn 2011): 205–33.

———. *On Speed: The Many Lives of Amphetamine*. New York: New York University Press, 2008.

Riesman, David. *The Lonely Crowd: A Study of the Changing American Character*. New Haven, CT: Yale University Press, 1950.

Ritchie, Elspeth Cameron. "Psychiatry in the Korean War: Perils, PIES, and Prisoners of War." *Military Medicine* 167 (November 2002): 898–903.

Rivas-Rodriguez, Maggie, ed. *Mexican Americans & World War II*. Austin: University of Texas Press, 2005.

Rohde, Joy. “Gray Matters: Social Scientists, Military Patronage, and Democracy in the Cold War.” *Journal of American History* 96 (June 2009): 99–122.

Rooney, Andy. *My War*. New York: PublicAffairs, 2000.

Rosales, Steven. “Soldados Razos: Chicano Politics, Identity, and Masculinity in the US Military, 1945–1975.” PhD diss., University of California, Irvine, 2007.

Rosen, Daniel. “Medical Care Information System of the Veterans’ Administration.” *Public Health Reports* 83 (May 1968): 363–71.

Ruger, William, Sven E. Wilson, and Shawn L. Waddoups. “Warfare and Welfare: Military Service, Combat, and Marital Dissolution.” *Armed Forces and Society* 29 (Fall 2002): 85–107.

Sato, Akihiko. “Methamphetamine Use in Japan after the Second World War: Transformation of Narratives.” *Contemporary Drug Problems* 35 (Winter 2008): 717–46.

Saxe, Robert F. *Settling Down: World War II Veterans’ Challenge to the Postwar Consensus*. New York: Palgrave Macmillan, 2007.

Saywell, Shelley. *Women in War*. New York: Viking Penguin, 1985.

Schell, Emil D. “The Role of Automatic Programming for UNIVAC.” *The Programmer* 3, no. 4 (July 1956): 8–15.

Schreiber, E. M. “Enduring Effects of Military Service? Opinion Differences between US Veterans and Nonveterans.” *Social Forces* 57 (March 1979): 824–39.

Scott, Wilbur J. “PTSD in DSM-III: A Case in the Politics of Diagnosis and Disease.” *Social Problems* 37 (August 1990): 294–310.

Scuteri, Gina M. “Casualties of War and Research: A Case Study of US Women Veterans of Vietnam.” PhD diss., Purdue University, 1993.

Seeley, Robert A. *Handbook for Conscientious Objectors*. Philadelphia: Central Committee for Conscientious Objectors, 1982.

Segal, David R., and Mady Wechsler Segal. “America’s Military Population.” *Population Bulletin* 59 (December 2004): 1–40.

Shafer, D. Michael, ed. *The Legacy: The Vietnam War in the American Imagination*. Boston: Beacon Press, 1990.

Shapely, Deborah. *Promise and Power: The Life and Times of Robert McNamara*. Boston: Little, Brown, 1993.

Shatan, Chaim F. “The Grief of Soldiers: Vietnam Combat Veterans’ Self-Help Movement.” *American Journal of Orthopsychiatry* 43 (July 1973): 640–53.

Sheehan, Neil. *A Bright Shining Lie: John Paul Vann and America in Vietnam*. New York: Vintage House, 1988.

Sherman, Janann. "They Either Need These Women or They Do Not: Margaret Chase Smith and the Fight for Regular Status for Women in the Military." *Journal of Military History* 54 (January 1990): 47–78.

Sherrod, Robert. *Tarawa: The Story of a Battle*. New York: Duell, Sloan and Pearce, 1944.

Shils, Edward A., and Morris Janowitz. "Cohesion and Disintegration in the Wehrmacht in World War II." *Public Opinion Quarterly* 12 (Summer 1948): 280–315.

Shin Huey Chong, Silvia. "Restaging the War: 'The Deer Hunter' and the Primal and the Primal Scene of Violence." *Cinema Journal* 44 (Winter 2005): 89–106.

Shultz, George P., and Kenneth W. Dam. *Economic Policy beyond the Headlines*. New York: W. W. Norton, 1977.

Small, Melvin. *Antiwarriors: The Vietnam War and the Battle for America's Hearts and Minds*. Lanham, MD: SR Books, 2004.

Smith, Nicholas M., Stanley S. Walters, Franklin C. Brooks, and David H. Blackwell. "The Theory of Value and the Science of Decision: A Summary." *Journal of Operations Research* 1 (May 1953): 103–13.

Spitzer, Robert L, ed. *DSM-III: Diagnostic and Statistical Manual of Mental Disorders*. 3rd ed. Washington, DC: American Psychiatric Press, 1980.

Spitzer, Robert L., Miriam Gibbon, Andrew E. Skodol, Janet B. W. Williams, and Michael B. First, eds. *DSM-IV Casebook: A Learning Companion to the Diagnostic and Statistical Manual of Mental Disorders*. 4th ed. Washington, DC: American Psychiatric Press, 1994.

Spoont, Michele R., James Hodges, Maureen Murdoch, and Sean Nugent. "Race and Ethnicity as Factors in Mental Health Service Use among Veterans with PTSD." *Journal of Traumatic Stress* 22 (December 2009): 648–53.

Stacewicz, Richard. *Winter Soldiers: An Oral History of the Vietnam Veterans against the War*. Chicago: Haymarket Books, 1997.

Starr, Paul. *The Discarded Army: Veterans after Vietnam: The Nader Report on Vietnam Veterans and the Veterans Administration*. New York: Charterhouse, 1973.

Stein, Judith. *Pivotal Decade: How the United States Traded Factories for Finance in the Seventies*. New Haven, CT: Yale University Press, 2010.

Stevens, Robert W. *Vain Hopes, Grim Realities: The Economic Consequences of the Vietnam War*. New York: Franklin Watts, 1976.

Stewart-Winter, Timothy. "Not a Soldier, Not a Slacker: Conscientious Objectors and Male Citizenship in the United States during the Second World War." *Gender & History* 19 (November 2007): 519–42.

Stouffer, Samuel A., Arthur A Lumsdaine, Marion Harper Lumsdaine, Robin McWilliams, M. Brewster Smith, Irving L. Janis, Shirley A. Star, and Leonard S. Cottrell. *The American Soldier: Combat and Its Aftermath*. 2 vols. Princeton, NJ: Princeton University Press, 1949.

Strain, Christopher B. "'We Walked like Men': The Deacons for Defense and Justice." *Louisiana History* 38 (Winter 1997): 43–62.

Summers, Harry G., Jr. *On Strategy: A Critical Analysis of the Vietnam War*. New York: Dell, 1982.

Suri, Jeremi. *Power and Protest: Global Revolution and the Rise of Détente*. Cambridge, MA: Harvard University Press, 2003.

Swofford, Anthony. *Jarhead: A Marine's Chronicle of the Gulf War and Other Battles*. New York: Scribner, 2003.

Terkel, Studs. *"The Good War": An Oral History of World War II*. New York: Pantheon Books, 1984.

Terry, Wallace. *Bloods: An Oral History of the Vietnam War by Black Veterans*. New York: Random House, 1984.

Thomas, William. "The Heuristics of War: Scientific Method and the Founders of Operations Research." *British Journal for the History of Science* 40 (June 2009): 251–74.

Timberg, Robert. *The Nightingale's Song*. New York: Simon and Schuster, 1995.

Toland, John. *Battle: The Story of the Bulge*. New York: Random House, 1959.

Tracy, Sarah W., and Caroline Jean Acker, eds. *Altering American Consciousness: The History of Alcohol and Drug Use in the United States, 1800–2000*. Amherst: University of Massachusetts Press, 2004.

Trujillo, Charley. *Soldados: Chicanos in Viet Nam*. San Jose, CA: Chusma House Publications, 1990.

Turner, Sarah, and John Bound. "Closing the Gap or Widening the Divide: The Effects of the G.I. Bill and World War II on the Educational Outcomes of Black Americans." *Journal of Economic History* 63 (March 2003): 145–77.

Uris, Auren. *Developing Your Executive Skills*. New York: McGraw-Hill, 1955.

Uyeki, Eugene S. "Draftee Behavior in the Cold-War Army." *Social Problems* 8 (Autumn 1960): 151–58.

Valentine, Janet G. "The American Combat Soldier in the Korean War." PhD diss., University of Alabama, 2002.

Waller, Willard. *The Veteran Comes Back*. New York: Dryden Press, 1944.

Watson, George M. "'Whiz Kid': Robert S. McNamara's World War II Service." *Air Power History* 50 (Winter 2003): 4–15.

Wecter, Dixon. *When Johnny Comes Marching Home*. Cambridge, MA: Riverside Press, 1944.

Welton, Harry. *The Third World War: Trade and Industry—the New Battleground*. New York: Philosophical Library, 1959.

Wiest, Andrew, Mary Kathryn Barbier, and Glenn Robins, eds. *America and the War in Vietnam: Re-examining the Culture and History of a Generation*. New York: Routledge, 2010.

Willbach, Harry. "Crimes and Veterans." *Journal of Criminal Law and Criminology* 38 (January–February 1948): 501–8.

Willis, John. "Variations in State Casualty Rates in World War II and the Vietnam War." *Social Problems* 22 (April 1975): 558–68.

Wood, Effie M. *G-I Joe—Three Years After*. Publication no. 44. Chicago: Research Council for Economic Security, 1948.

Woodward, Luther E., and Thomas A. C. Rennie. *Jobs and the Man: A Guide for Employers, Supervisors, Interviewers, Counselors, Foremen, and Shop Stewards in Understanding and Dealing with Workers—Veterans and Civilians*. Springfield, IL: Charles C. Thomas, 1945.

Worland, Rick. "The Other Living-Room War: Prime Time Combat Series, 1962–1975." *Journal of Film and Video* 50 (Fall 1998): 3–23.

Wynn, Neil A. "The 'Good War': The Second World War and Postwar American Society." *Journal of Contemporary History* 31 (July 1996): 463–82.

Ybarra, Lea. *Vietnam Veteranos: Chicanos Recall the War*. Austin: University of Texas Press, 2004.

Young, Marilyn B. "Now Playing: Vietnam." *OAH Magazine of History* 18 (October 2004): 22–26.

———. "The Post-war War." *History Workshop Journal* 51 (Spring 2001): 112–26.

Young, Victoria I. *Evolution of the US Army Force Structure*. 2 vols. McLean, VA: Science Applications International, 1989.

INDEX